Women's Ways of Worship

Teresa Berger

Women's Ways of Worship

Gender Analysis
and Liturgical History

A PUEBLO BOOK

The Liturgical Press Collegeville, Minnesota

A Pueblo Book published by The Liturgical Press

Design by Frank Kacmarcik, Obl.S.B.

Library of Congress Cataloging-in-Publication Data

Berger, Teresa.
    Women's ways of worship : gender analysis and liturgical history /
    Teresa Berger.
        p.   cm.
    "A Pueblo book."
    Includes bibliographical references and index.
    ISBN 0-8146-6173-4 (alk. paper)
    1. Women in public worship—Catholic Church—History.   2. Catholic
    Church—Liturgy—History.   I. Title.
    BX1970.25.B37   1999
    264'.02'0082—dc21   98-34348
                                                                                CIP

For Peter Ludwig Berger (*February 15, 1996),
whose birth interrupted the beginnings of this book
and whose life continues to "interrupt" mine
in the most wonderful ways

Contents

Preface   xi

Introduction   1

Chapter 1   Reconstructing Women's Ways of Worship:
            In Search of Methodological Principles   5

Principle 1: "Gender" as an Analytical Tool   6
Principle 2: A Preferential Option for Liturgical Historiography
            "from below"   8
Principle 3: A Temporary Abstention from Naming Constants   9
Principle 4: Re-Configuring the Canon of Sources   11
Principle 5: Re-Visioning Liturgical Periodization   13
Principle 6: Re-Defining Ritual Centers of Gravity   14
Principle 7: Re-Considering Liturgical Prohibitions   16
Principle 8: Re-Interpreting Anthropological Basics   18
Principle 9: Respecting Differences   20
Principle 10: Re-Gendering the Saints   21
Principle 11: Re-Interpreting Liturgical Texts   23
Principle 12: Re-Claiming the Liturgical Narrative for Women   24
Principle 13: Continuing the Methodological Quest   25

Chapter 2   Liturgical History Re-Constructed (I):
            Early Christian Women at Worship   27

1. Women at the Jewish Roots of Christian Worship   28

2. The Greco-Roman Cultural Matrix   29

3. Women in the Earliest Christian Communities   32

3.1. Inclusive Initiation   32

3.2. Women's Space as Liturgical Space   33

3.3. Christian Table Practice: Gender-Inclusive and/yet
     Gendered?   34

3.4. Gender Differentiation in Worship   36

3.5. Women's Liturgical Ministries   37

3.6. Feminine Imagery in the Liturgy   38

4. "Patriarchal" or "Liberating"?   39

5. Women at Worship in the Church of the Empire   40

  5.1. Women as Liturgical Practitioners   40

      5.1.1. Increasing Liturgical Marginalization   40

      5.1.2. Increasing Liturgical Genderization   41

      5.1.3. Discerning Women in Worship   42

      5.1.4. Liturgical Prohibitions and Practices   43

  5.2. Women's Liturgical Patronage   44

  5.3. Women in a Liturgy Gone Public   46

      5.3.1. Gender-Specific Constraints on Public "Appearance"   47

      5.3.2. Women-Problems at Public Worship   49

      5.3.3. Women's "Publicity" on the Fringes   50

      5.3.4. Christian Women and Rival Ritual Powers   52

  5.4. The Genderization of Liturgical Space   54

  5.5. Liturgical Taboos   56

  5.6. Women as Bearers of Liturgical Tradition   59

  5.7. The Liturgical Singing of Women   59

  5.8. Women's (Liturgical) Communities   60

  5.9. Women on the Way   61

  5.10. The Veneration of Women   63

      5.10.1. Women and Their Feasts   64

      5.10.2. Women and Their Churches   65

      5.10.3. Women Saints and Gender Identification   65

      5.10.4. Women-Sermons   66

6. Early Christian Women—Early Christian Worship:
   An Attempt at a Summary   67

**Chapter 3   Liturgical History Re-Constructed (II):
             Women in the Twentieth-Century Liturgical Movement   69**

1. The Scholarly Construction of the Liturgical Movement   72

2. Women and "Woman" in the Liturgical Movement:
   A Re-Construction   73

3. The Cultural Context of the Liturgical Movement   77

4. The Liturgical Movement: Moved by Women   81
   4.1. Women as Subjects of the Liturgy   81
        4.1.1. Women as Bearers of Liturgical Traditioning   82
        4.1.2. "Liturgical Experiences" of Women   84
   4.2. The Liturgy as a Script for Womanhood   89
   4.3. Liturgical Ministries of Women   93
        4.3.1. The Priesthood of Women   94
        4.3.2. The Diaconate for Women   97
        4.3.4. Lay Liturgical Ministries for Women   98
   4.4. Women's Liturgical Communities   98
        4.4.1. The Benedictine Convent Ancilla Domini on the
               Mont-Vierge, Belgium   99
        4.4.2. The Benedictine Abbey of the Holy Cross at
               Herstelle, Germany   100
        4.4.3. The Convent of the Sisters of the Most Precious Blood
               in O'Fallon, Missouri   101
   4.5. Liturgical "Women's Studies"   103

5. The Liturgical Movement: "Androcentric" and "Liberating"   106

**Chapter 4   Liturgical History in the Making:
             The Women's Liturgical Movement   109**

1. Narrating the New   109

2. The Emergence of a Women's Liturgical Movement   111
   2.1. Cultural Context and Social Location   111
   2.2. Birthing a New Liturgical Movement   113

3. The Problem Identified: "Man's Liturgy"   116

   3.1. Women's Liturgical Disillusionment   116

   3.2. A Range of Responses   118

4. Feminist Liturgies: Re-Inventing Women at Worship   121

   4.1. Women as Authoritative Liturgical Subjects   122

   4.2. Liturgical Tradition and Liturgical Innovation   124

      4.2.1. The Tension of Tradition and Crisis   124

      4.2.2. Ritual Recipes   124

      4.2.3. Consciously Contextual   125

      4.2.4. Feminist Liturgies and the Liturgy of Life   126

   4.3. The Pleasure of Symbols   126

      4.3.1. The Ordinary as Sacred   126

      4.3.2. The Redefinition of Sacred Space   128

   4.4. Women's Liturgical Language: Inclusive and Imaginative   129

   4.5. Liturgical Themes: "Women's Experiences"   130

   4.6. Re-Defining (Liturgical) Tradition   133

      4.6.1. Biblical Women   133

      4.6.2. A New Communion of Women Saints and Heroines   135

   4.7. Naming and Confronting Evil   137

   4.8. Healing and Hallowing Creation   139

   4.9. She Who Is Worshiped   140

   4.10. The Feminist Liturgical "Oikoumene"   143

5. Gendered Resistance: The Paradox of the Women's Liturgical
   Movement   143

Epilogue: Worship Beyond Gender?   151

Bibliography   157

Index of Names   176

Preface

I begin this book on women's ways of worship with an act of eucharist. I give thanks and celebrate my communion with

—the women who accompanied me while I was writing this book and remained my friends throughout, especially Ann Hoch, Mary McClintock Fulkerson, Kristin Herzog, Priscilla Pope-Levison, and Carol Voisin;

—the women who offered professional help as well as friendship: Roberta Schaafsma, my friend and wonderfully able reference librarian, and Mary Deasey Collins, my colleague who translated an early draft of the second chapter from German into English, generously read every chapter of this book, and gave me much encouragement on the way;

—Rosanna Panizo, my friend, colleague, teacher (always) and student (sometimes), who continues to break open for me the bread of Latin American Feminist theologies and liturgies.

A special thank you is due David McCarthy, my very able and dedicated graduate assistant. It has been a joy to work with David.

There are many others who generously extended professional help, among them Brother David J. Klingeman, O.S.B., archivist of St. John's Abbey, Collegeville, Minnesota; the staff of the Abbot Vincent Taylor Library of Belmont Abbey, North Carolina; and the women of WATER in Silver Spring, Maryland.

I thank the Divinity School of Duke University and especially its former dean, Dennis M. Campbell, for granting me a sabbatical leave in the fall of 1997. To Russell E. Richey I owe thanks for many years of friendship and for his reading of the first chapter of this book.

Lastly, I include in my eucharistic celebration someone with whom I have shared not only many actual eucharistic liturgies but also some of the other sacraments of life: Peter Ludwig Berger, my son. I dedicate this book to him, in hope.

TERESA BERGER

Introduction

"Women and Worship"—this is the (all too simple) title of two bibliographies that map the burgeoning literature at the intersection of liturgical theology and women's voices.[1] Behind the literature stand not only scholarly interests but also new liturgical practices, namely, a liturgical renewal movement among women that emerged, in the Roman Catholic Church,[2] after the Second Vatican Council. The broader context of the literature mapped by these bibliographies is the recent attention to women as distinct ritual practitioners.

Within the Church alone, to begin with, millions of women worship on any given Sunday. But women can be found at worship much more often than on Sunday mornings. There are women who pray the Liturgy of the Hours and attend Mass daily. Women go on pilgrimage, and women join in Corpus Christi processions. Women gather in Base Ecclesial Communities, and women worship in Feminist liturgy groups. In the lives (and deaths) of individual women a ritual moment can catch worldwide attention. The funeral of Mother Teresa provides a case in point (not to mention the funeral of the supposed woman "icon" of our day just prior to Mother Teresa's). All these incidents exemplify women's manifold ways of worship.

The literature of the two bibliographies referred to above consequently maps a great variety of these ways of worship. As these bibliographies show, scholarly attention to women's ways of worship has burgeoned over the last thirty years. By now this literature constitutes an identifiable sub-field within liturgical studies. Distinct

[1] See Berger, "Women and Worship," 96–110, and "Women and Worship: A Bibliography Continued," 103–117.

[2] For the most part, I confine my exploration of women's ways of worship to my own ecclesial tradition, Roman Catholicism. The justification for this limitation is the sheer wealth of materials, which defy any thought of comprehensiveness.

voices emerge, lines of development become visible, new conceptualizations appear, internal critiques develop, and external critiques are addressed. With all this vibrancy, however, the emphasis in this sub-field clearly lies in the area of contemporary Feminist reconstructions of liturgical practices and concepts. Other areas within liturgical studies remain largely untouched by Feminist reconceptualizations. A quick overview of the literature at the intersection of women and worship shows this development quite clearly. Scholarly interest concentrates on contemporary practice, reflection, and construction.

Particularly noteworthy, on the other hand, is Feminist scholarship's lack of impact on liturgical historiography. In fact, in liturgical historiography, the rift between the traditional liturgical narrative and the ever-growing study of women's history is becoming a noticeable problem. This development does not come as a complete surprise. With the rapid growth of women's studies as an academic discipline in the early 1970s and the first attempts to engage its challenges within liturgical studies in the 1980s, this rift appeared on the horizon. Today the richness of research into women's history is mirrored in only a handful of book-length liturgical studies and a small number of articles.[3] The mainstream narrative of liturgical history remains virtually untouched by the discoveries and revisionings of the new scholarship on women (which itself, unfortunately, has shown a marked disinterest in women's liturgical lives).

This state of affairs is troublesome for the "truth" and credibility of liturgical historiography, and it is increasingly so as the study of women's history unearths more material that challenges the traditional liturgical narrative. The present study seeks to respond to this problem. In addressing the narrative of liturgical history from the perspective of women's ways of worship, this study belongs to the larger sub-field of women's studies within liturgical studies. At the same time, the study responds to a specific lacuna of this sub-field as it has developed so far.

---

[3] See the following books: Procter-Smith, *Women in Shaker Community and Worship: A Feminist Analysis of the Uses of Religious Symbolism* (1985); Berger and Gerhards, *Liturgie und Frauenfrage* (1990); Berger, *Liturgie und Frauenseele. Die Liturgische Bewegung aus der Sicht der Frauenforschung* (1993); Muschiol, *Famula Dei. Zur Liturgie in merowingischen Frauenklöstern* (1994).

In the last analysis, only a continuous narrative of women's ways of worship throughout history will do justice to the challenges of Feminist reconceptualizations to liturgical historiography. Unfortunately, such a narrative, much as it is needed today, remains a project of the future. The present book is a modest beginning that sketches some of the contours of a history of women at worship, both in terms of methodological presuppositions and also in terms of material reconstruction. For the latter, I have chosen two for women's ways of worship crucial examples, namely, the earliest centuries of Christian liturgy and the twentieth-century liturgical renewal.

The earliest centuries of Christianity created dynamics that shaped women's ways of worship for centuries to come. An analysis of these dynamics is imperative for any history of women at worship. With the twentieth century, a new interplay of women and worship developed that fundamentally challenged the traditional liturgical script for women. Narrating this development is another crucial element of any history of women at worship.

Two distinct foci dominate this development in the twentieth century, and we will devote a separate chapter to each. The first focus of liturgical renewal is the classical Liturgical Movement of the first half of the century. The second such focus is a case of "history-in-the-making," namely, the Women's Liturgical Movement, as it emerged in the second half of the twentieth century and affects contemporary liturgical life in manifold ways.

Obviously, many centuries passed between the earliest Christian communities at worship and the twentieth-century liturgical renewal. Although the present study cannot attend to these, I hope to provide, with the time periods I have chosen for my reconstruction, at least the beginnings and the end for a continuous historical narrative of women's ways of worship.

As far as methodological presuppositions are concerned, the first chapter of the book will attend to these. This chapter presents thirteen interpretive strategies for reconstructing women's ways of worship. As such, the chapter clarifies the methodological principles on which the following narrative of women at worship is based.

Chapter 1

Reconstructing Women's Ways of Worship: In Search of Methodological Principles

The starting point for any reconstruction of women's ways of worship is the acknowledgment that, on the one hand, Christian worship has historically been deeply gendered, but that, on the other hand, liturgical historiography has all but ignored this fundamental gender differentiation. This double acknowledgment does not aim at a separate world of women at worship with a concurrent liturgical historiography that puts a "herstory" alongside the traditional histories. Rather, this acknowledgment aims at the revisioning of the whole (*seemingly* un-gendered) mainstream narrative of the liturgy. In other words, the methodological starting point of liturgical historiography from the perspective of women is not to add the previously missing, but to question the shape of liturgical historiography as a whole.

The mainstream historical narrative of the liturgy has been shaped substantially by the invisibility and/or exclusion of women. How "truth"-ful and credible can this narrative be with so much of the Body of Christ (to speak theologically) or the participants in these rites (to speak ritually) missing? The missing, however, cannot be righted simply by adding women here and there into the framework of the traditional narrative. Looking at the history of the liturgy from the perspective of women forces one to look with different lenses than those operative in traditional liturgical historiography. The reconstruction of women's ways of worship, therefore, inevitably entails a certain amount of deconstruction of the established narrative.

Before claiming too much for the "truth" of a women-focused liturgical narrative, let me quickly add the following. All historiography, including a gender-based narrative, is a form of interpretation. Liturgical historiography on the basis of gender analysis, then, is not about the one and only reality of women's ways of worship; it is, rather, a reconstruction of some aspects of women's liturgical lives through the lens of gender analysis. Needless to say, this gender-based reconstruction is a "construct." It is shaped, in the present case, by my own social location (gender included) and its particular strengths and weaknesses. These particulars impact the reconstruction, just as the social location of more traditional liturgical historians impacted their reconstruction (the invisibility of women in past histories of the liturgy is no accident).

It is therefore of crucial importance to make transparent at the beginning the methodological presuppositions that shape a particular narrative. This clarification of interpretive strategies is the task of the present chapter. In what follows, I want to explore thirteen methodological principles[1] of a women-focused liturgical narrative. This exploration of methodological presuppositions provides the immediate preparation for the more material accounts of women's ways of worship in the following chapters.

PRINCIPLE 1: "GENDER" AS AN ANALYTICAL TOOL

Fundamental for the revisioning of liturgical historiography from the perspective of women is the recognition of the category "gender" as an analytical tool. To put it simply, there is no such thing as a generic worshiper. The gender of a worshiper fundamentally shapes that person's liturgical life. Gender here does not primarily refer to a biological fact but to a historically, socially, and discursively constituted reality (which is not to say that "biological fact" is not also socially and discursively constructed).[2]

Obviously, gender is as variable a liturgical category as the different contexts in which it is being "done."[3] The liturgical life of a Roman matron who had become a Christian in the northern town of Colonia Agrippina in the fourth century differed from the liturgical

---

[1] Bradshaw helpfully talks of a set of "proposed interpretative principles" in his *Search for the Origins of Christian Worship*, 63. I am, however, trying hard to avoid constructing a (traditional) "decalogue," as Bradshaw did.

[2] For the liturgy, see Karle, "Nicht mehr Mann noch Frau," 25–35.

[3] See McClintock Fulkerson, "Gender—Being It or Doing It," 188–201.

life of one of the imperial women in Constantinople in the sixth century. Both women worshiped differently than a Chinese convert to the East Syrian Church in the seventh century or than a French woman serf in the thirteenth century did. All these women confronted a liturgy different from that of an Inca woman in sixteenth-century Peru or an African-American slave girl "belonging" to a monastery in the southern United States before the Civil War. And none of these women imagined what some of their daughters in the faith are celebrating today in Feminist liturgical communities.

All this goes to say that the liturgical performance of gender and liturgical gender scripts vary. In light of the widely differing contexts shaping the lives of women at worship throughout history, plural categories will capture the truth of the matter better than any singular one will. There is no one "feminine way of worship," just as there is no such being as a "universal woman" (nor, indeed, is there such a thing as "universal worship"). Women's ways of worship have been shaped in a multitude of ways by geographical location, class, ethnic origin, ecclesial affiliation, time, age, marital status, sexual orientation, etc. Gender constructs and relations, therefore, are complex and fluid categories, in the liturgy as elsewhere. A gender-focused reconstruction of liturgical history, then, has to be conceptualized not on the basis of a simplifying gender dualism; rather, gender is to be seen as one thread—and one that constantly changes color, for that matter—in a whole web of socially constructed relations. It is, though, the one thread in the web that claims most of my attention in the present study.

I have so far interpreted gender analysis in liturgical historiography to mean primarily "women at worship." What about the (gendered) liturgical lives of men throughout history? The most straightforward answer to this question is, very simply, that they are not the subject of this study. This does not mean that a study focusing on both genders or with a gender-specific focus on men at worship would not also be important. But it is not the topic I have chosen to address. At the same time, any form of gender analysis focusing on women will by necessity have to acknowledge that its subject is constituted by the fact that there is an "other," in this case, another gender. Even if poststructuralist Feminist theory has taught one to be wary of stable sexed identities and of gender dualism, much of the liturgy has, historically, been shaped by exactly that way of constructing gender relations. I have therefore chosen to follow this historical pattern in my study.

This does not mean, however, that men at worship can be excluded from the narrative. In the present study, men at worship will necessarily at some points have to accompany women at worship. Three of these points are worth identifying at the outset.

First, some things said about women's liturgical lives apply in some measure to men too. I will, however, usually not spell these out in any detail. One example is the early Church regulations concerning clothes, hairstyle, and make-up for women at worship. To a lesser degree, men's appearance was also subject to gender-specific regulations, but the details of these regulations are not the subject of the present study.

Second, there are gender differentiations operative in worship that can only be described for both genders simultaneously. The genderization of liturgical space is a case in point. Where women found themselves positioned in worship can only be described meaningfully in relation to where men were positioned. At points like these, my narrative obviously has to include both genders.

Third, there are gender-specific constraints in worship that are exclusive to women, such as the taboos surrounding menstruation and birth. Analogues that are gender-specific to men can be found (e.g., liturgical restrictions after nocturnal emissions), but again, a more detailed reconstruction of these analogues must be left to another study. My focus will stay with women at worship.

PRINCIPLE 2: A PREFERENTIAL OPTION FOR LITURGICAL HISTORIOGRAPHY "FROM BELOW"

As women's studies research has amply documented, women do not become visible if (liturgical) history continues to be written as a history of traditional institutions and rites, their male leaders, and their writings, including liturgical texts. This kind of historiography renders women, their institutions and ritualizations, their leadership and their writings (in a broad sense) invisible. Women's studies research has therefore opted for a historiography "from below," focusing particularly on the lives of so-called "ordinary" women.

Even with the new focus on ordinary women's lives and after decades of research in this field, we are still lacking vital pointers to the *liturgical* lives of most women. How, for example, did peasant women in the eleventh and twelfth centuries (when nine-tenths of Christians in the West were peasants[4]) live the liturgy, given their cultural context and horizon of expectations? How did other women worship—beggars, prostitutes, artisans, witches, traveling entertainers, concubines? The reality of their liturgical lives is all but unknown. And what did it mean, for example, for rites around pregnancy and birth in the early Church that five to ten percent of all pregnancies resulted in the death of the mother?[5] Or what did it mean for worship in Carolingian times that the average life-expectancy of women was thirty-six years of age, and only just over one-third of women (compared to fifty-seven percent of men) lived to be forty years old?[6] How was a liturgical assembly shaped by these facts, and how was worship molded by these realities? What did it mean for individual rites?

The questions could be multiplied *ad infinitum*. Nevertheless, as my study will show, there is, despite innumerable lacunae that a gender-based liturgical narrative faces, more than enough material at hand to break the pervasive silence about women at worship in traditional liturgical historiography.

PRINCIPLE 3: A TEMPORARY ABSTENTION FROM NAMING CONSTANTS

It is unhelpful to label the whole of liturgical history "patriarchal" and "oppressive" or to narrate it solely as a history of women's exclusion and invisibility. Claims of such constants of exclusion and invisibility can, of course, function powerfully in expressing women's pains at certain liturgical developments, but they are ultimately not helpful in the actual reconstruction of women's ways of worship.

There are several reasons for this. First of all, these generalizations simply do not correspond to the complex realities of women's ways of worship. Many women consistently and generously inscribed themselves into the liturgy despite its asymmetrically gendered nature and

---

[4] See L'Hermite-Leclercq, "Feudal Order," 230.

[5] See Rousselle, "Body Politics in Ancient Rome," 298f.

[6] See Fonay Wemple, "Women from the Fifth to the Tenth Century," 182.

found space for their encounter with God in, against, despite, and because of the liturgy. However we position ourselves as women at worship today, we need to acknowledge that multitudes of women before us considered themselves grace-fully confronted and nurtured by the Living God in the worship of the Church. A gender-focused reconstruction of liturgical history, then, needs to attend to the intricate ways in which the performances of gender and liturgy have been related rather than leveling these intricacies with quick generalizations.

Second, it is detrimental to the accuracy of a gender-focused narrative of the liturgy to name constants too quickly. Without more sustained research, it is better to abstain from such a naming of constants. Indeed, whether there are any constants and what they might be in a narrative of women's ways of worship seem to be open questions. I say this, having myself argued for such constants some years ago. I had in mind then such seeming universals as women's exclusion from ordained ministries and liturgical consequences of the menstrual taboo.[7] For now, I am more aware of the dangers that an early determining of such constants can entail. Claiming, for example, the exclusion from ordained ministries as such a constant will make it difficult to credit new research that revises the traditional picture of women's exclusion from such ministries.[8] If at all, constants will best be named at the end of a gender-focused reconstruction of liturgical history rather than at its beginning.

Third, defining liturgical history from the outset as oppressive and patriarchal masks ways in which women themselves were accomplices in the liturgical marginalization of other women. A white mistress in the nineteenth-century South, sending her slave girl to the slave gallery during worship, made herself an accomplice in the liturgical marginalization of her African-American slave.

Constants, then, are not immediately obvious in a reconstruction of women's ways of worship. In any case, the specifics of women's liturgical lives throughout history and the claim that these specifics add up to a reality *sui generis* may have to be substantiated along other lines than those of historical constants. Possibly the specifics of

[7] See Berger, *Liturgie und Frauenseele*, 18f.

[8] A good overview of the research can be found in Kraemer, *Her Share of the Blessings*, 183–187.

women's ways of worship are best described as the sum of innumerable liturgical gender performances by women throughout the history of worship. This question, however, will best be decided toward the end of a gender-focused reconstruction of liturgical history. It is too early for theoretical meta-generalizations.

PRINCIPLE 4: RE-CONFIGURING THE CANON OF SOURCES

One of the problems of traditional liturgical historiography when confronted with gender analysis is the accepted canon of sources and their interpretation. Four issues deserve particular attention here.

First, there are few first-hand accounts of the liturgical lives of women that could serve as sources for the construction of a narrative of women's ways of worship. This lack of women's narratives is particularly true for earlier time periods but remains more or less the case until the writings of women in the Women's Liturgical Movement in the second half of the twentieth century.

Second, though, the traditional liturgical sources do yield gender-specific information if only asked to do so. A case in point, chosen rather randomly, is the *Didascalia Apostolorum*. This Syrian Church order of the early third century begins with detailed remarks about gender relations, and just prior to its rules for the ordination of bishops, presbyters, and deacons, provides instructions to women about veiling and the use of public baths.[9] Moreover, the *Didascalia* also contains specifically liturgical material relevant to women's lives. It warns against baptism by women but does accept the liturgical ministries of widows and deaconesses. The example of this Church order shows that traditional liturgical sources can yield gender-specific material if only asked. The same is true for non-liturgical sources. A recent collection of Syrian hagiographic traditions of women gives fascinating glimpses at the liturgical lives of women outside the empire. There is the description of a prostitute's conversion during worship and her subsequent baptism, and accounts of women teaching their daughters the psalms, praying liturgical texts, and reading the Scriptures to other women.[10]

[9] For the latter see Schöllgen, "*Balnea Mixta*," 182–194.
[10] See Brock and Ashbrook Harvey, *Holy Women of the Syrian Orient*, 47–53, 126–128, 155.

There is a third source that a history of women at worship can and must draw on. An example will best illustrate what source I have in mind. Cyprian, bishop of Carthage in the middle of the third century, received a letter from his colleague Firmilian, bishop of Caesarea in Cappadocia. In this letter, Firmilian mentions a woman who baptized and celebrated the Eucharist, using the Church's own liturgical materials:

"And that woman . . . employing a by no means despicable form of invocation . . . would pretend to sanctify the bread and celebrate the Eucharist, and she would offer the sacrifice to the Lord not without the sacred recitation of the wonted ritual formula. And she would baptize many also, adopting the customary and legitimate wording of the baptismal interrogation. And all this she did in such a way that she appeared to deviate in no particular from ecclesiastical discipline."[11]

This and other reports cannot be ignored on the basis of the women mentioned being "heretics." Especially with women's liturgical practices being contested and eyed with suspicion, a reconstruction of women's ways of worship cannot take at face value every designation of women's liturgical practices as "out of order." Firmilian's letter, like many other writings, provides a glimpse of the manifold liturgical lives of women throughout history, and as such this description is a legitimate and important part of a gender-focused reconstruction of liturgical history.

Fourth, there is the importance of both non-classical literary and also non-literary sources for a reconstruction of women's ways of worship. To take the latter first: mosaics, images, statues, but also gravestone inscriptions or devotional objects yield valuable information about the liturgical lives of women that literary sources do not necessarily provide. Epigraphic and papyrological evidence, for example, has been turned to good use recently for a fuller picture of women's ecclesiastical offices in early Christianity.[12]

With the mention of non-classical literary sources I wish to point to the rich resource of women's occasional writings for the reconstruc-

---

[11] Quoted in Jensen, *God's Self-confident Daughters*, 183.
[12] See Ute E. Eisen, *Amtsträgerinnen im frühen Christentum. Epigraphische und literarische Studien* (1996).

tion of women's ways of worship. This resource will become particularly important, for example, when reconstructing the presence of women in the Liturgical Movement. By the first half of the twentieth century, women had gained some access to the world of liturgical writing and publishing. Consequently, brief articles by women appear in pastoral liturgical publications, as well as descriptions of liturgical "experiences," published letters and reflections, leaflets and booklets. All these are a crucial source of information for reconstructing women's presence in the Liturgical Movement.

PRINCIPLE 5: RE-VISIONING
LITURGICAL PERIODIZATION

A different focus and a different lens through which to look at the history of worship (namely, by way of women worshipers) and a redefined canon of sources demand a reassessment of the traditional narrative of liturgical development. Reconstructing the history of the liturgy from the perspective of women means narrating liturgical flourishing and decay, new ritual developments, and traditional ways of worship from an angle different from that of mainstream liturgical historiography.

Two examples from the present study illustrate this point. First, the fourth century in traditional historiography is typically seen as a watershed of liturgical development. With the so-called Constantinian revolution, the Church emerged publicly and its liturgy became a *cultus publicus*. Elaborate rituals flourished, and liturgical celebrations more and more became the ritual focus of surrounding society. This shift in liturgical celebration, however, was deeply—and specifically—problematic for women. Socially, women were mostly connected with the "private" sphere. In an underground liturgy, this private sphere had been privileged as sacred space for the Christian community, but in a public liturgy it was not. On the contrary, what now became sacred space, namely, the public arena of Christian ritual (basilicas, etc.) was a space culturally not immediately hospitable to women. Public space in Greco-Roman times was clearly gendered, and that to the distinct disadvantage of women. If, then, the fourth century was indeed a watershed for worship, it has to be narrated as deeply problematic especially for women worshipers, who found themselves in a cultural context that put considerable constraints on most women's public presence.

A second example involves the assessment of the twentieth-century Liturgical Movement. Was this Liturgical Movement, when viewed from the perspective of women, really the decisive renewal movement it is generally assumed to have been? It did not, after all, challenge the fundamental genderization of the liturgy it sought to renew. How renewing, then, was it for women, for whom the traditional genderization in many ways spelled marginalization? Is not the defining liturgical moment of renewal for women in the twentieth century rather the Women's Liturgical Movement, of which the classical Liturgical Movement then has to be narrated as a precursor? These questions and the two examples as a whole illustrate how a narrative of women's ways of worship evokes suspicion about traditional conceptions of liturgical development.

PRINCIPLE 6: RE-DEFINING RITUAL CENTERS OF GRAVITY

A liturgical narrative focused on women has to locate itself where its subject matter is found. In traditional liturgical historiography, women typically are relegated to the margins of ritual centers of gravity. If women are noted at all in the center of the traditional narrative, they are depicted either as passive recipients of the liturgy of the Church or as troublemakers. This characterization might be an accurate picture when one narrates liturgical history narrowly around the formation of certain key rites (the "key" question, of course, being: whose?). This, however, is a limited and limiting view of liturgical history. Looked at from another vantage point, women become visible as liturgical practitioners in their own right and rite. They assume ritual power and exercise ritual expertise. What I am suggesting here is, of course, that for a history of women at worship, one will have to relocate and redefine what "ritual center" means. The following three examples serve to illustrate this point.

There are, to begin with, liturgical practices which might not have seemed of fundamental importance in traditional historiography but whose significance in the lives of women is clear. I am thinking, for example, of the whole area of pilgrimage and its particular meaning for gender relations. If pilgrimage is read as a moment of suspending the traditional liturgical performance of gender (holy places usually were equally accessible to both men and women), then pilgrimage is one moment when women experience their gender not as a basis for ritual marginalization. In a gender-focused liturgical narrative, this ritual practice will therefore have to come to prominence in ways it did not in the mainstream narrative.

A second example is the whole field of ritual (in the past referred to as "paraliturgical") practices initiated by women. The wealth of devotional initiatives taken by women is astounding, especially since only a few of those practices with time were integrated into the dominant liturgical framework. (I am thinking, for example, of the Feast of Corpus Christi, behind which stand two women, Juliana of Cornillon and Eva of St. Martin.) Suffice it to name but one small example of this wealth of women's devotional initiatives. Teresa Enríquez (d. ca. 1456), a Castilian woman married to a high government official, used much of her influence and money to promote her own particular devotional wishes and initiatives.[13] She pressured even the pope to allow Viaticum to be carried to the sick openly, that is, not hidden under the priest's clothing, as was the custom, but with a *velum*, lit candles, and accompanying attendants. The pope, in granting her request, described Teresa as *ebria sacramenti*, "drunken with the sacrament."[14] Teresa also saw to it that every night a bell would toll to remind the faithful to pray for the souls in purgatory.

But these devotional initiatives are only part of a much larger picture. Teresa endowed monasteries, established hospitals, cared for wounded soldiers, and provided and mended liturgical vestments for poorer parishes. All these initiatives, of course, Teresa Enríquez was able to support through her considerable financial means, her influence by reason of status, and the help available to her through servants.

Teresa is not alone. One could fill volume after volume with (both laudatory and derogatory) accounts of women's liturgical initiatives. Such a regrouping of liturgical materials—not by rite or time or place but by the gender of the practitioner—would quickly provide a new set of ritual centers in the development of the liturgy.

Gender alone, however, is not a sufficient analytical tool. As mentioned above, gender intersects with other cultural practices to form

[13] A brief description of her devotional practices can be found in Dobhan, "Der Name Teresa," 144f.

[14] See Dobhan, "Der Name Teresa," 145.

an intricate web of power relations. Liturgical initiatives of women well illustrate this point. Generally, the more power and influence a woman had, the more likely she was to see her initiative succeed in proximity to the established ecclesiastical center of liturgical gravity. Women on the margins of society and at its root were more likely forced to embody devotional practices distanced from the established center. There were also women's ritual practices, for example in relation to midwifery, that almost routinely caused ecclesiastical suspicion. Ecclesiastical critics then and the traditional liturgical narrative until very recently would label these practices "magical."

This observation leads to another point: With the redefinition of liturgical centers of gravity comes the question whether a liturgical narrative from the perspective of women will want to accept the distinction of ritual practice into "liturgical" on the one hand and "magical" on the other. If the liturgical realm successively marginalizes women, and many women's ritual activities consequently become located "at the margins" of this realm, one may need other ways to describe this ritual "margins-become-center" for women than by naming it "magic." I will suggest in the following chapter that the notion of rival spheres of ritual power is helpful in this context.

A third example of shifting centers of gravity between traditional and gender-based liturgical narratives is women's religious communities. Within a women-focused narrative, these communities take on special significance. They embody, after all, a crucial and intense interplay of women with liturgy. In women's religious communities, "women's liturgies" were celebrated daily and for centuries before such liturgies came to prominence in the wake of the Women's Movement. These religious communities, then, and the women found at worship in them, deserve the sustained attention of a gender-based liturgical narrative.

PRINCIPLE 7: RE-CONSIDERING LITURGICAL PROHIBITIONS

Traditional liturgical scholarship has usually read authoritative-sounding prohibitions as descriptions of what never was allowed to be. In this scenario, liturgical sources, seemingly, constantly guard against women on the brink of transgressing what should never be transgressed. Women seem to be natural liturgical troublemakers.

16

Another, more fruitful interpretation views these prohibitions as pointers to women's liturgical practices that were contested and debated, sometimes repeatedly and at length.[15] These prohibitions, in other words, are attacks on existing practices:

"Regulations provide excellent evidence for what was actually happening in local congregations, not by what is decreed should be done but by what is either directly prohibited or indirectly implied should cease to be done. That such regulations were made at all shows that the very opposite of what they were trying to promote must have been a widespread custom at that period. Synodical assemblies do not usually waste their time either condemning something that is not actually going on or insisting on the firm adherence to some rule that everyone is already observing."[16]

If, then, "legislation is better evidence for what it proposes to prohibit than for what it seeks to promote,"[17] there is manifold evidence for women active in a great variety of liturgical ministries throughout the history of the Church. For example, the continuous insistence by the fourth century on forbidding women to baptize and teach, to enter the sanctuary in ministerial functions, to exorcise, to bless, to anoint, and to heal has to be read as pointing to liturgical functions women did, in fact, exercise. Even if these practices were contested, the very protests against them show that women did baptize and teach, exercise liturgical leadership, exorcise, bless, anoint, and heal. Only at a point when liturgical prohibitions against women's ministries cease and when there are no other indications of such ministries is it legitimate to speculate that women were no longer active in these ministries. How fascinating it would be to write a history of women in liturgical ministry on the basis of all that women have been forbidden to do at various times in the history of the Church. What a rich picture of women's actual liturgical functions such a history would provide!

[15] See Bradshaw, *Search for the Origins of Christian Worship*, 67f. In Bradshaw, though, this interpretation of liturgical prohibitions does not have a gender-specific focus.

[16] Ibid., 69.

[17] Ibid., 68.

PRINCIPLE 8: RE-INTERPRETING
ANTHROPOLOGICAL BASICS

When gender is introduced as an analytical tool, the way in which anthropological basics of worship, such as space and time, have been narrated must be critically assessed. In contrast to traditional constructions of liturgical *time*, a gender-focused liturgical narrative will pay close attention to the markers of time peculiar to women.[18] Women's life cycles are shaped in gender-specific ways by menarche, menstruation, menopause, and, for vast numbers of women, pregnancy, giving birth, and post-birth periods. These gender-specific experiences had a multitude of liturgical consequences, as sources since the third century amply document. In traditional historiography, however, gender-specific shapers of liturgical time do not become visible. In the mainstream liturgical narrative, something like a menstrual taboo in worship would have been noted as an abstruse and isolated incident, if not denied altogether. For much of women's liturgical lives, however, it was of fundamental importance. Menstruation could lead to a delay of a woman's baptism, exclude her from worship at least once a month, deny her a place in proximity to the altar, prevent her from receiving the Eucharist, and stop her from participating in communal prayer with her sisters. It is hard to conceive of many other time factors that had a similar impact on women's ways of worship.

Women-specific markers of time, however, are not the only focus of a gender-based liturgical narrative. Such a narrative also must attend to the traditional markers of time and analyze how these were gendered in particular ways. The lives of men and women historically have differed significantly, and this impacted the way liturgical time was experienced. For a turn-of-the-century, middle-class housewife and mother, for example, a holy day did not necessarily mean a day of rest. In fact, work inside the house tended to increase when work outside the house ceased. There were festive meals to prepare, and that without the help of servants, who had the day off. Husband and children, at home rather than at work or school, had to be attended to. Guests had to be entertained, and the house had to be prepared for that. Worship, when located within the context of such a "holy" day of strenuous domestic

---

[18] Whether women *experience* time differently than men, as some Feminists have claimed, might also be an interesting field of exploration for a women-focused narrative of liturgical time.

work for the woman of the house, takes on a different meaning than it had in the male context of leisure for the same day.

The construction of liturgical *space* in the mainstream narrative also is problematic. The traditional narrative all but leaves invisible the starkly gendered nature of this fundamental aspect of Christian worship. A history of women's ways of worship will have to narrate anew. The construction of the new narrative deserves close attention, since liturgical space is a crucial expression of liturgical ordering, of inscribing liturgical power and privilege. Indeed, if one could choose only one aspect of the liturgy to map women's ways of worship, liturgical space—and particularly the positioning of women relative to the altar—would be a good candidate. I therefore want to sketch here what a gender-focused narrative of this particular spatial arrangement might include.

The earliest Christian communities grew in a cultural context where space was clearly gendered. Initially, Christian communities met in a space typically associated with women, that is, in private homes, and they used that sphere's language, namely family-centered language, to describe themselves. "In church" was synonymous with "in the home." With the fourth century, the Church emerged publicly in a sustained way. But the public sphere of the time was not one inherently hospitable to, and welcoming of, women. A clear indication that Christianity's going public worked to the liturgical disadvantage of women is the fact that women began to find themselves in disadvantaged public worship space. They were, for example, distanced from the altar and the presiding celebrant, in some cases more so than lay men.

With the Middle Ages, a gender-focused narrative of liturgical space becomes difficult to sustain, due in part to increasing diversification depending on geographic and social location, and due in part to the lack of research. Given these constraints, one fact nevertheless is clear: women continued to be distanced spatially from the liturgical center, the sanctuary. If by the thirteenth century women in some monastic communities could not even *see* the altar during the celebration of the Eucharist,[19] this visual dislocation was only one sharp marker of a pervasive trend, namely, to distance women spatially from the center of the liturgy.

[19] For examples, see Bruzelius, "Hearing Is Believing: Clarissan Architecture," 83–91. See also Gilchrist, *Gender and Material Culture*, 104f., 109.

19

There were exceptions to this trend, as usual. We know of women who were sacristans[20] and therefore responsible for ringing bells, for liturgical candles, for the care of the corporals, and for providing hosts. These women sacristans must have had access to the sanctuary. The same applies to a *trésorière* witnessed to in a fourteenth-century manuscript of a Benedictine convent in northeastern France. The manuscript functioned as a liturgical handbook for the "treasurer," who oversaw liturgical ceremonies, choreographed processions and the Easter play, and disposed of altar furnishings. She obviously also had access to the altar and the sacristy.[21]

The examples of these women show that there were exceptions to the distancing of women from the sanctuary. Exceptions for status reasons are later established in the *Pontificale Romanum* (1596). The rule that women must not enter the sanctuary did not apply in the case of the consecration of abbesses, queens, and virgins, or the coronation of a queen. These rare exceptions signal just how pervasive the separation of women and sanctuary had otherwise become. This gender-based spatial separation was in place for almost another four hundred years. It was not called into question until well into the second half of the twentieth century. At that point, however, liturgical space became a focus and marker of the Feminist redefinition of women's place in worship.[22]

PRINCIPLE 9: RESPECTING DIFFERENCES

A gender-focused liturgical narrative must guard against the temptation to read its evidence "universalistically." Even if the canon of sources established by its own reading practices is constituted around the notion of, broadly speaking, liturgical gender performances or, more narrowly, women's ways of worship, what might mean "women" in one liturgical context can differ substantially from "women" in another context. In other words, the suggested constant in a women-specific liturgical narrative must not be allowed to become too constant, if the narrative is to stay true to the diversity of

---

[20] See Moor, "Role of the Female Sacristan Prior to Trent," 306–321, and Gilchrist, *Gender and Material Culture*, 20.

[21] See Hamburger, "Art, Enclosure and the *Cura Monialium*," 119.

[22] See, for example, Kathleen M. Henry's statement that "the altar has come to symbolize patriarchy and hierarchy, for many" (Henry, *The Book of Ours*, V).

women's actual liturgical lives. The seeming constant "woman" will have different meanings in different contexts and, moreover, itself is fluid, depending on status, age, ethnicity, and other factors. A "lady" is a different kind of woman from a "mistress." What being a woman at worship means, then, is not only played out against widely differing cultural contexts but will have different meanings, depending on what other factors shape this "woman being" at a given point in time, what structures she is embedded in, what conflicting issues are present, and, last but not least, how "manhood" is defined at the time.

Even something as women-specific as a menstrual taboo, for example, is never relevant to all women always and everywhere (there is no liturgical Vincentinian canon for women's ways of worship). Girls before menarche, women after menopause, pregnant and anorexic women are personally untouched by liturgical menstrual taboos. Even where actually menstruating women in widely differing contexts are all subject to liturgical menstrual taboos, these taboos might have different meaning and weight within the overall framework of these women's lives.

This can also be true for women within the same cultural context but of differing status within their shared culture. Concretely, the same liturgical menstrual taboo affected an aristocratic woman's liturgical life differently than that of a serf. Although both women might abstain from attending Mass the same Sunday during their menstruation, the aristocratic woman had far more opportunities to "make up" her missing Mass (by traveling a distance a few days later, by attending Mass in a convent she had endowed, by going to her private chapel) than the woman serf, whose liturgical opportunities were essentially tied to the liturgical offerings of her local parish.

In light of all these variables, the best a liturgical narrative of women's ways of worship can hope to be is appropriately cautious, authentically particular, intentionally "non-universal," and able to allow every conceivable difference as well as a fair amount of ambiguity and inconsistency in its own subject matter.

PRINCIPLE 10: RE-GENDERING THE SAINTS

Since this is a vast area of reconstruction of women's ways of worship, suffice it here to sketch some fundamentals. First, there is the simple fact that the Christian liturgy knows liturgical feasts centering on holy women and including readings of women's lives and homilies on women (or "woman"). All these provide liturgical points of gender identification for women in a space that again and again marks their gender as "problematic."

Second, and related to the liturgical veneration of women saints, is the dedication of churches to particular women. Mary, the Mother of God, is the most obvious example, but there are many others. It is worth exploring how these woman-defined churches relate to women's actual lives (for example, are these churches particularly attractive to women worshipers?).

A third area of regendering devotion to the saints is attention to the veneration of particular objects related to women's lives. The robe and cincture of the Virgin Mary in Constantinople, the Virgin's veil, and her milk are examples of woman-specific (secondary) relics. Again, these provide specific points of gender identification for women. Other relics and rituals could be mentioned. The swaddling clothes of Jesus, one of the relics kept at the cathedral of Trier, Germany, probably had an immediacy of relevance to women—in whose hands traditionally lay the care of infants—that it did not have for men. And the ritual of *Kindelwiegen*, the liturgical rocking to sleep of the infant Jesus in an actual cradle as it developed in the Middle Ages, would also generate particular gender identification for women. It comes as no surprise that this ritual was particularly encouraged in women's religious communities.[23]

The type of relics related to women and their lives deserves closer attention. These relics are likely bearers of powerful gender scripts. It is surely no coincidence that the Virgin's *veil* became a focus of attention, that rituals and items associated with child-care turned into devotional foci, and that statues of the pregnant Mary were found particularly in women's communities. These are, at least in part, witnesses to a liturgical sanctification of traditional female roles.

Women saints in the liturgical calendar, the dedication of churches to particular holy women, the veneration of gender-specific objects, and homilies on women—these are all areas of the veneration of women saints that deserve careful mapping in a narrative of women's ways of worship. These aspects of devotion to the saints,

---

[23] See John, "Kindelwiegen," 552–555.

after all, had profound implications for the liturgical lives of women.[24]

I want to lift up, in conclusion, one such implication in particular. Women in the past had a host of gender-specific problems with which usually only heavenly powers could help: infertility, abusive husbands, life-threatening pregnancies, complications at birthing, high infant mortality rates, etc. Before domestic abuse hotlines, infertility treatments, and pediatric emergency rooms, women sought divine intervention as a primary way of responding to the crises in their lives. Asking female saints as well as women friends and relatives for help was a crucial part of a woman's network of support. It is not surprising, then, to find particular women saints called upon for particular "women's problems," and certain places of pilgrimage focusing especially on women's concerns.

PRINCIPLE 11: RE-INTERPRETING LITURGICAL TEXTS

An important task for a gender-focused narrative of the liturgy is the analysis of liturgical texts as gender scripts. This is particularly the case in texts that make women the object of discourse. The traditional liturgy contained many of these, from hymns to the Mother of God to prayers over the bride, from texts in the churching of women to collects on the feast days of women saints.

Even if the relationship between women as objects of discourse and women's actual liturgical practices is not immediate, liturgical texts about women must not be neglected as "imaginary." There are obvious connections, for example, between women being stereotyped as naturally weak and essentially sinful in liturgical texts and women's actual presence in the liturgical assembly being marked as problematic in a variety of ways. Gender analysis reads liturgical texts (and rites) as powerful gender scripts. One example is the traditional nuptial blessing, with its clear message of the subordination of woman to man. Especially in the liturgy with its performative character, there are no "mere" texts; liturgical texts "do," and they make participants "perform" gender roles in powerful ways. A woman veiled, given away by her father, and singled out for special prayer in

[24] Of course, women's devotions to a *male* saint are also gendered in specific ways. For a fascinating example of this, see Robert A. Orsi's study *Thank You, St. Jude: Women's Devotion to the Patron Saint of Hopeless Causes* (1996).

the traditional marriage rite *em-bodied* a position of dependence and weakness.

PRINCIPLE 12: RE-CLAIMING THE LITURGICAL NARRATIVE FOR WOMEN

Lest the traditional liturgical narrative by now seem disposable, I want to emphasize the importance of reclaiming the whole of liturgical history for women. There are two points to this reclamation. The first point involves laying claim even to the "absences," that is, those areas of liturgical history that seem marked by women's "real absence" rather than any form of presence. This is the case, for example, for the development of official liturgical texts, for rites of ordination in later centuries, and for much of liturgical legislation.

Rather than foregoing these areas as part of a women-focused liturgical narrative, however, I suggest reclaiming these absences as crucial forms of liturgical genderization. In other words, the very absence of women in these texts, rites, and legislative practices is an integral and constitutive part of the existence of these practices. Indeed, one could say that wherever women are most absent in liturgy, gender as an issue is most powerfully present.[25] The clearest example of this principle is, in all likelihood, priestly ordination. Where actual women seem most absent, the issue of gender is most virulently present. For a gender-based liturgical narrative, then, women's presence also has to be located in its absence, everywhere.

This introduces the second point, the reclaiming of the whole of liturgical history, traditional elements included, for women. "Our heritage is our power," the artist Judy Chicago claimed in creating her "Dinner Party." Chicago is right in pointing to the empowerment of women through the memory of other women's lives. Her "Dinner Party," however, might suggest that the remaining heritage is "man's." Or, putting this point in the context of the present study, only the women-specific elements of a liturgical narrative would have meaning for women today.

I want to suggest an alternative interpretive strategy, one that envisions and encourages the reclaiming of the whole of liturgical history for women. This interpretive strategy owes its basic conceptualization

[25] My thinking at this point owes much to Briggs, "A History of Our Own," 170–175.

to the theologian Kathryn Tanner.[26] Tanner has recently suggested that on the basis of poststructuralist social theory, the theological enterprise can be understood as a form of cultural struggle over symbolic resources. Translating her insight into the field of liturgical theology, any narrative of liturgical history can be read as a form of struggle over the meaning and organization of the past for the present. This past, however, is never fixed, even if there are dominant interpretations of it in the present. The individual elements of these dominant interpretations are always susceptible to being newly aligned.

A narrative of women's ways of worship, then, does not have to function with the largest possible amount of distance between itself and the traditional narrative. On the contrary, it needs to (re)claim the largest number of elements possible from the traditional narrative and realign them within a gender-based narrative of women's ways of worship. The Eucharist can serve as an example here. Rather than foregoing a Eucharistic focus because of the particular alignment this sacrament has had in the traditional narrative, a Feminist reconstruction will realign the centrality of this sacrament in the life of the Church with central features of its own narrative, for example, the women-specific intensity of Eucharistic devotion.[27]

With this kind of interpretive strategy, the whole of liturgical history is open to being reclaimed as women's heritage, not only overtly women-specific elements in it. This openness, to be sure, is only created in struggle, in "wrestling with the patriarchs."[28] It comes as the result of a contest over meaning, in this case the meaning of the liturgical past for the liturgical present and future.

PRINCIPLE 13: CONTINUING THE
METHODOLOGICAL QUEST

The material exploration in the following chapters is only one side of the continuing quest for a narrative of women's ways of worship.

---

[26] See Tanner, "Social Theory and the Practice of Feminist Theology," 179–197.

[27] Walker Bynum has mapped the Eucharistic devotion of women mystics in the thirteenth century; see her "Women Mystics and Eucharistic Devotion," 119–150. For an earlier example, see Anderson, "Holy Women and the Cult of the Eucharist in the Early Irish Church," 49–107.

[28] This is the title of Lee McGee's book on retrieving women's voices in preaching (1996).

Further work is also needed on the methodological side. For one, criteria will have to be developed to distinguish long-term patterns from short-term occurrences. The fact, for example, that the Celtic Church counted among its places of worship a church where women, together with other female "animals," were denied entry is in all likelihood an isolated incident.[29] Behind this spectacular case, however, lurks a long-term pattern of distancing women from the Holy, which expresses itself in manifold ways throughout the history of the liturgy.

Second, a gender-focused narrative of liturgical history is constantly open to revisioning its own position, particularly in dialogue with refined theories and tools in gender studies or, more specifically, women's studies.[30] Women's studies as a field has experienced vibrantly new conceptualizations of its subject matter ever since it came into being, and there is no reason to think that the field will ossify in the near future. A liturgical narrative in dialogue with women's studies must therefore be open to reconceptualizations in the very process of constructing its own narrative.

In conclusion, gender analysis in liturgical historiography is a multifaceted enterprise, encompassing not only the human beings who worshiped but liturgical time and space, texts and structures of rites, as well as constant reflection on the conceptualization of its subject matter. The present study can only be a beginning. It is by no means an exhaustive account of what a gender-focused liturgical narrative looks like. As such, the study demands a multitude of choices: of time periods, of geography, of rites, of sources, of women to present. Given the many limitations of the project, I at least hope to make transparent along the way why I have made certain choices and why these choices are appropriate ones.

The following two chapters will display how gender analysis reshapes liturgical historiography for two crucial time periods: early Christianity and the twentieth-century Liturgical Movement.

---

[29] See Warren, *Liturgy and Ritual of the Celtic Church*, 136f.

[30] For an intriguing reflection on historiography, see E. A. Clark, "The Lady Vanishes: Dilemmas of a Feminist Historian after the 'Linguistic Turn,'" 1–31.

Chapter 2

Liturgical History Re-Constructed (I): Early Christian Women at Worship

I begin my gendered reading of liturgical history at the point where most histories of the Christian liturgy begin, namely, with the earliest Christian communities of faith. This beginning can be justified not only in terms of chronology but also in relation to the sources. The closer one comes to modern times, the more sources are available to Feminist reconstructions of history. Early Christianity, therefore, is arguably the most difficult time period for a historical narrative of women's ways of worship. It is conceivably also the most crucial, since it is constitutive for the later interplays of ritual and gender in the Church. If the importance of gender analysis can be established for this time period, it will have ramifications for the history of the liturgy as a whole.

The task of reconstructing the liturgical lives of early Christian women has to attend to the social, cultural, and religious context of the earliest Christian communities. For women in these communities, this context is the multifaceted world of women in antiquity. The first female Christians were, after all, initially Jewish, Greek, and Roman women. Their contexts need to be highlighted in a liturgical historiography interested in the women who came to worship the Christian God. Who were they—from the handful of women around Jesus to the hundreds of thousands, even millions, of women in the Church by the fourth century?[1]

---

[1] MacMullen, *Christianizing the Roman Empire*, 85, suggests that there were five million Christians in 312 C.E. If that number is correct, there must have been over two and a half million Christian women at that point in time. Stark, *Rise of*

1. WOMEN AT THE JEWISH ROOTS
OF CHRISTIAN WORSHIP

In most descriptions of the Jewish roots of Christian worship, Jewish women's ritual practices remain all but invisible. The authors tacitly describe Jewish ritual as if the description applies equally to men and women: initiation by circumcision, the twice daily recitation of the *Shema*, the yearly pilgrimage for Passover. Jewish women, however, were not necessarily included in any of these rituals. In rabbinic Judaism, women were technically excused or excluded from the study of Torah, from the annual pilgrimages to Jerusalem, from the recitation of the *Shema*, from putting on phylacteries, etc. It is a mistake to assume that Jewish ritual practices can be described through the religious lives of Jewish males.

To make things worse, most histories of Christian liturgy simply ignore gender-specific ritual practices of Jewish women, such as the separation of dough, the lighting of the Sabbath candles, the ritual purity laws surrounding menstruation and birth, the maintenance of a kosher household, the cleansing of the home for the annual Passover meal, the preparation of the dead for burial. All these practices were religious activities in the hands of women. Many of these ritual practices were located in the domestic sphere; so, too, were the earliest beginnings of Christian worship. It is, therefore, a grave mistake to assume that the domestic (women's) sphere is irrelevant for the development of early Christian worship.

But the ritual lives of many Jewish women were not confined to the domestic sphere alone. Neither are they best described on the basis of rabbinic sources. By the time the earliest Christian communities emerged, most Jews, including Jewish women, lived in the Diaspora. For the Diaspora, however, there is hardly any evidence of the presence of rabbis in Jewish communities. It is not surprising, then, that recent Feminist reconstructions of "women's Judaism"[2] in the Diaspora world show that the lives of Jewish women were varied and

---

Christianity, 3–7, would lead one to estimate the number of women as high as three to four million. Stark's methods of reconstruction, however, have come under severe criticism from some.

[2] See Kraemer's succinct treatment of the subject in her "Jewish Women in the Diaspora World of Late Antiquity," here 48. For women in Palestine, see Ilan, *Jewish Women in Greco-Roman Palestine*, 176–184.

by no means as "domesticized" ritually as had been thought on the basis of rabbinic sources. Jewish women were more frequently present at public religious functions, such as synagogue worship, than rabbinic sources suggest.[3] Women even functioned as synagogue leaders and elders of their communities.[4] And, contrary to previous assumptions, there is no conclusive evidence from antiquity that women and men were spatially separated in synagogue worship.

These complex aspects of Jewish women's ritual lives must be attended to in a description of the Jewish roots of Christian worship. The first women converts to Christianity, after all, were shaped by them. The complexity of Jewish women's ritual lives at the same time falsifies an image of Christianity as the ritual liberator of women over and against Judaism, as some earlier Christian Feminist reconstructions had suggested.

2. THE GRECO-ROMAN CULTURAL MATRIX

Both Judaism and its offspring, Christianity, existed for centuries in the Greco-Roman cultural matrix. Christianity spent its first formative centuries within it. It should therefore not come as a surprise that Christianity has deep roots in the Greco-Roman cultural construction of "woman." The new religion was by no means as innovative regarding women's lives as has previously been imagined. The recent scholarship on women in antiquity has reshaped more traditional perceptions of early Christianity by giving us key insights into the lives of its women, including such data as women's life expectancy, medical problems, marriage patterns, statistics of mothers' death in childbirth, infant mortality, contraception, division of labor, employment, financial dealings, love between women, etc.[5]

Unfortunately, this massive new research on women in early Christianity has all but bypassed the liturgical lives of these women. No prolonged arguments are needed, however, to establish that the details of Greco-Roman women's lives influenced the worship of the Church. They shaped, after all, the lives of at least half of the

[3] See Kraemer, *Her Share of the Blessings*, 106–127.

[4] See Bernadette J. Brooten's ground-breaking study, *Women Leaders in the Ancient Synagogue* (1982).

[5] For a survey, see, for example, Rousselle, "Body Politics in Ancient Rome," 296–336.

Christian worshipers. The new scholarship on women in antiquity has shown, for example, that there was no generic "Greco-Roman woman." The differences of status, between, say, an aristocratic Roman matron and a "foreign" slave girl were stark. What happened when both the influential, affluent, educated matron and her powerless, illiterate slave attended a Christian worship service is a good question! We do not have the answers yet. The one unifying element in the lives of both these women was that no woman was perceived as equal to a man of her status.[6]

The *ritual* practices of non-Christian women in antiquity are obviously of particular interest for a history of Christian women at worship. The situation is complex and defies facile categorization. In ancient Greece, religious observance was the one public activity in which women could participate in Greek society. They were excluded, however, from blood sacrifices. At the same time, we know of the existence of women priests in ancient Greece.[7]

In the Roman Empire, women were excluded (with exceptions, for example, the vestal virgins) from presiding at public priestly functions and sacrifices.[8] They were, however, obliged to participate in the imperial cult. Rituals within the home were largely in the hands of the *pater familias*, although women were expected to take an active role in these domestic devotions. The gods of the house might well include female figures, for example Fortune, in front of whose stone statue women would pray.[9] There were also rituals specific to women, often connected to fertility, pregnancy, and birth. And a wide array of different "exotic" cults, myths, and rituals was present in the Roman Empire. Some of these had a distinctively female following. The popular cult of the Egyptian goddess Isis is a case in point.[10] A description of an elaborately choreographed procession in honor of Isis gives us a very lively picture of this worship of a goddess. The

[6] See Sawyer, *Women and Religion in the First Christian Centuries*, 31.

[7] See Bruit Zaidman, "Pandora's Daughters and Rituals in Grecian Cities," 338–376.

[8] See Scheid, "Religious Roles of Roman Women," 377–408.

[9] The Christian hymn writer Prudentius (348–ca. 410) describes such a scene in the first book of his *Contra Symmachum*.

[10] See, for example, Reginald E. Witt's study *Isis in the Ancient World* (1971, 1997).

description comes from the second-century author Apuleius of Madaura. Apuleius describes the procession as follows:

"At the head [of the procession] walked women crowned with flowers, who pulled more flowers out of the folds of their beautiful white dresses and scattered them along the road; their joy in the Saviouress appeared in every gesture. Next came women with polished mirrors tied to the backs of their heads, which gave all who followed the illusion of coming to meet the Goddess, rather than marching before her. Next, a party of women with ivory combs in their hands who made a pantomime of combing the Goddess' royal hair, and another party with bottles of perfume who sprinkled the road with balsam and other precious perfumes; and behind these a mixed company of women and men who addressed the Goddess as 'Daughter of the Stars' and propitiated her by carrying every sort of light—lamps, torches, wax candles and so forth. . . . Then followed a great crowd of the Goddess' initiates, men and women of all classes and every age, their pure white linen clothes shining brightly. The women wore their hair tied up in glossy coils under gauze head-dresses; the men's heads were completely shaven, representing the Goddess' bright earthly stars, and they carried rattles of brass, silver and even gold, which kept up shrill and ceaseless tingling."[11]

It is tempting to wonder what Christian women did with a procession like this. Would they have known? Yes, this was a public event. Would they have been horrified? Yes, in all likelihood. This was "idolatry." Would they have cared to watch? Probably not, at least not with a good conscience. But possibly they did. Some writers of the time (Tertullian is a good example) castigate Christians for attending the theater, the circus, gladiatorial fights, and chariot races. Were there women in the Christian communities who had come from such ritual traditions as the cult of Isis? There must have been. The women who became Christians at this time did not come from a "ritual no woman's land"; there was no such thing.

Looking at one key city of earliest Christianity, Philippi,[12] we are confronted with a number of women-oriented ritual traditions from

[11] Quoted in Fantham's sourcebook *Women in the Classical World*, 382.

[12] The detailed reconstruction by Lilian Portefaix is of fundamental importance here; see Portefaix, *Sisters Rejoice*, esp. 126–128.

which non-Jewish converts to Christianity would have come. Women at worship in Philippi would have been particularly involved in the cults of Diana, Dionysius (a priestess was in charge of his local oracle), and Isis. With what ritual heritage and expectations would Philippian women have become Christians, and how did their backgrounds shape their Christian liturgical lives? At this point the only answers to these questions are informed guesses.

The ritual lives of Greco-Roman women, as will be evident from the above, spanned a broad spectrum, from the state religion on the one hand to non-Roman religions on the other.[13] The spectrum was fluid, as the fate of Christianity itself best illustrates. Christianity started as a small non-Roman religion in a corner of the empire and by the fourth century had become the state religion. Women were found at worship throughout this development.

3. WOMEN IN THE EARLIEST CHRISTIAN COMMUNITIES

Early Christian liturgy was celebrated in and shaped by the Greco-Roman cultural context. How will a liturgical history from the perspective of women, conscious of this context, narrate the development of the liturgy in this time period? There is at least some material available for a history of women at worship in the earliest centuries of Christian liturgy. But the data is incomplete, diverse, sometimes contradictory and, above all, in need of a systematic treatment. My sketching of the first contours of such a systematic treatment is as follows.

3.1. Inclusive Initiation

The earliest Christian liturgical assemblies were made up, unquestioningly, of both women and men. The same rite, baptism, initiated all into the community of faith. It is worth noting that this basic initiation rite into the worship of the Church was powerfully inclusive of both genders. Christian communities did not practice gender-specific or gender-exclusive initiation. The baptismal confession in Galatians 3:28 is a reminder of this: "There is no longer Jew or Greek, there is no longer slave or free, there is no longer male and female; for all of you are one in Christ Jesus." In other words, in Christian

---

[13] See Sawyer, *Women and Religion in the First Christian Centuries*, 128.

baptism, race, status, gender, and marital status become dethroned as fundamental markers of identity for the Christian assembly.

3.2. Women's Space as Liturgical Space

Another characteristic feature of early Christian worship is worth noting. The earliest ecclesial and therefore liturgical space was women's space. "The home, a domain traditionally associated with women, was the place where the *ekklesia* gathered."[14] This particular gathering space was home to Christian communities for well over two hundred years, until the middle or end of the third century.[15] It was a context congenial to the active participation and leadership of women. Women formed new churches in their homes and functioned as heads of these house churches.

This development was certainly aided by the existence of the particular form of the private "household workshop," that is, extended households that could include shops, some of them the workplace of women (wooldressing, embroidery, hairdressing, beautification, gold-leaf and ivory work, etc.). These household workshops were "an important arena for conversion in early Christianity [that] facilitated the work of women evangelists."[16] In fact, pagan opinion of earliest Christianity connects the new religion in a particular way with women's spaces, as Margaret MacDonald has recently shown:

". . . early Christianity is [seen as] a religion of women's spaces. Religion which should properly be tied to the public domain of men has become privatized and feminized. Church groups are offensive because in them the public sphere is swallowed up by the private and women play a major role in defining the new ethos. The true purpose of the home is negated when it shelters church meetings and male responsibilities in public affairs are ignored or subverted."[17]

The earliest Christian liturgies, then, were celebrated in what the cultural context considered "women's spaces." The other side of this coin is the fact that some early Christian women left their own

---

[14] MacDonald, *Early Christian Women and Pagan Opinion*, 217.

[15] See Snyder, *Ante Pacem*, 166.

[16] MacDonald, *Early Christian Women and Pagan Opinion*, 121.

[17] MacDonald, *Early Christian Women and Pagan Opinion*, 112f. Mattila, "Where Women Sat," 268f., challenges the view of the house church as a private space.

domestic spheres behind for various forms of ministry. The New Testament mention of Phoebe and the narrative of Thecla serve as two examples. These women crossed boundaries into the predominantly male world of public space, a crossing that soon became contested.

3.3. Christian Table Practice: Gender-Inclusive and/yet Gendered?

Initiation into the Christian community and the space in which this community gathered were hospitable to women. But what happened when the community actually gathered, especially when it shared its festive meal? What about the table practice of the earliest Christian communities? From all we know, this table practice was clearly gender-inclusive. Women were not excluded from the Eucharistic meal because of their gender. How far the earliest Christian meal practices nevertheless were gendered in particular ways is another question.

On the basis of earliest Christian sources alone, this question is impossible to answer. These sources simply do not yield any information on elements of genderization in earliest Eucharistic practices. In fact, the only clues of possible forms of genderization come from the wider social context. At the time the earliest Christian communities came into being, Greco-Roman meal practices had undergone some significant changes. Formal public meals were beginning to make room for the presence of women, that is, women other than the musicians, dancers, and prostitutes who would customarily have been present at a banquet with men anyway.[18] Social criticism of women's presence at banquets continued nevertheless, largely making an association between women's presence and the entertainment of men: "Women associated with banquet settings were seen in the popular imagination as prostitutes."[19]

If, indeed, the earliest Christian communities adapted wider Greco-Roman meal traditions for their own gatherings, the inclusion of women at the Christian table needs to be assessed in that light. This inclusion of women would have been noteworthy and "progressive" for the surrounding culture but not unique.[20] It was shared, for

[18] I am indebted to Kathleen E. Corley's research here; see her *Private Women, Public Meals: Social Conflict in the Synoptic Tradition* (1993).

[19] Ibid., 63.

[20] See ibid., 24.

example, with some Roman groups and with Hellenistic Jewish communities. Nevertheless, this inclusion of women at the Christian table was noteworthy enough for Christians to come to some public attention for sharing meals together.

Another example of interpreting earliest Christian meal traditions in their social context and through the lens of gender comes with the question of table etiquette, particularly of seating practices and seating patterns. Did women at Christian meals simply do what women did at meals in the Greco-Roman world? Did married women sit at their husbands' feet, as was the social etiquette? Did the women recline, as the men did? Did they recline separately? These issues are not discussed in earliest Christian literature. Should we therefore assume that Christians followed standard practice? After all, if they had introduced novel, highly unusual and contested practices, this break with tradition would have left traces.

An interesting light is thrown on these questions by a fresco in the Catacomb of Priscilla in Rome. The late first-century fresco shows seven women (no figure is clearly male) reclining together at a Eucharistic (?) meal.[21] Rather than this being a proto-Feminist group, it is probably a witness to the Greco-Roman meal practice of separate seating for men and women. Other frescos that show only men at the (Eucharistic) meal would support this. Possibly we have here the roots of the later stark genderization of liturgical space. The roots would then lie in the Christian acceptance of Greco-Roman meal etiquette as a formative factor in the development of the Eucharistic liturgy.

In conclusion, and with the caveat that we clearly have more questions than answers, earliest Christian table practice appears to have been both gender-inclusive *and* gendered in particular ways. Women were not excluded from the Eucharistic meal, but the seating arrangements at these meals probably had gender-specific features. To put it differently, the earliest Christian communities were not simply women-friendly, liberating, or proto-Feminist, as might appear when one first looks at issues like worship space and initiation into the community. In fact, at the heart of the Christian assembly, namely,

[21] For more, see Irvin, "Ministry of Women in the Early Church: The Archaeological Evidence," 76–86.

the Eucharistic meal, forms of genderization appear to be present from the start.

3.4. Gender Differentiation in Worship

Moreover, already in the New Testament we find indications of gender-specific liturgical regulations asymmetrically curbing the activities of women. Women were counseled not to abandon women-specific attire during prayer and prophecy (1 Cor 11:2-16). There were prescriptions regarding women's dress, coiffure, and jewelry, and exhortations to women on keeping silent in church (1 Tim 2:9-12). These prescriptions for women's presence at worship give us first glimpses at the importance of gender differentiation in worship.[22] They take on added significance against the background of the assembly as such being gender-inclusive. Some of the earliest communities obviously perceived a need clearly to differentiate men and women while uniting them in worship. It was women who bore the burden of the differentiation. This differentiation functioned more and more as a means of enforcing gender boundaries to the liturgical disadvantage of women. There is, to put it differently, evidence of a "liturgical muting" of women within the New Testament itself. Moreover, early evidence from other sources indicates suspicion surrounding the presence of women at Christian celebrations, a presence (together with men) that was viewed as not respectable.[23]

There is, however, no trace of women being excluded from such fundamentals of early Christian worship as the Sunday assembly, fasting, the breaking of the bread, or penitence. Regionally, these liturgical fundamentals were shaped in different ways. The liturgical lives of affluent women in the ancient metropolis of Rome were bound to differ from the liturgical lives of Jewish-Christian women in rural areas of Palestine.

---

[22] Schüssler Fiorenza, *In Memory of Her*, 230, however, reads 1 Corinthians 11:2-16 not as a reinforcement of gender differentiation, but as encouragement of the order and missionary character of the community. For a fascinating account of veiling as "prophylactic" in 1 Corinthians 11, see Martin, *Corinthian Body*, 229–249.

[23] See MacDonald, *Early Christian Women and Pagan Opinion*, 56.

3.5. Women's Liturgical Ministries

One key issue for a reconstruction of women at worship in the earliest Christian communities is the question of liturgical ministries.[24] There is a growing consensus now that in the New Testament women exercised a number of leadership functions, such as deacons, patrons of house churches, apostles, and missionaries.[25] Most historians of the liturgy do not reflect this growing consensus in their reconstruction of earliest Christianity. They will mention the development of the threefold office of deacon, presbyter, and bishop, and leave it at that. Many ignore the offices of widows and deaconesses, clearly attested to in the East by the third century (*Didascalia Apostolorum* 3; for deaconesses, the *Apostolic Constitutions* offers a prayer of ordination, ca. 380 C.E.).

For a history of women at worship, widows and deaconesses are of particular interest. They held a variety of liturgical functions (depending on geographic location and time), such as doorkeepers, ushers, overseers of other women at worship, and assistants at baptism. The prebaptismal anointing and postbaptismal instruction of women could be in the hands of a deaconess. Widows might have pastoral care of sick women, including prayer and laying on of hands. Tertullian reports that penitents seeking reconciliation would prostrate themselves in the center of the assembly before the widows and presbyters (*De pudicitia* 13,7). Widows, therefore, could—due to their privileged seating (?)—play a liturgical role in rites that in themselves were not focused on them.

Another point is worth mentioning here. When looking at women in prominent liturgical ministries in the earliest communities, it is important to consider the realities of social status of these women in ministry. Take as an example the earliest non-Christian reference to specifically Christian women.[26] It is found in the Governor Pliny's letter to Emperor Trajan, written around 110 C.E. Pliny describes his

[24] A book outdated in many of its interpretations and conclusions but nevertheless worth consulting because of the breadth of materials collected is Roger Gryson's *The Ministry of Women in the Early Church* (1976).

[25] The literature on the subject is substantial. Suffice it here to point to the magisterial study by Elisabeth Schüssler Fiorenza, *In Memory of Her*, 160–204.

[26] For a closer look at this letter, see MacDonald, *Early Christian Women and Pagan Opinion*, 51–59.

torture of two slave women who were "ministers" (*ministrae*), that is, they had prominent ministerial roles in the Christian community. Their slave status apparently was not a problem for the community (there is some ambiguity, though, in the differentiation between slave women, freedwomen, and freeborn working women in sources of the time).

When one realizes the specific situation of female slaves in the Greco-Roman world, the status of *ministra* in a Christian community is noteworthy. It implies a stark "status dissonance" for these women. In their daily lives they were legal nonentities. Both their labor and their bodies belonged to their masters, as did their children. For these women to rise to prominence within a Christian community involved a change of status that is hard to fathom. It speaks for the Christian community to which these slaves belonged that neither gender nor status indicators prevented its members from accepting the ministries of these women.

3.6. Feminine Imagery in the Liturgy

One last field of inquiry for a history of women at worship in earliest Christianity is worth mentioning. It is the vast domain of feminine imagery in connection with liturgical practices. Particularly noteworthy is baptism, which was associated early on with the image of birth (e.g., John 3:3-7). In the early Syrian and Armenian baptismal traditions, the Holy Spirit is imaged as mother.[27] The Eucharist also attracted feminine imagery. It was imaged as God's milk, with Jesus Christ as the nursing breasts of the Father. The liturgical practice of the benediction of a chalice with milk and honey for the neophytes at the baptismal Eucharist (in Egypt, North Africa, and Rome) is a ritual expression of this image.[28] This image and its ritual expression are particularly significant, since the metaphor of nursing for the saving activity of a deity is present in one of the women-centered ritual traditions surrounding early Christianity, the worship of Isis.[29]

[27] For more, see Winkler, "Überlegungen zum Gottesgeist als mütterlichem Prinzip," 7–29.

[28] See Betz, "Eucharistie als Gottes Milch in frühchristlicher Sicht," 1–26, 167–185.

[29] Gail Paterson Corrington has pursued this subject further in "The Milk of Salvation: Redemption by the Mother in Late Antiquity and Early Christianity," 393–420.

Not only were individual Christian rites associated with feminine imagery but the Church itself was routinely represented through such imagery. The most widely used symbol in emerging Christian art was a female figure with arms stretched above her head in prayer, the *Orante*.[30] Christianity took over this symbol from the surrounding culture but gave it an ecclesial and liturgical orientation. The *Orante* stood no longer simply for *pietas* but for the Christian Church at worship. That this Church mirrored itself in the image of a woman at prayer is worth noting.

Feminine imagery for liturgical realities became an influential part of liturgical tradition throughout the centuries. We do well to attend to its earliest beginnings in this time period. Care, of course, has to be exercised when interpreting this imagery. It does not necessarily reflect or embody existing gender relations and should not be read as such. On the other hand, liturgical imagery and liturgical reality are intertwined in myriad ways and may never completely be separable.

4. "PATRIARCHAL" OR "LIBERATING"?

So much for basic elements of a reconstruction of the liturgical lives of women in the earliest Christian communities. Clearly, any facile label such as "liberating" on the one hand, or "patriarchal" on the other, does not do justice to the complex realities of women's liturgical lives in the earliest Christian communities. This judgment holds especially true if one takes into account the varying ritual traditions from which women became Christians and the status these women occupied in the larger society. For a slave girl to take up a leadership position within a Christian community certainly spelled forms of freedom and ritual authority she had not known. For her mistress to join the same Christian community might have meant losing some of the authority and status she had within her own domestic community. On the other hand, for a slave woman to attend Christian gatherings did not add much in terms of her freedom of movement outside of the domestic sphere. For her mistress, the opportunities to go out in public were more restricted. Attending a Christian gathering, therefore, posed peculiar problems for her but also enlarged her range of movement.

---

[30] The literature is vast. For a summary, see Snyder, *Ante Pacem*, 19f.

Being part of a Christian community at worship, then, meant different things to different women in earliest Christianity. This, however, does not negate gender-specific shapers of worship in these communities. These shapers became much more explicit as time went on. The following reconstruction of women at worship in the Church of the empire will show this.

5. WOMEN AT WORSHIP IN THE CHURCH OF THE EMPIRE

The second phase in traditional histories of the liturgy typically came with the development of worship in the "Church of the empire," that is, in the decades and centuries immediately following the emperor Constantine. Beginning with Constantine, Christianity became the dominant religious power in the Roman Empire. It thereby also became the dominant ritual context for women.[31] With this ascendancy to dominance came a number of significant shifts in the liturgical lives of Christian women. In what follows, I will highlight ten areas of particular importance in shaping the ritual lives of women in this time period.

5.1. Women as Liturgical Practitioners

5.1.1. Increasing Liturgical Marginalization

Of fundamental importance is the issue of women as subjects and agents of liturgical celebration. What did women actually do in worship in the Church of the empire? Where were they active subjects and participants in the liturgy? These questions are not easy to answer.

A first key task toward the formulation of an answer is the collection of possible shreds of evidence from differing cultural contexts across the empire and beyond. The contours of the picture emerging from these shreds of evidence point in the following direction: in the Church of the empire, we witness an increasingly diverse liturgical marginalization of women. Pointers to this growing marginalization are the demise of specifically female liturgical ministries in some

[31] Two points, beyond the characteristics of Roman women's lives, deserve more attention than I can give here: first, the lives of women in the Germanic tribes that gained growing influence in the West; and second, the lives of women in the East (including Christian women beyond the confines of the empire, for example, Coptic, Syrian, and Armenian women).

40

areas (widows and deaconesses), the exclusion of women from the sanctuary and ministries in proximity to it, the growing front against liturgical singing by women, the diversification of forms of menstrual, sexual, and birthing taboos, an intensification of the (quite literal) silencing of women in worship, and elaborate regulations surrounding women's presence at worship. Taken together, these elements add up to a picture of a growing asymmetrical genderization of worship in the Church of the empire, a genderization to the ritual disadvantage of women. As mentioned before, if liturgical historiography from the perspective of women sees a need to reconfigure traditional ways of periodization, here is a prime candidate for a key element in the reconfiguration.

An area worth investigating further at another point is the role of women in Christian domestic devotions and private prayers. Was there a genderization of these devotional practices similar to the one that occurred in public worship? Was the domestic singing of psalms and hymns, daily prayer, and meditation on the Scriptures influenced and shaped by the gender of the Christian engaged in them? And if not, why did public worship become gendered in particular ways while domestic devotions did not? Was the "publicity" of worship the reason for its more starkly gendered nature?

5.1.2. Increasing Liturgical Genderization

The question of women as subjects of liturgical celebration cannot be treated negatively alone. Worship in the Church of the empire continued to see women included in baptism, public prayer, the Sunday assembly, fasting, the Eucharist, and penitence. There are indications, though, of some of these liturgical fundamentals being gendered in particular ways, and this even well before the Constantinian revolution. Baptism is a case in point. Women were, of course, baptized. But, to simply take the *Traditio Apostolica* as an example here, women were baptized after the men, not during their menstruation, and with gender-specific instructions, such as to unloose their hair prior to their baptism. In other words, the baptism of a woman followed a different choreography than the baptism of a man. How much this was also true of other rites is difficult to ascertain for this time period. Nevertheless, a detailed reconstruction of the genderization of seemingly gender-neutral liturgical rites will be one of the fundamental tasks of an in-depth history of women at worship.

5.1.3. Discerning Women in Worship

As regards women as liturgical practitioners, there is evidence by the sixth century of women becoming the focus of liturgical rites that were openly and intentionally gender-specific. This was the case, for example, in the veiling of the bride during nuptials, in the nuptial blessing, and in the veiling of virgins. It was also the case for the so-called churching of women, a rite marking the end of a woman's period of abstention from worship after having given birth. The earliest extant texts for the rite come from the Middle Ages, but its roots lie in taboos surrounding birth as witnessed to in much earlier Jewish and Christian writings.

These examples show that "discerning women in worship" must not be equated with women becoming liturgical subjects in their own right and with their own ritual power. In the women-specific ritual elements that developed, for example, in Christian marriage, woman was the focus of attention as the subordinate and weaker one who needed special prayer. And in the rite of churching, a woman who had given birth was essentially seen as in need of "purification," and therefore in need of a specific liturgical rite centering on her. Ritual significance, then, must not be equated with ritual power in the hands of women. On the contrary, the ritual significance of women is not incompatible with a position of disempowerment.

But women were also explicit subjects and agents of liturgical celebrations on their own initiative. This was the case, for example, when they themselves organized public prayers and vigils in time of war.[32] Other, easily overlooked references must be noted here. The Arabic version of the *Canones Apostolorum*, an (Egyptian?) Church order of the end of the third century, for example, knows of women lectors (can. 53) as well as deaconesses and subdeaconesses. Syrian Monophysites in the fifth century had "diaconal abbesses" who, in the absence of a priest, gave the Eucharist to their sisters and to children. At non-Eucharistic celebrations in their monastic communities, these diaconal abbesses read the epistle and the gospel.[33]

[32] See Muschiol, *Famula Dei*, 55.
[33] See Ansorge, "Diakonat der Frau," 40.

42

These examples may, of course, be dismissed as isolated incidents in corners of the Roman Empire and beyond. But every detail of women at worship contributes to our better understanding of the liturgical lives of Christian women throughout history. Attending to these details also prevents from oversimplification, as if women at worship were a uniform reality. Rather, we are confronted with a broad spectrum of possibilities of women as liturgical practitioners, and the two ends of the spectrum may not even be in sight yet.

5.1.4. Liturgical Prohibitions and Practices

Another area of women's liturgical practices emerges if all the negative exhortations are read as pointers to existing practices. These exhortations yield a picture of women teaching, baptizing, presiding and otherwise ministering at liturgical celebrations, healing, exorcising, receiving confessions, and absolving. Of course, early Christian writers frequently connected these activities with "heretical" groups. But there were enough prohibitions of such ritual activities by women also within the narrower confines of the Church Catholic to prevent us from linking women's liturgical activities primarily with communities "on the fringes."

Taking negative exhortations concerning women's exercise of ritual power as pointers to actual practices is especially justified if other supporting evidence for such practices can be found. In the case of women as agents of baptism, for example, we have the story of an Antiochene martyr named Sara. Sara is supposed to have died during the Diocletian persecutions at the turn of the third century. Her story is told in the Arabic-Jacobite *synaxarion*, that is, a liturgical book containing hagiographical writings for reading in worship. The narrative of Sara in essence attempts to validate a woman's baptism by depicting God as the author of the act. Sara, the wife of a non-Christian husband who did not want to see his children received into the Church, baptizes her two children in an emergency, during a storm at sea (which God is seen as bringing about). The story describes the baptism in great detail. Sara prays, then makes the sign of the cross on the foreheads of her children and over their hearts with her own blood. She then dips the children into the seawater, baptizing them in the name of the Father, the Son, and the Holy Spirit. When a bishop later on tries to baptize the children, God validates

Sara's baptism by letting the water freeze, thus preventing the bishop from attempting baptism.[34]

Whatever the historical merits of the story of Sara's baptism of her children, the fact that such a story was told is one indicator (we have others) of the struggle surrounding the issue of women baptizing. The story of Sara is one that clearly wants to validate such a baptism, since it depicts Godself as initiating it.

As will be obvious, the subject of women as liturgical practitioners in the Church of the empire is a complex one. Three trends, though, are clear. There is growing liturgical marginalization, growing liturgical genderization, and growing contestation surrounding liturgical practices by women. What follows will provide further illustration of these features of women at worship in the decades and centuries following Constantine.

5.2. Women's Liturgical Patronage

A second subject matter shaping the liturgical lives of women develops naturally from the first. Women's influence on the liturgy in this time period tended to crystallize around other points than ministerial leadership functions. One such point of influence was women's patronage and giving.[35] This obviously was primarily the domain of affluent and influential women such as Helena (d. 330), the mother of Emperor Constantine, who financed the building and decoration of numerous churches in Palestine and Asia Minor, or the Empress Galla Placidia (d. 450), whose name is forever connected with churches in Ravenna, or the Empress Pulcheria (d. 453), who had churches built and decorated, and donated liturgical vessels and vestments.

The growing visibility of women's liturgical patronage and giving has to be located in its proper social context. Two points are of importance here. First of all, women's patronage was nothing new in the Church of the empire. We know of women as patrons of ecclesial communities from the earliest times (that is, of house churches). Second, though, with the Christianization of the Roman aristocracy,

[34] The story is narrated and interpreted by Synek, *Heilige Frauen der frühen Christenheit*, 191–198.

[35] See E. A. Clark, "Patrons, Not Priests: Gender and Power in Late Ancient Christianity," 253–273.

affluent and influential women joined the Church, and that at a point in time when traditional avenues for patronage were closing for these women (patronage began to be linked to high governmental offices, from which women were excluded). The Church and its liturgy benefited from this, since they became primary recipients of women's patronage. This patronage was especially generous, for many of the aristocratic women had embraced an ascetic lifestyle that encouraged them to renounce their possessions. As Elizabeth Clark puts it:

"The almost-unimaginable wealth of some of these aristocrats-turned-ascetics (recall that . . . Melania the Younger's annual income—not her entire fortune, to be sure—could have supported 29,000 persons for a year) was enthusiastically accepted by the Church, which with the expansion of Christianity in the post-Constantinian era and with the burgeoning ascetic movement, needed extensive income for its charity and construction operations."[36]

One particular area of women's liturgical patronage was the growing veneration of the saints. Examples abound of affluent women using their power and influence to "maneuver" a saint. It suffices to name three such examples here. The wealthy Pompeiana in 295 C.E. obtained the body of the martyred Maximilianus and initially kept it in her own home. Later on she buried the martyr's body in Carthage, in close proximity to her own future grave. Roughly a decade later, another wealthy Christian woman named Asclepia built a shrine above the grave of a martyr in Salona, Dalmatia. The building was designed to hold her own tomb also. And a Spanish aristocrat living in Carthage in the early fourth century, by the name of Lucilla, owned the bone of a martyr. Lucilla had developed the devotional practice of kissing this bone before receiving the Eucharist. At one point a deacon rebuked her for this practice, which she subsequently stopped.[37]

Ecclesiastical authorities were trying to prevent these various forms of individualistic patronage that placed the control of "liturgical

[36] E. A. Clark, "Ideology, History, and the Construction of 'Woman' in Late Ancient Christianity," 179.

[37] Peter Brown narrates and interprets these examples in his well-known *Cult of the Saints*, 33f.

material," in this case relics, in the hands of wealthy patrons. But priests and bishops did encourage wealthy women to take an active part in the liturgical veneration of the saints—under the control of ecclesiastical authorities. Bishops needed this kind of wealthy patrons to celebrate with increasing ceremonial splendor the liturgy of the Church of the empire. It is telling that the nickname of one of the bishops of Rome, Damasus (d. 384), came to be *auriscalpius matronarum*: "The Ear-Tickler of Noble Ladies."[38]

As far as women's liturgical patronage is concerned, we know of gifts also from non-aristocratic and non-affluent women, particularly widows.[39] The question as to whether there were gender-specific interests in liturgical giving (e.g., as far as patron saints were concerned, specific relics, the subject matter of mosaics, architectural particulars, etc.) deserves further attention. From what we know, gender-specific liturgical gifts are indeed discernible. There is, for example, mention again and again of women donating fabric and clothes. The production of these in antiquity lay almost exclusively in the hands of women. Indeed, in Greek the term "women's work" refers not to housework but to fabric-making, which included spinning, weaving, and decorating cloth.[40] The ritual importance of fabric as the possession of women should not be underestimated: "A splendid robe was a woman's most natural gift to a god."[41] The fabrics donated by Christian women were used liturgically, for example, for altar coverings and hangings.[42] But we also know of clerics having (liturgical?) vestments made for themselves and cleaned by women,[43] a form of "participation" in the liturgy that for centuries quite literally was in women's hands.

5.3. Women in a Liturgy Gone Public

A third and crucial area is that of worship as a *public* space for women in early Christianity. For understanding the importance of

[38] Quoted by Brown, *Cult of the Saints*, 36.

[39] See Krause, *Witwen und Waisen im frühen Christentum*, 93–108.

[40] For more, see the helpful summary account in G. Clark, *Women in the Ancient World*, 12–14.

[41] Ibid., 13.

[42] See G. Clark, *Women in Late Antiquity: Pagan and Christian Life-styles*, 105–118.

[43] See Krause, *Witwen und Waisen im frühen Christentum*, 65 n. 80.

this, a closer look at the cultural context shaping women's public presence is indispensable.[44]

In antiquity, the social division that located women primarily in the "private," domestic sphere and identified men with the "public" sphere was a powerful shaper of women's lives. But there were marked differences among women, depending on their status and their location. Geographically, one can contrast "Athenian seclusion" with "Roman freedom" for women.[45] This "freedom" of Roman women meant that they could go to shops and the marketplace, attend public places of worship, go to hear speeches, see exhibitions, be present at public banquets, and visit friends. The women were usually "chaperoned" when going out, that is, they were escorted by men of the family or by slaves. Obviously, the focus is on wealthy women here. Women of the poorer classes, and particularly female slaves, were more visible in public throughout.

Christianity and its liturgy grew in this cultural context. But, as noted previously, they initially grew in the sphere dominated by women, that is, houses. When Christianity went "public" on a large scale in the fourth century, it entered a sphere where, in varying degrees in the larger culture, women were marginalized. A public liturgy, therefore, almost inescapably entailed some measure of marginalization for women in Christian worship. The sources bear this out in myriad ways. There are numerous indications of the public presence of women at worship being a problem or, conversely, of presence at worship being a problem for women in the Church of the empire.

5.3.1. Gender-Specific Constraints on Public "Appearance"

First, the public presence of women at worship became "fenced" by detailed regulations concerning their clothing, coiffure, make-up, and jewelry (these regulations, incidentally, give us valuable information about women's fashions of the time; they also provide us with clear liturgical gender boundaries). It was women who constantly

[44] A brief overview is provided by MacMullen, "Woman in Public in the Roman Empire," 208–218.

[45] See G. Clark, *Women in the Ancient World*, 17–20. For a more nuanced interpretation of the status of Athenian women, see D. Cohen, "Seclusion, Separation, and the Status of Women in Classical Athens," 134–145.

had their presence put under liturgical constraints by being admonished what to wear, how to do or not to do their hair, etc. Clothes, coiffure, and jewels were status indicators, for sure. And women were used to dressing up for religious festivals in the surrounding culture. The justification given by Christian writers for admonitions concerning women's attire at worship was, however, usually that of modesty, decency, and order. The effects on women's lives were clear constraints on their liturgical presence and participation. The following will illustrate this.

The *Traditio Apostolica* (21), for example, stipulates that women have to remove all golden jewelry and unloose their hair at the point of their baptism.[46] The *Didascalia Apostolorum* (3) enjoins women to receive the Eucharist with their heads covered. The fourth-century Egyptian *Canones Hippolyti* (can. 17; special material) prescribe that women attending worship come without jewelry, not wear their hair loose, not receive the Eucharist with a "perm," and refrain from talking and laughing during worship. Ambrose of Milan warns virgins against sighing, clearing their throats, coughing, and laughing while the liturgy is being celebrated (*De virginitate* III.3, 13). He addresses a similar request to women neophytes (*De sacramentis* VI.3, 15 and VI.3, 17). In the same vein, Cyril of Jerusalem, in the middle of the fourth century, admonishes women catechumens to pray silently in public worship, that is, to move their lips but without making a sound (*Procatechesis* 14).

And repeatedly, early Christian sources encourage women to come to worship veiled. Since there were different ways of veiling, it is not always certain which form a particular author wanted to encourage or prescribe (see, for example, the discussion in Tertullian, *De virginibus velandis* 16). One trend is discernible: exhortations to veil lessen the farther west one traveled in the empire. Women in the East were more likely to be encouraged to come to worship veiled than were their Western sisters.[47]

---

[46] For more on gender-specific baptismal practices in early Christianity, see Miles, *Carnal Knowing: Female Nakedness and Religious Meaning in the Christian West*, 24–52. For a later time, see the important article by Vincie, "Gender Analysis and Christian Initiation," 505–530.

[47] See Küchler, *Schweigen, Schmuck und Schleier*, 490f.

As far as women's actual ways of attending worship are concerned, early Christian sources provide some interesting glimpses into that reality. From the letters of Jerome, for example, we know that Roman aristocratic women toward the end of the fourth century might come to worship accompanied by their eunuchs (Ep. 22, 32) and have their own footstools at church (Ep. 22, 27).[48] This show of status and wealth within the liturgical assembly attracted the sharp criticism of Jerome. From non-Christian sources we know that affluent women were used to attending religious festivals in festive dress, arriving at the place of worship in their own carriages, and accompanied by large numbers of household slaves.[49]

5.3.2. Women-Problems at Public Worship

The public, mixed-gender nature of the liturgical assembly also explains why worship could be a dangerous space for women. As one recent researcher puts it: "the usual setting for rape was a festival crowd (and Christian martyr-feasts . . . were not much better). Going out was asking for trouble."[50] A saintly man in those days could pride himself on never having had a sexual encounter even though he had attended many festivals of the martyrs in his youth.[51] Sozomen, in his ecclesiastical history written in the fifth century, mentions a woman in Constantinople who accused a deacon of having raped her in church during her penitential exercises (*Historia ecclesiastica* VII.16). A fourth-century homily warns virgins not to attend vigils, funerals, and other liturgical events, since even public worship can bear dangers for them.[52] In a similar vein, Jerome warns that a daughter should stay close to her mother during vigils and not visit churches and the martyrs' graves on her own (Ep. 22, 17; Ep. 107, 9; Ep. 130, 19; see also Ambrose, *De virginitate* II.2, 9). In another letter, Jerome praises the Roman aristocrat Marcella, who frequently visited the martyrs' graves privately but shunned public assemblies

[48] Jerome's letters to ascetic women are available in the collection *Handmaids of the Lord*, 101–279.

[49] See Sawyer, *Women and Religion in the First Christian Centuries*, 24.

[50] G. Clark, *Women in the Ancient World*, 17.

[51] See Brown, *Body and Society*, 326, with reference to Theodoret, *Historia Religiosa* 20.2.

[52] See G. Clark, *Women in Late Antiquity*, 127, and Brown, *Cult of the Saints*, 43.

(read "public worship"; see Ep. 127, 4; cf. Ep. 128, 4). Some of these last prescriptions are certainly based on the topos of an ascetic retreat from the world. Nevertheless, they need to be taken seriously in a history of women at worship. They shaped, after all, the liturgical lives of women in the fourth century.

Within the ascetic movement, the situation was especially problematic. The simple presence of women at worship could be construed as a problem. Monks asked themselves whether it would not be better to stay away from worship than to risk encountering a woman.[53] In the same vein, Palladius mentions in his *Historia Lausiaca* (59) that some women ascetics voluntarily abstained from public worship so as not to lead men into temptation.

But the issue of the public presence of women in church was not only a problem within the ascetic movement. An imperial edict issued in the 320s forbade women to come to church together with men and, indeed, discouraged them from attending worship at all.[54] Whether this edict was ever put into practice is another question, but the simple fact of its existence shows that the public presence of women in the worship of the empire was perceived and treated as a problem.

5.3.3. Women's "Publicity" on the Fringes

These examples indicate the ambivalence that public worship could hold for women. To what extent women found public ritual space *hospitable* to them is an interesting question. From a sermon by Basil of Caesarea (Hom. 14, 1: "Against Drunkenness"), we know of women who danced at martyrs' graves outside of the city on Easter morning. Basil castigates these women because they danced unveiled and "publicly," that is, before the eyes of men. Women dancing before men was not unusual in antiquity, but its location was typically entertainment, the brothel, or the circus, with the dancers usually being female slaves and prostitutes.

Basil gives us a glimpse at a ritual space that women seem to have found hospitable, namely, cemeteries. Cemeteries were spaces that in Basil's time had become the center of an extensive redefinition of pub-

---

[53] See Thraede, "Frau," 259f.

[54] See Muschiol, "Reinheit und Gefährdung," 44, with reference to Eusebius, *Vita Constantini* 1.53.

lic space by Christianity. From being on the outskirts of the city, and therefore on the fringes of public life in antiquity, they became one of the foci of Christian ritual presence. The primary reason for this redefinition was the rising devotion to the martyrs and saints, and by extension to their graves and shrines.

But already prior to this development, cemeteries seem to have been women-friendly spaces: "For women in the ancient world, the cemetery areas had always been a zone of 'low gravity,' where their movements and choice of company were less subject to male scrutiny and the control of the family."[55] The new Christian shrines of the martyrs and saints therefore were located in a space originally hospitable to the presence of women. These shrines can thus be interpreted as one ritual space conducive to women.

Monica, the mother of Augustine, might serve as an example of a woman attracted to this space. While still in North Africa, she was in the habit of bringing a basket full of meal-cakes and bread and wine to the shrines of the saints on their memorial days. She would consume some of the food herself at the shrine of the saint and give the rest away. When Monica moved to Milan, she found that this ritual practice of her North African Church was discouraged by Ambrose. In fact, a doorkeeper prevented Monica from following her usual devotional routine in this regard (*Confessions* VI.2). The incident as reported by Augustine gives us an interesting glimpse at forms of ecclesiastical control over women at worship in the Church of the empire.

This small example of ecclesiastical control of women's visits to cemeteries is part of a larger picture. There was growing suspicion of women's visits to cemeteries and consequently mounting constraints surrounding these visits.[56] An early example is a canon of the Synod of Elvira, held in Spain at the beginning of the fourth century. The canon stipulates: "Women are forbidden to spend the night in a cemetery since often under the pretext of prayer they secretly commit evil deeds" (can. 35).[57] The canon in all likelihood targets women's

---

[55] Brown, *Cult of the Saints*, 44.

[56] Ibid., 147f.

[57] I am quoting from the translation by Laeuchli, *Power and Sexuality: The Emergence of Canon Law at the Synod of Elvira*, 130. Laeuchli devotes a section of his study to "The Clerics and Women"; see 97–101.

participation in all-night vigils, as numerous other texts do also. To point to just one other example: in the East, the famous canons of Patriarch John III of Constantinople (d. 577) threatened excommunication for women visiting family graves and playing tambourines and dancing there.[58]

These regulations of women's visits to cemeteries become more intelligible against the background of cemeteries initially being ritual spaces conducive to the public presence of women. At a time of growing marginalization of women in Christian worship, however, constraints on the presence of women became visible across the whole range of sacred spaces.

5.3.4. Christian Women and Rival Ritual Powers[59]

The emerging ecclesiastical suspicion concerning women's visits to cemeteries could be interpreted as a reaction to an initially "rival" space to established liturgical power. There were other such rivals. Two deserve particular mention. There were, first, Christian women who attended ritual festivals other than Christian ones. Chrysostom, for example, gives us a fascinating glimpse of Christian women in Antioch who participated in a Jewish festival (probably Rosh Hashanah). Chrysostom, of course, sharply criticizes this participation.[60]

Second, we find indications of women's own spheres of ritual power within Christianity. These ritual spheres were centered around so-called "superstitious" or "magic" practices, often at the fringes of the liturgy. Particularly in relation to menarche, love, marriage, fertility, birth, and the lives of their children, women will come to be attacked again and again for making use of "magic," as many sources document.[61]

As mentioned in the previous chapter, it is important for a history of women at worship to find other ways of describing this female rit-

[58] See Quasten, *Music and Worship*, 86.

[59] This concept owes its existence to Peter Brown's interpretation of the conflict between rival systems of patronage in early Christianity; see Brown, *Cult of the Saints*, 33.

[60] His sermon is published in Kraemer, *Maenads, Martyrs, Matrons, Monastics*, no. 31.

[61] See Dienst, "Zur Rolle von Frauen im magischen Praktiken und Vorstellungen," 173–194.

ual power than by a priori labeling it "magic." At a time when the public liturgical realm successively marginalized women, women's ritual activities not surprisingly became located elsewhere, usually at the margins of the liturgical realm. This ritual "margins-become-center" for women must be interpreted in relation to "public-worship-become-a-problem" for women at this time. One possible reinterpretation is to see this as a conflict between rival systems of ritual activity and power: the one centered around public acts of worship and under the control of ecclesiastical authorities, the other largely in the hands of ordinary people and located at the fringes of the liturgy or in the private sphere.

We are far from knowing what this rival world of ritual power looked like for women, although we get glimpses of it from time to time in early Christian writings. Chrysostom, for example, criticizes a domestic ritual measuring the power of a name given to a child. A number of lamps would be assigned different names and then lit. The lamp burning the longest would thereby indicate the most promising name for the child. Chrysostom tries to propose distinctly Christian countermeasures to this domestic ritual, such as giving the child the name of an apostle, a martyr, or a bishop. In the case of a child falling gravely ill (a frequent and potentially life-threatening occurrence at the time), Chrysostom suggests making the sign of the cross over the child or hanging a small Gospel text around her neck.[62]

Domestic folk rituals such as the one Chrysostom describes must have been numerous. We can gather other evidence from the large number of ritual practices in relation to human reproduction, such as uterine spells, birth spells, etc.[63] That Christians themselves made use of such ritual practices is evidenced by amulets, spells, and curses with clearly Christian undertones. A collection of such texts from Christian Egypt has recently been made available. Let me quote a couple of examples. A healing amulet worn by a woman actually begins with a liturgical text, the *Sanctus*. The amulet dates from the fifth or sixth century and reads as follows:

[62] For this and more, see Leyerle, "Appealing to Children," 248–250. For more on women's practices of healing in early Christianity, see Larson-Miller, "Women and the Anointing of the Sick," 37–48.

[63] For more, see Aubert, "Threatened Wombs: Aspects of Ancient Uterine Magic," 421–449.

"Holy, holy, holy, lord . . . who has healed again, who has raised Lazarus from the dead even on the fourth day, who has healed Peter's mother-in-law, who has also accomplished many unmentioned healings in addition to those they report in the sacred gospels; Heal her who wears this divine amulet of the disease afflicting her, through the prayers and intercession of the ever-virgin mother, the mother of god."[64]

The text breaks off at that point. A more malignant example of such texts of ritual power is a curse against a woman and her children. The text dates from the fourth century and reads as follows:

"Holy god, Gabriel, Michael, do what is sufficient for me, Mesa. Lord god, strike Philadelphe and her children. Lord, lord, lord, god, god, god, strike along with her Ou . . . Christ, have mercy upon me and hear me, lord."[65]

Examples of such texts could easily be multiplied. Suffice it to say here that all these ways of exercising ritual power must be taken account of in a history of women at worship. The Church and its worship had to contend with such rival ritual powers throughout, some of them clearly in the hands of women.

5.4. The Genderization of Liturgical Space

A fourth area of fundamental importance to the liturgical lives of women in the empire is the growing genderization of liturgical space. As we have seen, in antiquity the public sphere was not inherently hospitable to women. What happened to the liturgy when it moved from "women's space" inside the home to much more public worship spaces? One response to this shift was a noticeable and growing genderization of public liturgical space. This genderization of space can be interpreted as another way of enforcing liturgical gender boundaries, as the following examples illustrate.

In the *Didascalia Apostolorum* (XII), a genderization of liturgical space is clearly before the eyes of the author. The assembly was ordered from east to west. To the east was the bishop's seat. Then came

[64] Meyer, *Ancient Christian Magic: Coptic Texts of Ritual Power*, 38.

[65] Ibid., 51f. The editors wrongly identify the liturgical text at the beginning as the *Trisagion*.

the priests, then the lay men. Farthest to the west—and away from the altar and the bishop's seat—the women had their place. Among themselves, these women were divided according to marital status: young girls, married women, and widows. A female newcomer to worship would be asked by a deacon to identify herself by marital status and then was led to the appropriate place.

A clearly gendered liturgical space is also visible in the *Testamentum Domini* (whether these sources reflect historical "facts" or merely the ideals of their author-compilers, a gendered liturgical space is visible in either case). Women entered the church through a special women's entrance (guarded by deaconesses?). They worshiped separated from the men. Widows and deaconesses had their own space in the sanctuary during the celebration of the Eucharist (in defiance of canon 44 of the fourth-century canons of Laodicea). These women, however, were not allowed to occupy this space during the time of their menstruation.

Of special importance for the further development of liturgical space was the separate worship space occupied by women and men to which these sources (and many others) witness. We know of three different arrangements in the early centuries. First, women's space was located behind that of the men, who directly faced the altar (*Didascalia Apostolorum*). Second, men stood on the right, women on the left side in church (*Testamentum Domini*). Third, women found themselves in a gallery above the main worship space (e.g., the Hagia Sophia in Constantinople).[66] Chrysostom, in one of his early homilies in Antioch toward the end of the fourth century, even mentions a grille or screen between men and women in church (Hom. 73 Matt. 3). He notes having heard from older men that such a partition was not used originally in worship.[67] This architectural expression of a gendered divide can also be found in later centuries.[68]

The origin of the various gender-specific arrangements of liturgical space is not immediately obvious. Possibly there is a connection to the liturgical separation of women in Judaism, but the references to

[66] See Gilchrist, *Gender and Material Culture*, 109.

[67] See Aston, "Segregation in Church," 238–240, and Mayer, "Dynamics of Liturgical Space: Chrysostom and his Audiences," esp. 108f.

[68] See Muschiol, "Liturgie und Klausur" (forthcoming).

this practice come from a later period. On the other hand, women in antiquity also had their separate (disadvantaged) space in the theater and the circus. A third possibility is to connect the developing genderization of liturgical space with earliest Christian meal etiquette. One possible arrangement for a public meal seated women and men separately. This form of meal etiquette could be seen to emerge as the dominant Christian table practice, particularly when Christian table fellowship came to be celebrated more and more publicly. But whatever its origins, the genderization of liturgical space obviously shaped women's experiences of the liturgy in fundamental ways.

5.5. Liturgical Taboos

A fifth area shaping women's liturgical lives in the Church of the empire is the ambivalence toward menstruation, sex, birthgiving, and midwifery as it left its imprint on worship. Liturgical menstrual taboos are a case in point.[69] In the third century, menstruation could mean the postponement of a woman's baptism[70] (*Traditio Apostolica* 20[71]; see also its reception history in *Canones Hippolyti* 19; *Testamentum Domini* II.6 suggests an additional day of prebaptismal preparation for menstruating women).

At the same time in Alexandria, menstruation entailed the exclusion of a woman from participating in worship—at least that is what Dionysius of Alexandria (d. 265) suggests in a letter to bishop Basilides.[72] Roughly a hundred years later, Timothy of Alexandria is stricter still. Not only should a menstruating woman not enter church or be baptized, but she should also not nurse her newly baptized

[69] For more on the menstrual taboo, see S. Cohen, "Menstruants and the Sacred in Judaism and Christianity," 273–299.

[70] One wonders how the need for this postponement was determined. Was there a prebaptismal interrogation for women concerning their menses? Were women expected to know not to come forward for baptism if the day of their baptism happened to coincide with their menses? How and by whom was this communicated to women? What if baptism had to be postponed several times? Alternatively, do we need to read these prescriptions as a baptismal menstrual taboo existing primarily in the mind of the author/compiler of the text?

[71] I am awaiting further discussion of Bradshaw's suggestions of "Redating the Apostolic Tradition," 3–17.

[72] The letter is easily accessible in Kraemer, *Maenads, Martyrs, Matrons, Monastics*, no. 26.

child except in cases of emergency, and she should refrain from kissing the hand of a priest.[73] The punishment for women who do not conform is severe. It is matched only by the punishments for murder and heresy: seven years of fasting on water and bread alone, exclusion from ever entering a church again, and excommunication to the end of life (I am, again, bracketing out the question whether we are confronted with codifications of existing practice or wishful prescriptions on the part of the author; in either case, menstrual taboos are visible).

In fifth-century Syria, menstruating widows and deaconesses might not be allowed to take their rightful place around the altar (*Testamentum Domini* I.23). And in the Western Church, many penitentials of the early Middle Ages witness to prohibitions for menstruating women to participate in worship and receive the Eucharist.[74] According to the *Institutio Sanctimonialium Aquisgranensis* of 816 c.e., a canonical rule for women's communities drawn up at the Synod of Aachen, nuns were not allowed to participate in the communal Liturgy of the Hours during the time of their menstruation.[75] Menstruation could also have liturgical ramifications beyond the taboos mentioned here. Thus Tertullian can urge that women not participate unveiled in public worship after menarche (*De virginibus velandis* 1; 11).

The times of pregnancy and birth also shaped liturgical practices in specific ways. In the *Testamentum Domini*, women who are sick because of pregnancy are subject to specific rules for fasting, and the Eucharist is brought to them at home at Easter by a deaconess (II.20). The *Canones Hippolyti* (can. 18; special material) envision, both for new mothers and midwives, a separation from the liturgical assembly after a birth. The women involved in the birthgiving should not attend worship for some time, according to these canons. If they did, they had to take their place with the catechumens(!). These canons, which by no means stand alone in the liturgical tradition,[76] consequently encourage a proliferation of midwives so that these women

---

[73] See Muschiol, "Reinheit und Gefährdung," 44.

[74] For Feminist research on the penitentials, see Krüger, "Überlegungen zum Quellenwert der irischen Bussbücher für historische Frauenforschung," 154–170.

[75] For more, see Muschiol, "Liturgie und Klausur" (forthcoming).

[76] See Roll, "The Churching of Women after Childbirth," 210f.

do not have to—as an occupational hazard—constantly forgo worship. Nevertheless, prior to the widespread availability of contraceptives, a quite substantial number of women would routinely be excluded from the liturgical assembly by such regulations.

The situation, however, was by no means uniform. There are early Christian sources that explicitly argue against the exclusion of women from worship during their menses or after having given birth. The *Didascalia Apostolorum* and the *Apostolic Constitutions* make a point of not censoring the liturgical participation of menstruating women. The same applies to the response of Gregory the Great to Augustine of Canterbury. When Augustine asked the bishop of Rome whether women should be allowed to enter church and partake of Communion at the time of their menstruation, Gregory answered in the positive. Many early medieval penitentials, however, show that Gregory's positive response did not become the general rule.[77] What the different voices pro and con show is that the issue of women's participation in worship at the time of their menses and after having given birth was contested.

But there was not only ambivalence towards menstruation, pregnancy, and birth. Even a liturgical rite such as marriage—or more precisely, its sexual consequences—could engender ambivalence and resulting liturgical taboos for women. Caesarius of Arles, writing in sixth-century Gaul, mentions the custom of women abstaining from worship for thirty days after their wedding (night). Caesarius wants to encourage the husbands to do the same.[78] Extant texts for a Mass on the thirtieth day after a wedding also have a decidedly penitential and purificatory tone.[79]

Taken together, these incidences of liturgical taboos reveal a ritual web of gender-specific constraints on women menstruating, having sex, being pregnant, giving birth, and lactating. Most women, prior to widespread forms of birth-control, were involved in one or several such activities for much of their lives. The consequences for their participation in worship were regular limitations or actual abstentions.

---

[77] See Meens, "Ritual Purity and the Influence of Gregory the Great," 31–43.
[78] See Leonard, "Rites of Marriage in the Western Middle Ages," 183.
[79] Ibid., 183.

5.6. Women as Bearers of Liturgical Tradition

A sixth area of women's liturgical lives in the Church of the empire is the role women played in the missionary expansion of Christianity and concurrently the handing on of liturgical traditions. The example of a woman prisoner of war who around 330 C.E. evangelized the Georgians well illustrates this point. As part of her evangelization, this anonyma, whom tradition calls "Nino," explained the "rite for the worship service *(colendi ritum),*" that is the "rite of prayer and the form for the worship [of God]"[80] to her converts. At the same time, she initiated the building of a church and gave detailed architectural advice on its construction. "Nino" surely is not the only woman in the history of Christian missions who took an active part in liturgical traditioning. We know, for example, that women played an important role in the missionary expansion of the early Middle Ages by their active participation in the process of bringing children to baptism.[81]

The contours of the ways women were involved in liturgical traditioning are barely visible as of yet. Here is an area that deserves careful attention, particularly for the centuries when sources about women's actual faith practices are more numerous.

5.7. The Liturgical Singing of Women

A seventh area shaping the liturgical lives of women in the Church of the empire is the struggle surrounding the liturgical singing of women. In the first two centuries, this simply was not a subject of debate. One can therefore safely assume that women did participate in whatever singing occurred in worship. With the third century, however, this active liturgical participation of women began to be seen as a problem. Whether the primary reason for this was the popularity of women's singing in non-Christian and Christian heterodox groups is worth questioning.[82] It may well rather have been a part of the general "muting" of women's voices in public worship at this time.

---

[80] Quoted in Jensen, *God's Self-confident Daughters,* 77.

[81] See Nolte, *Conversio und Christianitas,* 135–152.

[82] As Quasten assumes in his study of the subject, *Music and Worship,* esp. 85f. Quasten does not take sufficient account of other forms of the liturgical "muting" of women and therefore has to see the silencing of women's singing in the liturgy as a reaction to women's musical participation in heterodox communities.

Whatever the reasons, with the third century the liturgical singing of women began to be critiqued in different parts of the empire. By the fourth century it was clearly contested, with different Christian authors writing pro and con. Ambrose of Milan, for example, argued for allowing women to participate in the singing of the psalms in worship *(Ennaratio in Ps. 1)*. The Syrian theologian Ephraem (d. 373) even founded choirs of ascetic women in Edessa that sang his own hymnic compositions in worship on Sundays and feast days.[83] Some years later, the pilgrim Egeria in her travel diary (24,1) describes similar choirs of ascetic women participating in the liturgy in Jerusalem.

Liturgical singing by ascetic women continued to be acceptable, while liturgical singing by other women came to be contested and, in the end, often forbidden. Cyril of Jerusalem, for example, enjoined women to pray silently in public worship by moving only their lips but without making a sound *(Procatechesis* 14). In numerous texts, singing by women is forbidden, especially in connection with nightly vigils.[84] In the end, only women's ascetic groups and communities remained as privileged spaces for the continuing liturgical singing of women, as well as for their arranging and composing of music.[85]

5.8. Women's (Liturgical) Communities

This fact points to an eighth important area of women's liturgical lives. Ascetic life meant something quite different for women than it did for men, and not only in the realm of worship. For women, it could mean freedom from arranged marriages, a sexual double standard, frequent and often life-threatening pregnancies, and domestic abuse, which was rampant, as we know from sermons and other texts, for example, Augustine's *Confessions* IX.9. We know of groups of ascetic women living together by the time of Pachomius (d. 347). This "father" of cenobitic asceticism left the sister in his care with a group of women living a life of ascetic renunciation together (they deserve to be named the "parents" of cenobitism more so than Pachomius). Initially such women lived together in private homes,

[83] See Quasten, *Music and Worship,* 78f.

[84] See ibid., 86f.

[85] For more on this, see Bagnall Yardley, "'Ful weel she soong the service dyvyne': The Cloistered Musician in the Middle Ages," 15–38.

often as part of an extended ascetic family. We know little about their liturgical practices outside of the home, but something about their daily domestic devotions.

Macrina the Younger (d. 379), the "Cappadocian mother" as one might call her (she was the elder sister of Basil and Gregory of Nyssa and greatly influenced their spiritual development) is a good example.[86] Macrina moved from a communal ascetic life within the home to founding a monastic women's community proper. The devotional center of these women's daily lives was prayerful meditation and the singing of the psalms. The community, in fact, had a specific office of a "leader of the choir of the virgins," which in Macrina's lifetime was held by the deaconess Lampadion.[87]

The example of Macrina's community shows that worship was one realm where monastic life could spell freedom for women, and liturgical singing was one of its components. Other areas of liturgical free space for cloistered women have recently been brought to light by the important work of Gisela Muschiol, who has studied the liturgical life of women's communities in Romano-Merovingian Gaul. Muschiol shows that the center of daily life was a liturgy that the women themselves shaped and celebrated under the liturgical presidency of their abbess.[88] This daily liturgy included not only the singing of the psalms but also the reading of the Scriptures, prayers, confession of sins and absolution (by the abbess!), intercessions, and vigils. All these lay in the hands of the women themselves. They thus had a measure of control over their own liturgical lives far exceeding that of their sisters whose worship was centered in parish churches.

5.9. Women on the Way

A ninth aspect of women's liturgical lives in the Church of the empire is constituted by ritual practices which might not have seemed of fundamental importance in traditional historiography but whose importance in the lives of women cannot be denied. I am thinking, for example, of the whole area of processions and pilgrimages and

---

[86] *The Life of Saint Macrina*, written by her brother Gregory of Nyssa, is readily available in English translation in *Handmaids of the Lord*, 51–82.

[87] For more, see Ruth Albrecht's study, *Das Leben der heiligen Makrina* (1986).

[88] See Gisela Muschiol's magisterial study *Famula Dei* (1994).

their particular meaning for women.[89] As mentioned above, visits to the shrines of the saints, processions, and pilgrimages were ritual moments in which the traditional gender-based social divisions might temporarily be suspended. Holy places were usually equally accessible to women and men, who were found on the way together, "in a manner rare in a late-antique urban context."[90]

Pilgrimages by women are important for other reasons also. They give us travel descriptions and thereby writings by women at a time when such writings were scarce. For the time under consideration, there is one pilgrim who is of fundamental importance to liturgical historiography: Egeria. Her travel diary, which describes her pilgrimage in the years 380 to 385, is crucial for our knowledge of worship in the fourth century. Liturgical historiography at this point is in the unusual situation of drawing much of its data from a woman's writing. But the document has to be named and appreciated as such. A gender-specific reading of Egeria's diary will, for example, highlight points of the pilgrimage that focus on women in a particular way.

Egeria's visit to the shrine of Saint Thecla, the famous legendary companion of the apostle Paul, is a case in point. Egeria herself clearly counts this visit among the high points of her pilgrimage (23.3). The figure of Thecla was one of the "strong women" of earliest Christianity—teaching, healing, baptizing—whose fame had spread enough to attract devotees (particularly women?) to her shrine. Egeria, upon reaching the church, read the *Acts of Thecla* there. But her visit to Saint Thecla's shrine is memorable for another reason. There Egeria met her woman friend from her days in Jerusalem, the deaconess Marthana. Marthana seems to have functioned as one of the titular guardians of the shrine of Thecla. The network of women on pilgrimage that we get a glimpse of at this point is one of the noteworthy features of Egeria's travel diary. Here, then, is the description of Egeria's visit to the shrine of Saint Thecla and her reunion with Marthana in her own words:

"I arrived at a city called Seleucia of Isauria . . . Since it is around fifteen hundred feet from the city to the shrine of Saint Thecla, which

[89] A fascinating gender analysis of Muslim pilgrimage is provided by Young, "Ka'ba, Gender, and the Rites of Pilgrimage," 285–300.

[90] See Brown, *Cult of the Saints*, 43.

62

lies beyond the city on a rather flat hill, I thought it best to go out there to make the overnight stop which I had to make. At the holy church there is nothing but countless monastic cells for men and women. I met there a very dear friend of mine, and a person to whose way of life everyone in the East bears witness, the holy deaconess Marthana, whom I had met in Jerusalem, where she had come to pray. She governs these monastic cells of *aputactitae*, or virgins . . . there are many cells all over the hill, and in the middle there is a large wall which encloses the church where the shrine is. It is a very beautiful shrine . . . Having arrived there in the name of God, a prayer was said at the shrine and the complete Acts of Saint Thecla was read. I then gave unceasing thanks to Christ our God, who granted to me, an unworthy woman and in no way deserving, the fulfillment of my desires in all things."[91]

Two other points are noteworthy in appreciating Egeria's diary. First, the text was written for a group of women, and women with an intense interest in liturgical details. The possibility that these women were comparing Egeria's descriptions with their own liturgical practices is one plausible explanation for this interest.[92] Second, an important part of this naming of the travel diary as a *woman's* text will be the realization that Egeria was no female lone ranger. She stood within a larger company of fourth-century women who set out on pilgrimage to the holy places (and worshiped there, to add the obvious). Egeria was but one of them,[93] and others could readily be named, among them Helena, Melania the Elder, Paula and her daughter Eustochium, Fabiola, Poemenia, and Melania the Younger.

5.10. The Veneration of Women
A tenth and vast area of women's liturgical lives in the Church of the empire is the complex development of the liturgical veneration of holy women, including the burgeoning veneration of Mary, the mother of Jesus. There are several aspects of this veneration of

[91] Egeria, *Diary of a Pilgrimage*, 87.
[92] See Sivan, "Holy Land Pilgrimage and Western Audiences: Some Reflections on Egeria and her Circle," 528–535.
[93] See Sivan, "Who was Egeria?" 59–72; Douglass, "A New Look at the *Itinerarium Burdigalense*," 313–333.

women that deserve particular attention in the time period under consideration.

5.10.1. Women and Their Feasts

First, there are the beginnings of actual liturgical feasts centering on holy women. These feasts included the liturgical reading of women's stories, in earliest times usually martyrdom accounts, on the appropriate feast day. For women worshipers, female saints and their stories provided points of gender identification at a time when the female gender was again and again marked as a liturgical "problem."

Which saints and what stories women would have heard extolled in worship deserves closer attention. A preliminary glance at stories of women saints reveals that such stories clearly took into account their changing audience. They could be recrafted so that the heroine would serve as a role model for other women in other times.[94] The narrative of the martyrdom of Anastasia is a good example (especially since Anastasia is one of the women who came to be commemorated in the Roman Canon).[95] As recorded in the *Gesta Martyrum*, a collection of pious legends written in the fifth and sixth centuries in honor of Roman martyrs, the figure of Anastasia is constructed in such a way as to be relevant to women devotees who were married rather than living in ascetic virginity. Anastasia thus becomes "an example for the edification of all *matrons (pro aedificatione omnium matronarum)"*[96] rather than an exemplar primarily for ascetic women. From later centuries, we have collections of stories of women saints that were clearly designed particularly for the hands and ears of women, and there are indications that women's contexts shaped the reception history of women saints in particular ways.[97]

---

[94] For more, see Cooper, *Virgin and the Bride*, 116–143.

[95] The group of women mentioned in the Roman Canon (Perpetua and Felicity, Agatha, Lucia, Agnes, Cecilia, Anastasia) deserves closer attention and study. What liturgical image of "woman" is created by the choice of these particular women saints in the heart of the traditional Roman Eucharistic Prayer?

[96] Quoted in Cooper, *Virgin and the Bride*, 121 (italics mine).

[97] See Feistner, *Historische Typologie der deutschen Heiligenlegende des Mittelalters*, 249–257, 292–306.

5.10.2. Women and Their Churches

Related to the beginning liturgical veneration of women is, second, the dedication of churches to particular women saints. Mary is the most obvious example, but there are others. In Armenia, for example, the martyr Hripsime, who died at the turn of the third and fourth centuries, quickly came to be venerated liturgically. By the end of the fourth century, various forms of veneration are attested to, and in the middle of the fifth century, a church was dedicated to Hripsime.[98] Between, on the one hand, the innumerable churches dedicated to Mary, the Mother of God, and, on the other hand, the clearly localized veneration of the Armenian martyr Hripsime, there are countless other churches dedicated to holy women throughout the Christian world. A liturgical narrative of women's ways of worship does well to map the emergence of these women-defined churches.

5.10.3. Women Saints and Gender Identification

A third area related to the liturgical veneration of women that has gender-specific implications is the veneration of particular objects related to women's lives. As mentioned in the previous chapter, the robe and cincture of the Virgin Mary in Constantinople, the Virgin's veil, her ring, and milk are examples of such female (secondary) relics. Again, these would provide specific points of gender identification for women.

Another case of particular gender identification may be found in forms of veneration said to be typical of and for women. Epiphanius of Salamis (d. 403) provides an example of this in his *Panarion* (78.23; 79.1-9). Epiphanius was scandalized by a group of Christian women who, according to his description, on a certain day of the year baked bread, set it out on a festively decorated chair, offered it to Mary, and then partook of it together. Epiphanius accused the women of acting as priestesses (in imitation of the Christian Eucharist? in imitation of non-Christian offerings to goddesses?). What is of interest for a history of women at worship is the glimpse Epiphanius gives us of a woman-specific veneration of Mary, a veneration evidently on a collision course with ecclesiastically more acceptable forms of veneration.

---

[98] See Synek, *Heilige Frauen der frühen Christenheit*, 140.

5.10.4. Women-Sermons

A fourth important factor is that women become the focus of sermons on particular holy days. In the time period under consideration, we begin to have records of sermons women heard in church about holy women. For example, women heard Easter sermons pointing to Mary Magdalene from such preachers as Gregory of Nyssa and John Chrysostom.[99]

A concurrent negative homiletic stereotyping of women must, however, also be noted. The many women throughout history who had Eve preached at them are probably the best testimony to a homiletic gender stereotyping. Positive or negative, the varying scripts for women that sermons contain are worthy of further examination. Such a gendered reading of homiletic material is not limited to sermons about holy women alone. Other sermons, too, contain reflections of women's realities, from diatribes against make-up to condemnations of abortive practices.[100]

Two aspects are worth mentioning in concluding these reflections on the liturgical veneration of women. The first is the question of the continuity of women-centered sacred space. In some instances, Christian saints were (spatial) inheritors of devotion to pre-Christian female deities. The devotion to Saint Thecla near Seleucia, for example, was located at a point where a pre-Christian goddess was venerated. The tradition of the veneration of Mary in Ephesus connected with a strong veneration of the goddess Artemis/Diana in that city. Second, and in a different vein, it is worth noting that a discrepancy developed early on between the number of male and female saints who came to be venerated liturgically.[101]

More sustained research is needed before details of a picture of "women-veneration" really emerge. At this point, I simply want to draw attention to the fact that in the time period under consideration, we see the beginnings of a multifaceted liturgical "women-

---

[99] For more, see Synek, *Heilige Frauen der frühen Christenheit*, 40–52.

[100] See Cunningham, "Women and Preaching in the Patristic Age," 53–72.

[101] A first look at numbers is provided by Wittern, *Frauen, Heiligkeit und Macht. Lateinische Frauenviten aus dem 4. bis 7. Jahrhundert*, 9. For the kind of detailed work needing to be done, see Wilson, "Female Sanctity in the Greek Calendar," 233–247.

veneration" that will have provided particular gender-specific opportunities for women at worship.

6. EARLY CHRISTIAN WOMEN—EARLY CHRISTIAN WORSHIP: AN ATTEMPT AT A SUMMARY

What, then, can be said in summary about the liturgical lives of early Christian women? First of all, and at its most basic, simply this: they had one, and it needs to be noted by any historian of the liturgy interested in the fundamental question of who actually worshiped the Christian God. The collection of materials presented here is a first attempt to bring to life the earliest Christian women at worship. The liturgical lives of these women were shaped by dynamics that were complex and diverse. These dynamics range from earliest communities initially gathering in women-friendly spaces to women becoming increasingly distanced from the Holy of Holiest in the Church of the empire. But the development was by no means uniform or unidirectional. At the same time at which women lived through a period of growing marginalization in public worship, they also found new spaces of liturgical freedom in women's ascetic communities and in their own ritual practices in the vicinity of the liturgy (specific devotions, patronage, vestments, etc.).

Another point is important. We know little about how the liturgical dynamics described here actually affected women's own sense of worship. We have no access to how these women experienced the worship of the Church as part of their lives and faith practices. Unless sources written by women themselves miraculously appear in the future, the chances are slim that we will ever know. This, of course, is one more reason to look closely at anything we *can* still gather from other sources about these women at worship.

Chapter 3

Liturgical History Re-Constructed (II): Women in the Twentieth-Century Liturgical Movement

In the preceding chapter, I outlined a reconstruction of women's liturgical lives in early Christianity. The present chapter rather boldly jumps ahead to the twentieth century. Bypassing the many intervening centuries of women at worship does not mean that these centuries are devoid of either significance or much material to study. On the contrary, the very richness, variety, and complexity of the centuries following the early Church mitigate against their inclusion here. A continuous narrative of Christian women at worship from the earliest beginnings to our own day will have to await another time and more detailed research than can be presented in this one volume.

The present chapter focuses on a time period close to the present and of fundamental importance for the interplay of women and worship today.[1] The Liturgical Movement in the twentieth century has profoundly (re-)shaped liturgical lives in ways unthinkable at the beginning of the century. The focus in this chapter will be on the presence of women in this liturgical renewal movement as it grew in the Roman Catholic Church in the first half of the century.[2] If the preceding

[1] A preliminary version of the research for this chapter can be found in Berger, "The Classical Liturgical Movement in Germany and Austria: Moved by Women," 231–251. My book *Liturgie und Frauenseele* (1993) gives a more detailed account of the beginnings of the Liturgical Movement in Germany and Austria.

[2] Separate studies are necessary for women's ways of worship in other Churches. The starting point for the interplay between women and worship is different from that of the Roman Catholic Church. I am also not looking at women in the Liturgical Movement in the so-called Third World. This subject deserves close attention but needs a more competent narrator of the social location of the movement in the Third World than I am.

chapter provided an example of reconstructing the dynamics of women's actual liturgical lives, the focus in the present chapter is more specific. I want to reconstruct women's presence in one particular renewal movement within the overall liturgical life of the Church.

As far as their actual liturgical lives were concerned, women of the early twentieth century in many ways inherited trends that shaped the lives of Christian women at worship in the early Church. This continuity can be shown at a number of points. Women at the beginning of the twentieth century worshiped in a starkly gendered ritual world. The leadership of the liturgy was exclusively in the hands of men. Women themselves seldom took an active role in public liturgical celebrations. Some liturgical rites excluded women by virtue of their gender (such as various ordinations). Others focused on women because of their gender or its consequences (the blessing of the bride, the churching of women after childbirth). Liturgical space was clearly divided by gender, and women were all but excluded from the sanctuary—except for purposes of cleaning. Women's liturgical singing, where it was possible at all, was defined as non-liturgical. Most women did not know the language of the liturgy. Learning Latin was the prerogative of an educated elite, a group that for the most part still excluded women. And last but not least, women continued to be subjected to detailed regulations of their dress code and appearance.[3]

The Liturgical Movement did not challenge the basic asymmetrical genderization of worship. Yet, it did offer women a new vision of the liturgy, a vision that enabled women to claim this "wonderful world of the liturgy"[4] for themselves in new ways. In that sense, the Liturgical Movement served as a midwife of the *Women's* Liturgical Movement that took place in the second part of the century. Together,

---

[3] The bishop of Paderborn, Germany, for example, in 1926 instructed his priests: "Persons of the female sex can only be admitted to the holy sacraments, especially Holy Communion and Confirmation, if their dress covers their knees, is tightly closed up to the neck, is not made of transparent materials, and has sleeves which at minimum cover the elbows. Priests are encouraged to simply pass by without explanation anyone who with their dress signals a lack of respect for the Almighty." In the 1980s, women in the diocese of Paderborn created a facsimile of this episcopal instruction and included it in a pamphlet on the situation of women in this diocese. See Berger, *Liturgie und Frauenseele*, 164, n. 592.

[4] Lina M., "Wie ich zur Liturgie kam," 324.

these two liturgical renewal movements signal a "reconquest" of liturgical space successively lost to women in preceding centuries.[5]

Methodologically, with the Liturgical Movement one enters a world different from that of early Christianity. This world differs especially as far as sources are concerned. There is, for the Liturgical Movement, a substantial body of materials written by women themselves. Other records also provide insight into women at worship at the time of the Liturgical Movement, records that are not available for earlier times. This applies, for example, to photos and films. Moreover, there are still close links to the world that the women of the Liturgical Movement inhabited. In some lucky instances, it is possible to speak in person with a woman active in the Liturgical Movement (during the initial research for this chapter, I had the privilege of talking to Josepha Fischer [b. 1900], who worked with Romano Guardini at Burg Rothenfels in the 1920s; in the latter stages of my research, I enjoyed several sustained conversations with Therese Mueller [b. 1905], a key figure of the North American Liturgical Movement). Even where such personal contact is no longer an option, the world that shaped these women's liturgical lives for the most part still exists. The chapel used for worship at Burg Rothenfels; the Benedictine Abbey of Herstelle; St. John's Abbey, Collegeville, Minnesota; and Grailville in Loveland, Ohio—these all can be entered and provide important insights into women's lives in the first half of the twentieth century.

What, then, about women's presence in the Liturgical Movement at this time? Looking at the traditional image of the Liturgical Movement, one has to start with women's absence. An example is provided in the preface to the first volume of the prestigious *Jahrbuch für Liturgiewissenschaft*, one of the key journals of the movement. The editor, Odo Casel, O.S.B., wrote the following: "The liturgy is not an intellectual construct of a world of speculations far away from earthly concerns; it is the worship of the Church, born out of historical facts, out of the life and suffering of Christ, and developed

---

[5] The militance of the term "reconquest" is not inappropriate here. The Women's Liturgical Movement, by necessity, is marked by a certain militance vis-à-vis the traditional world of the liturgy. Militance, of course, was also a notable feature of the women's suffrage movement; see Cott, *Grounding of Modern Feminism*, 26, 35f., 53ff.

through the mind and prayer of the Church and its great men, in whose soul the Spirit of God dug and found gold."[6] When Casel speaks of the "great men" of the Church, he refers, in his native German, exclusively to male human beings. Casel was right, of course. If one looks at traditional liturgical historiography (which was the historiography available to Casel), the worship of the Church seems indeed to have been born (!) out of the prayer of the Church and its great men.

As far as early Christianity is concerned, I hope I have put this traditional picture to rest in the preceding chapter. In the present chapter, I want to put it to rest for another period of liturgical development, that of the Liturgical Movement. In the first part of this chapter, I want to deconstruct the scholarly reception history of the Liturgical Movement and show how the movement came to be (mis-)represented as a male enterprise. The second part of the chapter will focus on women and their voices in the Liturgical Movement. The chapter as a whole will display how the image of the Liturgical Movement, created through a selective reception history, rendered invisible what was present in the movement itself, namely, women, women's voices, and an intense concern with women's issues of the time.

1. THE SCHOLARLY CONSTRUCTION OF THE LITURGICAL MOVEMENT

A quick glance at the major histories of the Liturgical Movement leads one to believe that this movement was a male enterprise. Although *the* authoritative history of the Liturgical Movement does not yet exist, the short form of such a history is readily discernible. The canon of significant names usually includes the following "fathers" of the movement. The French Benedictine monk Prosper Guéranger (1805–1875) and the British liturgical scholar Edmund Bishop (1846–1917) typically are mentioned as nineteenth-century forerunners of the Liturgical Movement. Lambert Beauduin (1873–1960) from the Benedictine Abbey of Mont César in Belgium marks the actual beginnings of the movement with his address at a conference in Malines, Belgium, in 1909. In the 1920s, a center of the

---

[6] Casel, "Zur Einführung," 2.

movement came to be located in German-speaking countries. The Benedictine Abbey of Maria Laach in Germany, with its abbot Ildefons Herwegen, O.S.B. (1874–1946), and its monk Odo Casel, O.S.B. (1886–1948), was one of the foci. The priest and scholar Romano Guardini (1885–1968) is also invariably included in any history of the Liturgical Movement. Other names usually mentioned are Pius Parsch (1884–1954) at Klosterneuburg, and Josef Andreas Jungmann, S.J. (1889–1975), of Innsbruck, Austria, as well as Johannes Pinsk (1891–1957), university chaplain and parish priest in Berlin.

On this side of the Atlantic, Virgil Michel, O.S.B. (1890–1938), of St. John's Abbey at Collegeville, Minnesota, is clearly the key figure of the beginning Liturgical Movement in North America. After a visit to Benedictine centers of liturgical renewal in Europe in the mid-twenties, Michel began a liturgical apostolate of amazing proportions, which soon blossomed into a movement. Suffice it to mention one aspect here: together with the Jesuit Gerald Ellard, S.J. (1894–1963), and the priest Martin Hellriegel (1891–1981), Michel in 1926 founded the central organ of the North American Liturgical Movement, the journal *Orate Fratres*, today known as *Worship*.

This cluster of names provides the framework for most histories of the Liturgical Movement. In accordance with their own specific foci and interests, writers might add various other names to this canon. One characteristic of these histories, however, is immediately obvious: nowhere do women become explicitly visible in this "master narrative."

2. WOMEN AND "WOMAN" IN THE LITURGICAL MOVEMENT: A RE-CONSTRUCTION

Looking beyond the standard reception history back to the Liturgical Movement itself, one quickly begins to question this invisibility of women. Even prior to any in-depth gender analysis, women and women's issues are plainly visible in the movement. There are, for example, the Benedictine women's communities on the Mont-Vierge in Belgium and at Herstelle in Germany. The community on the Mont-Vierge began in the early 1920s with the express purpose of introducing the "modern woman" to the riches of the Church's liturgical life. The Abbey of the Holy Cross at Herstelle was the home of liturgical authors such as Aemiliana Löhr, O.S.B. (1892–1972). It was also the convent to which Odo Casel was called in 1922 as chaplain and spiritual director. Casel remained in this office until his death in 1948. The Abbey of the Holy Cross at Herstelle and its women liturgical authors, however, are rarely mentioned in histories of the Liturgical Movement, and then usually in footnotes that give these women the appearance of being utterly dependent on Casel. Aemiliana Löhr became known primarily as "Casel's master pupil."[7] Her wide range of liturgical publications, totaling over three hundred articles, poems, and books, have only now begun to be studied in their own right.[8]

With regard to Casel, not much attention has been paid to the fact that his *Mysterientheologie* found one crucial expression in his regular talks to a women's community. Most scholars have likewise ignored the fact that in Casel's writings, "much of importance is said about the Christian image of women in our times," as one of his confreres put it.[9] Lastly, it is rarely noticed that the *Jahrbuch für Liturgiewissenschaft*, edited by Casel, contains an unusual number of reviews by or about women and their liturgical writings.

The case of Odo Casel, who was chaplain in a women's community for twenty-six years and therefore regularly spoke to women and/or on women's issues, is not an isolated one. For one, he has a counterpart on this side of the Atlantic. Martin Hellriegel was chaplain to the Sisters of the Adoration of the Most Precious Blood in O'Fallon, Missouri, for twenty-two years. He therefore also developed much of his liturgical reflection in the context of a women's community.

But a concern with women's issues can be demonstrated with other "fathers" of the Liturgical Movement, as a quick overview of the literature shows. Abbot Ildefons Herwegen, for example, encouraged one of his monks at Maria Laach, Athanasius Wintersig, O.S.B. (1900–1942), to write *Liturgy and Woman's Soul*, without a doubt the most explicit discussion of women's issues within the Liturgical Movement. This book alone, appearing in the famous series *Ecclesia Orans*, raises the question of why a movement apparently untouched by women would generate a book on such a subject. But *Liturgy and*

---

[7] Thus Theodor Schnitzler in a review of Löhr, "Die Heilige Woche," 126.

[8] Helen McConnell is completing a dissertation at The Catholic University of America entitled "Aemiliana Löhr's Theology of Liturgical Worship."

[9] See Neunheuser, "Vorwort," 17.

Woman's Soul does not stand alone, since a little Belgian volume on the same topic predates Wintersig's by three years. *The Christian Woman and the Liturgical Renewal* was published by Abbé Auguste Croegaert in 1922 (Virgil Michel drew on this little book for his article "The Christian Woman").

Several other facts prove the conventional wisdom on the invisibility of women in the Liturgical Movement as a misreading of the evidence. To point to Herwegen again: in 1931, the Abbot presented a paper to Catholic teachers, all women, entitled "Church and Woman." Ten years later he contributed a remarkable preface to a book by the Benedictine nun Maura Böckeler. In this book Böckeler attempted to describe "woman" as a symbol of the Divine, more specifically, as a symbol of the Holy Spirit.

Two other significant figures in the Liturgical Movement in Germany also discussed women's issues, namely, Romano Guardini[10] and Johannes Pinsk. In 1921, Guardini presented a thoughtful talk on "women's nature and mission" to a group of women active in the Catholic Women's Movement. This talk was later published in a leading Catholic women's journal. One of Guardini's close friends played a key role in the Catholic Women's Movement, Gerta Krabbel (1881–1961), the president of the Catholic German Women's Association. Krabbel belonged to Guardini's inner circle of friends since the 1920s. Johannes Pinsk likewise had a particular interest in women's concerns, especially the professional life of women. Pinsk was a regular contributor to various women's journals and wrote extensively on women's issues. After his death in 1957, a book on women and the workplace was published as a posthumous collection of his writings.

The Liturgical Movement in Austria was no less interested in women's issues than its German counterpart. One obvious example is Pius Parsch, with his numerous articles about or for women. Parsch's *Klosterneuburger Hefte* contain a number of issues devoted exclusively to women, including one issue on women around Jesus and one on the biblical "heroine" Judith. Above all, Parsch provides many references to women in the concrete work of the liturgical

---

[10] For a detailed account, see Gerl-Falkovitz, "'dass die Frau sich wirklich selbst finde.' Romano Guardinis Wahr-nehmung der Frau," 127–141.

apostolate. These references show that in the kind of liturgical apostolate Parsch championed, women made up the majority of activists.

Across the Atlantic, women and women's issues were no less present in the Liturgical Movement, as has most recently been demonstrated by Keith Pecklers, S.J., in his study of the Liturgical Movement in the United States of America between the years 1926–1955. Virgil Michel himself consistently supported the leadership of women.[11] Justine Ward (1879–1975), an expert on Gregorian chant,[12] for example, served on the first editorial board of *Orate Fratres*. Michel also cooperated closely with women on some of his numerous projects. A case in point is the Dominican Sisters of Grand Rapids, Michigan. Together with them (they stayed at St. John's Abbey in the summer of 1929), Michel devised a series of religion textbooks for grade school children. Sister Jane Marie Murray, O.P., was one of Michel's main collaborators.[13] It is hardly surprising that Michel also addressed the topic of women and worship in his journal *Orate Fratres* ("The Liturgy and Catholic Women" appeared in 1928/29, "The Christian Woman" in 1938/39). Michel's articles drew on materials he presented in an address to a joint session of the Catholic Central Verein and the Catholic Women's Union held at St. Cloud, Minnesota, in August 1928. The address was entitled "The Liturgical Movement and the Catholic Woman." Women also participated in the North American Liturgical Movement beyond the immediate confines of Virgil Michel's benevolent orbit. As shown below, women missionized and organized, lectured and taught, and above all, worshiped with intensity and joy.

In addition to the "fathers" of the Liturgical Movement showing deep interest in women's issues, and women's active involvement in the liturgical apostolate, one also finds women active in writing and publishing on matters liturgical, especially women in religious communities. But other women authors also emerged in the Liturgical Movement, including Florence Berger, Dorothy Coddington, Therese Mueller, Mary Perkins Ryan, and Mary Fabian Windeatt in North

[11] See Franklin and Spaeth, *Virgil Michel: American Catholic*, 86f.

[12] For more, see the study by Pierre M. Combe, *Justine Ward and Solesmes* (1987).

[13] Murray wrote a tribute to Virgil Michel in the January 1939 commemorative issue of *Orate Fratres*, 107–112.

America,[14] and Edith Hegemann[15] and Maria Louise Lascar[16] in Germany. Regular contributions written by women appeared in liturgical journals such as *Orate Fratres, Bibel und Liturgie,* and *Liturgische Zeitschrift.*

3. THE CULTURAL CONTEXT OF THE LITURGICAL MOVEMENT

A look at the cultural context of the Liturgical Movement further strengthens these findings by showing why women's issues came to the forefront of attention with such force and needed to be addressed by any movement that wanted to be relevant to its own times. The early decades of the twentieth century forced the "woman question" (thus the terminology of the time) on the Liturgical Movement. The movement, however, also found attention to this question congenial with its own theological presuppositions, concepts, and images.

Three factors in particular shaped the "woman question" within the broader cultural context of the Liturgical Movement in Europe and North America. The first such factor was the emergence of a strong Women's Movement, or more accurately, "Woman Movement," in the nineteenth century.[17] The second factor was the various setbacks this movement faced in the 1920s with the end of the suffrage movement. The most marked of these setbacks occurred in Germany and Austria under the National Socialist regime, in Italy with Mussolini's dictatorship, and in Spain with General Franco. There were, however, other noticeable setbacks, as data from the Great Depression in America shows. Third, a distinctive Women's Movement emerged within the Catholic Church in the decades just preceding the Liturgical Movement.

---

[14] More information on all these women is readily available in the two volumes of *How Firm a Foundation,* edited by Kathleen Hughes and Robert L. Tuzik respectively, and in Pecklers's study, *The Unread Vision: The Liturgical Movement in the United States of America: 1926–1955* (1998).

[15] See, for example, her publications "Zu einem Aufsatz über 'Das Priestertum der Frau,'" and "Liturgische Gedanken zur Enzyklika *Quadragesimo Anno.*"

[16] See, for example, her publications "Abendländische und griechisch-orthodoxe Mönchsprofess als Tauferneuerung," "Die Sorge der Kirche für Mutter und Kind," and "Von der Würde und Weihe der christlichen Jungfräulichkeit."

[17] For more, see Cott, *Grounding of Modern Feminism,* 3, 16.

The beginnings of an organized Women's Movement lie in the nineteenth century. By the beginning of the twentieth century, the "woman question" had become a crucial social and political topic, as women entered educational, public, and professional life in rapidly growing numbers. The attention the "woman question" commanded indicates the depth of crisis of traditional women's roles and the intensity of struggle over new interpretations. One of the defining moments of the Women's Movement came with the end of the First World War, when women gained the right to vote in several countries. In the United States, the suffrage amendment was passed by the Senate and ratified by the states in 1919/20. In Germany, (legal) equality of the sexes was in principle guaranteed by the constitution of the Weimar Republic in 1918, the same year that saw the publication of a key book of the nascent Liturgical Movement, Romano Guardini's *The Spirit of the Liturgy*.

Whether the First World War really was a watershed for women is debatable. For some, for example young, middle-class professional women, it certainly was. For others, such as working-class mothers, it was much less so. On the whole, the war resulted in a conservative reaction to changing gender relations. After 1918, two notable developments set in: a "demobilization" of women, especially in relation to women entering professions and academia, and an intensification of "gender warfare."[18] An example of the latter is the mounting vehement critiques of feminism and of emancipated women. These critiques came from various quarters, the Church included (with voices of the Liturgical Movement playing their part[19]). An example of the first, namely, the demobilization of women, is Germany, where the Women's Movement faced drastic setbacks in the 1930s. At the beginning of that decade, women comprised nearly a third of the work force. During the economic crisis of the following years, however, women were increasingly pushed back into the home. When the National Socialists seized power in 1933, they placed quotas on the number of women who could study (no more than 10 percent of the student body), and through various governmental programs, women were strongly encouraged to concentrate on home and family. For the

[18] Thébaud, "The Great War and the Triumph of Sexual Division," 67.
[19] For more, see Berger, *Liturgie und Frauenseele*, 130–136.

National Socialist regime, the Women's Movement was an enemy. Not surprisingly, National Socialism pronounced as one of its goals the "emancipation from women's emancipation." In the United States the situation was very different and yet evidenced some similarities as far as women's lives were concerned. Here also, the economic depression of the 1930s curtailed women's professional lives and fueled critiques of the "modern woman" of the 1920s.

A third issue shaping the way the Liturgical Movement perceived the "woman question" was the emergence of a distinct Women's Movement within the Catholic Church. Catholic women's organizations had mushroomed in the second half of the nineteenth century. Some clearly depended on the ecclesiastical hierarchy, but others were more independent, with control in the hands of women themselves. The membership was comparatively large. In Germany alone, almost two million women belonged to various Catholic women's organizations in the mid-twenties.[20] In America, the National Council of Catholic Women began in 1920. Within a decade, fifty diocesan women's organizations and at least sixteen national women's societies affiliated with it.[21] A number of significant movements led by women also flourished together with the Liturgical Movement. In some cases, strong links existed between these movements and the Liturgical Movement. Dorothy Day and the Catholic Worker Movement, as well as Catherine de Hueck Doherty and the houses she founded, are cases in point. So is the Grail Movement, transplanted from the Netherlands to the United States by Lydwine van Kersbergen.[22] These women leaders all participated in the Liturgical Movement, which in turn benefited from the influence of committed women with apostolates of their own.

Women's issues, then, had come to the forefront of attention in society and the Church during the rise of the Liturgical Movement. The traditional historiography of the movement, however, simply ignores

[20] See Sack, "Katholische Frauenbewegung, katholische Jugendbewegung und Politik in der Weimarer Republik," 121.

[21] See Cott, *Grounding of Modern Feminism*, 92.

[22] For a history of the Grail movement in America, see Alden V. Brown, *The Grail Movement and American Catholicism, 1940–1975* (1989). For a recent interview with Lydwine van Kersbergen (b. 1905), see O'Brien and Miller, "A Woman of Vision," 95–106.

women and reflections on women's issues. The "master" narrative thus renders invisible an important element of the original movement. The historiographic consensus that women were of little relevance in the Liturgical Movement, is, of course, not established through lengthy arguments; rather, it is created through silence. None of the traditional narratives of the Liturgical Movement mention the intense debates over women's issues that raged in society at the time. Few accounts make reference to the women's religious communities that played an important role in the movement. Never are the numerous publications by women noted.

This consensus of silence in the reception history of the Liturgical Movement is all-embracing. It marks such early descriptions as that of the Protestant theologian Walter Birnbaum (1926, 1966) and that of Waldemar Trapp (1939). It permeates the book of the Belgian Benedictine Olivier Rousseau (1945) and the theological analysis of Ernest Benjamin Koenker (1954). It characterizes the works of Louis Bouyer (1955), Ferdinand Kolbe (1964), and Lancelot Sheppard (1967). It exists in the memoirs of Bernard Botte (1973). It colors the detailed research of Theodor Maas-Ewerd (1969, 1981). And it still dominates the recent narrative of the development of the Liturgical Movement by John Fenwick and Bryan Spinks (1995). If authors refer to women at all in these histories of the Liturgical Movement (one writer calls women active in the movement "liturgical ladies"[23]), they often do so in a subtly negative context, depicting women as the ones clinging obstinately to praying the rosary while liturgically enlightened priests attempt communal celebrations of the Mass.

These histories may lead to the assumption that the invisibility of women arises from the fact that women themselves have not shaped the writing of this history. This assumption, however, is too simplistic, as a recent work dealing in part with the Liturgical Movement demonstrates. In her book *In Her Own Rite* (1990), Marjorie Procter-Smith compares the Liturgical Movement with the Women's Movement. She characterizes the Liturgical Movement as begun and led exclusively by men, mostly priests; in stark contrast, the Women's Movement clearly is a women's initiative.[24] Procter-Smith, who em-

[23] Rusch, "Erinnerungen an Pater Jungmann," 123.
[24] See Procter-Smith, *In Her Own Rite*, 1–35; cf. Northup, *Ritualizing Women*, 17f.

ploys a Feminist methodology, obviously does not want to marginalize women, yet she supports such a marginalization through her characterization of the Liturgical Movement. She joins a host of other writers in rendering invisible the many women and their voices in the Liturgical Movement. The roots for Procter-Smith's unintentional marginalization of women lie in an uncritical acceptance of a mainstream liturgical historiography blissfully ignorant of women's ways of worship. Such an uncritical acceptance is misplaced.

One indication that this mainstream narrative of the Liturgical Movement is beginning to change is provided by the two volumes *How Firm a Foundation* and by the recent study of Keith F. Pecklers. These books introduce some of the pioneers of the Liturgical Movement and their writings. The first volume of *How Firm a Foundation, Voices of the Early Liturgical Movement,* includes fourteen women among the seventy "voices," all of them from the North American side of the movement. No European women are included, however, although many European men are. Even Aemiliana Löhr is missing.

Deconstructing the traditional historiography and reconstructing the presence of women and women's issues in the Liturgical Movement demand renewed attention to the movement as a whole, not only to select women who happen to be more visible than the others. In the last analysis, the marginalization of women and women's issues in the reception history of the Liturgical Movement can be corrected only through a renewed hearing of the original voices of the Liturgical Movement itself, not through a simple critique of secondary works. What follows, then, will analyze the Liturgical Movement as it was shaped and "moved" either by women or by women's issues.

4. THE LITURGICAL MOVEMENT: MOVED BY WOMEN

4.1. *Women as Subjects of the Liturgy*

The Liturgical Movement at its heart was a rediscovery of the communal celebration of the liturgy as *the* fundamental act of the Church. The movement thus signaled a break with a ("Tridentine") understanding of liturgy that primarily centered around a conglomeration of individual rites and rubrics. The rediscovery of the local assembly as the subject of the liturgy led directly to Pius Parsch's succinct question "How is a woman a subject of the liturgy?" Parsch posed this question in a 1933 article entitled "Woman's Participation in the Liturgical Movement." The article was based on a talk he gave at an "important liturgical meeting for women" (according to the later description in his journal *Bibel und Liturgie*).

In answering his own question, Parsch stressed that women, as baptized and confirmed members of the Church, are indeed full subjects of the liturgy. Women participate in the priesthood of all believers "in the same complete measure as a man."[25] Parsch found biblical support for his claim in Galatians 3:28, which he interpreted to mean that "Christ eliminated any inferiority that might have existed previously. In Christ, both man and woman are considered absolutely equal as far as their being subjects of the liturgy is concerned." In parentheses, he quickly added "with the exception of the ordained ministry."[26] Despite this disclaimer, it is clear that in the Liturgical Movement the rediscovery of the whole Church as the subject of the liturgy included the recognition of women as bearers of the liturgy.

Was this recognition primarily theoretical? For an answer, one needs to look beyond the key writings of the fathers of the Liturgical Movement. Other sources, particularly those reflecting liturgical life at the (parish) base, yield the crucial clues. Women are more readily visible as active participants and shapers of the Liturgical Movement in the local parish than they are in the great monastic, clerical, and scholarly centers. A number of women's activities in the parish-centered Liturgical Movement deserve particular attention.

4.1.1. Women as Bearers of Liturgical Traditioning

There is, to begin with, the role of women as liturgical educators. This catechetical role of women had been exercised primarily within the family (and schools), but with the Liturgical Movement it clearly moved beyond, particularly into parishes. Promoting the catechetical role of women, of course, was no invention of the Liturgical Movement. In preceding centuries, women's educational and "civilizing" powers had often been noted ("the hand that rocks the cradle holds the world"). In the Liturgical Movement, these "powers" took on a liturgical direction. Women, for example, initiated other women

---

[25] Parsch, "Die Mitarbeit der Frau in der liturgischen Bewegung," 440.
[26] Ibid.

into a fuller understanding of the Latin liturgy, distributed liturgical texts in their parishes and neighborhoods, led parish classes introducing people to the use of the missal, pushed for the rediscovery of the blessing of homes among parish members, integrated the liturgical year into their duties as kindergarten teachers and homemakers, and accompanied children of the parish in their preparation for the sacraments.[27] In all these activities, women clearly "moved" the Liturgical Movement at the parish level.

Another facet of women's active part in the Liturgical Movement was the growing number of devotional books on the liturgy, particularly the Mass, that were directed toward women as their audience. These devotional books written specifically for women often had women as their authors. These little books and pamphlets do not capture the attention, never mind the admiration, of liturgists today, but they are a visible indicator of a vibrant link between women and worship in the Liturgical Movement.

A third aspect of women's presence in the parish-based Liturgical Movement is found in the liturgical base communities that sprang up in the wake of the movement. These groups, usually known as "liturgical study clubs," were largely made up of women[28] and frequently were initiated and led by women.[29] The structure of these groups resembled in many ways what today would be called "base ecclesial communities," small groups that meet to pray, sing, reflect, and act together. Such groups mushroomed as part of the Liturgical Movement. In 1932, for example, Mrs. John W. Clendenin, then the executive secretary of the Catholic Action Committee of Women, reported in *Orate Fratres* that in the Wichita diocese alone, sixty-five such clubs existed, with the expectation that many more would be formed.[30]

These clubs accomplished two things in particular. They empowered women in matters liturgical through a deepened understanding of the liturgy, and they provided women with a liturgical apostolate outside the traditional domestic sphere. In other words, women active

[27] For more, see Berger, *Liturgie und Frauenseele*, 112f.

[28] See, for example, the note "Catholic Women are Studying the Liturgy," *Orate Fratres* 7:30f.

[29] See, for example, the description by Dorcas, "Nothing Ventured," 492–495.

[30] See *Orate Fratres* 7 (1932) 523.

in the Liturgical Movement were neither confined to the home nor to the traditional liturgical role of spectators. Being active in the Liturgical Movement for women meant embracing an apostolate much wider than the domestic sphere. With its concentration on the liturgy of the Church, the Liturgical Movement offered women the possibility of a public ecclesial apostolate of sorts. The possible tension between women's domestic tasks and this liturgical apostolate was noticed early on. Pius Parsch, for example, cautioned women against attending Mass every morning if this infringed upon their domestic duties. The Mass had to take second place if the husband and children were waiting for breakfast.[31]

Taking together the avenues women found to educate themselves in matters liturgical and the roles they fashioned for themselves as liturgical activists, one can easily imagine how these women, implicitly or explicitly, posed a challenge to the traditional liturgical omnicompetence and power of the parish priest. The Liturgical Movement nurtured a form of liturgical leadership of women in its midst, even if this was not always appreciated, either by the parish priest or by other women. One woman activist was admonished by a woman parishioner: "You're monkeying with things only the priest has a right to know about . . . and you'll have to tell it in confession."[32]

4.1.2. "Liturgical Experiences" of Women

What the "new wonderful world of the liturgy" meant to women becomes clear in the narratives of "liturgical experiences" written by women. Pius Parsch's journal *Bibel und Liturgie* had a regular column with exactly that title. *Orate Fratres* contained a column entitled "The Apostolate" and a section called "Communications," which regularly described the ways in which the liturgy could shape the daily lives of laypeople. These two liturgical journals thus provide important insights into the interplay between women and worship in the Liturgical Movement.

In many cases, the commitment of women to a life shaped by the liturgy was intense. The Catholic Women's Union in the United

---

[31] See Parsch, "Liturgie und Familie," 166. This admonition to women to skip early morning Mass if it conflicted with family breakfast was no invention of the Liturgical Movement; see McDannell, "Catholic Domesticity," 56f.

[32] Dorcas, "Nothing Ventured," 494.

States, for example, passed a series of resolutions entitled "Liturgical Movement and Catholic Women," which expected the following of a Catholic woman: making the Eucharist the center of her spiritual life, use of the missal, reading of the liturgical texts before Mass, joining a liturgical study club, receiving the Eucharist at every Mass attended, bimonthly or monthly confession, supporting the priest in the reintroduction of liturgical celebrations such as the Liturgy of the Hours, promoting congregational singing, and carrying the spirit of the liturgy into the home.[33]

Not every woman active in the Liturgical Movement followed this regimen, but women's narratives of their liturgical experiences show the deep imprint of the liturgical renewal. A first trait these narratives share is the passionate conviction women had of their liturgical apostolate. Emphatic commitments such as "We want to be apostles" or "We want our liturgical apostolate to be grounded in a deep knowledge of the liturgy" appear over and over.[34] This deep consciousness of a liturgical apostolate was rooted in a new sense of ownership of the liturgy on the part of women active in the movement. Again and again these women emphasized how important it was to them to "co-pray and co-celebrate" the liturgy. An author identified only as Lina M. wrote in *Bibel und Liturgie*:

"I remember very well the first time I went to Mass with my *Schott* [a German-language missal]. A day earlier, my sister had initiated me into the mysteries of the priest's Mass. . . . So, courageously, I began to pray the Mass together with the priest. The beginnings, of course, were very difficult, and I had to leave out many a thing to even keep up half-way with the celebrating priest. I was glad when Mass was over. . . . Today, I cannot imagine a Mass any more in which I do not really join in the prayers and co-celebrate. . . . I am deeply grateful to all those who led me into this new wonderful world of the liturgy."[35]

The importance of "co-celebrating" the liturgy is also evident in the exhortation of Mary Frioux, an American laywoman, to priests:

[33] See "Liturgical Movement and Catholic Women," 565f.
[34] For but one example see Loley, "Liturgische Exerzitien in Poysdorf," 306f.
[35] Lina M., "Wie ich zur Liturgie kam," 324.

"You fail to realize that you do not offer alone. . . . Do not consider us incapable of taking complete part in it [the Mass]. We can, reverend Fathers, we can . . . we are a royal priesthood too. . . . Give us the Mass, dear Fathers."[36] The insistence of women on *"co-celebrating"* easily attracted the suspicion of the hierarchy, as an incident involving the Grail and Archbishop Samuel A. Stritch of Chicago illustrates. The Grail had advertised its first summer program in the United States in 1942 with a flyer announcing, "Together, we will celebrate the Holy Mysteries." Lydwine van Kersbergen was promptly informed by the Archbishop that "the faithful assist at Mass . . . but they do not celebrate Mass, which essentially consists in acts of exclusively priestly power."[37] The Archbishop would not have been pleased to hear another Grail member, Janet Kalven, assure a group of diocesan women in the Midwest in the same year that they were "co-offerers of the Holy Sacrifice of the Mass."[38]

Second, many women's narratives share a liturgical discourse clearly shaped by the distinct "language game" of the Liturgical Movement. To quote one example:

"My awaking in the morning is a turning to the *parousia* of the Lord's grace, which will again be granted to me today in the holy sacrifice of the Mass. While getting dressed, I allow the introit, or another part of today's Mass which has captured my attention . . . to resonate in my soul. I also reflect on the fact that I now clothe myself in the mystery dress [*Mysterienkleid*] of this day."[39]

The ease with which women, for better or worse, appropriated for themselves the linguistic world of the Liturgical Movement was, in all likelihood, due to the liturgical formation taking place in the study clubs.

Third, this quote and many others like it show how intensely women of the Liturgical Movement allowed their daily lives to be shaped by the liturgy of the Church. A telling example of the way in which women's *domestic* lives were "liturgized" is found in the fasci-

---

[36] Frioux, "Lay Woman Speaks Up," 225f.
[37] Quoted in Campbell, "Heyday of Catholic Action," 241.
[38] Ibid., 242.
[39] Anonyma, "Leben mit der Kirche," 411.

nating little book by Florence S. Berger entitled *Cooking for Christ: The Liturgical Year in the Kitchen* (1949). Florence Berger (1909–1983) was one of the key figures of the North American Liturgical Movement, the Catholic Women's Movement, and the National Catholic Rural Life Conference. *Cooking for Christ* wove these three commitments together into a collection that turned out to be far more than simply a cookbook. *Cooking for Christ* provided a continuous narrative of liturgical catechesis, biblical and theological reflection, traditional devotional practices, personal and family anecdotes, and, of course, recipes. Most of the latter had their origin in traditional European dishes connected in one way or another with liturgical feasts and seasons, among them German "Easter sweet bread" and Dutch "bishopwyn," French "pâté de Noël," and "St. Michael's waffles." In all of this, Berger wrote with great ease and confidence, whether she was quoting liturgical texts, drawing on the wisdom of Josef Andreas Jungmann, relating an anecdote about Martin Hellriegel, or advising the (female) readers to use a pressure cooker[40] for the Christmas plum pudding and not cook it for ten hours, as the generation of their grandmothers had still done. A quote from the preface to *Cooking for Christ* gives a "taste" of Berger's book:

"Of all the rooms in a house, the friendly, comforting kitchen is mother to us all. It is the source of our food, our learning and our virtue. . . . There is, I believe, a reason for this, and it lies in the woman who is mistress of that kitchen. Cook, you may call her. I prefer to call her 'Christian in Action.' She herself is Christ-centered because she brings Christ home to her kitchen and, in corollary, her kitchen reflects the Christ within her. To some it may seem sacrilegious

---

[40] This tiny example reveals another divide (beyond gender) in the Liturgical Movement, a divide that still awaits scholarly attention. I am thinking of the analysis of such factors as class and race. At a point in time when, for example, fewer than three-fifths of white tobacco workers' households and fewer than two-fifths of the black workers' households around Durham, North Carolina, had electricity (Cott, *Grounding of Modern Feminism*, 145), Berger's assumptions of her readers' context clearly reveal a middle-class audience. The larger issue looming behind this example is the "class appeal" of the Liturgical Movement. To put it differently, one could ask whether there was a Liturgical Movement in, for, by, and with disenfranchised white and black workers, Native Americans, working class children. What did it look like?

to connect cookery and Christ, but that is exactly what this book means to do. If I am to carry Christ home with me from the altar, I am afraid he will have to come to the kitchen because much of my time is spent there. . . . Liturgists have called us back to a vision of early Christian worship and have begged for more active lay participation in the Lord's service. . . . Now perhaps mothers and daughters can lead their families back to Christ-centered living and cooking. Foods can be symbols which lead the mind to spiritual thinking."[41]

As a cookbook, Berger's little volume was not alone. For example, the *Feast Day Cookbook* by Katherine Burton and Helmut Ripperger and the *Cookbook for Fridays and Lent* by Irma Rhode both appeared in 1951. These two books were less colored, though, by the influence of the Liturgical Movement than Berger's. As a little monument of one woman's "liturgizing" of her daily (kitchen) life, *Cooking for Christ* stands by itself (on its right hand stands Florence Berger's companion volume *Cooking for Christ: Your Kitchen Prayer Book*). Through this process of "liturgizing," women shaped traditional female activities into an important part of the liturgical apostolate. These women activists of the Liturgical Movement grasped the whole of their lives, including meal preparation, as in need of a liturgical stamp.

Another good example of the phenomenon of "liturgization" is the text from the Catholic Women's Union alluded to above. In 1933, this organization adopted a series of resolutions at its annual convention in Missouri that were published in *Orate Fratres* under the title "Liturgical Movement and Catholic Women." The text outlines a detailed "liturgization" of a woman's life, especially the domestic sphere: from the removal of "unworthy pictures" from the walls and the blessing of a home by a priest to holy water fonts in individual rooms; from the making of the baptismal garment to the abolishing of birthday parties for the sake of celebrating the children's saints' days and baptismal anniversaries; from cultivating a "Catholic Saturday evening spirit" to "[s]upernaturalizing" the Christmas Eve celebration.[42]

---

[41] Berger, *Cooking for Christ*, Preface.
[42] See "Liturgical Movement and Catholic Women," 564–568.

One last point related to women's involvement in the Liturgical Movement is worth mentioning here. It concerns the making of liturgical vestments, traditionally a woman's task. In the journal *Bibel und Liturgie,* for example, one finds over the years quite a few articles on this subject. A good number of them were written by women. Many issues of this journal also included embroidery models for liturgical vestments. Their target audience clearly was women engaged in the making of liturgical vestments. With the help of these women, the Liturgical Movement pointedly struggled against lace as part of liturgical vestments. Lace was seen as "worldly, effeminate, and feminine,"[43] which is why the "effeminate lace constantly growing in breadth"[44] had no rightful place in the embroidering of liturgical vestments. It is one of the smaller ironies of the history of women at worship that this liturgical battle against a supposedly effeminate piece of cloth was in practice waged by women.

4.2. The Liturgy as a Script for Womanhood

Women in the Liturgical Movement do not only receive theoretical recognition as full subjects of the liturgy, nor is their presence described exhaustively by various women-specific activities. The Liturgical Movement also had an intense interest in interpreting the liturgy as an authoritative script for gender roles, particularly that of "woman." The liturgy, in short, came to be claimed as a "prayed ideal of womanhood."[45] There was, then, in the Liturgical Movement a conscious attempt to develop a specifically liturgical version of "woman."

The social location of the movement made such an attempt a necessity. As mentioned above, the time period of the Liturgical Movement was characterized by an intense debate and reinterpretation of women's roles in society and the Church. The Liturgical Movement joined in this debate by trying to define the nature of woman *on the basis of the liturgy.* The question never raised by the movement was whether the liturgy was an adequate place for defining "women's nature" (that there is such a thing, no one doubted). In the Liturgical Movement, one is confronted with something like a

---

[43] Parsch, "Paramentenschule," 19–22, 60–63, 246f., 345–347, here 20.
[44] *Bibel und Liturgie* 7 (1932/33) 291.
[45] Parsch, "Die Mitarbeit der Frau in der liturgischen Bewegung," 436.

liturgical hegemonism: the liturgy becomes the ultimate reference point for the whole of life, including gender roles.

The liturgical ideal of "woman" that the Liturgical Movement proposed had its basis in the image of the *Ekklesia* in the liturgy. As Aemiliana Löhr put it: "In the image of the Church, as it radiantly becomes visible in the liturgy, each Catholic woman recognizes her specific calling according to God's will: to be a vessel, to be receptive. . . . This is the nature of woman. . . . In the liturgy, then, woman sees herself in the image of the *Ekklesia*."[46]

This equation "Woman—Church"(!) is true not only on the textual level but also in terms of imagery. Illustrations in publications of the Liturgical Movement often depict the Church as a stylized, timelessly beautiful woman. Not surprisingly, this woman regularly takes on the figure of the early Christian *Orante*. The "awakening of the Church in the souls," which, according to Romano Guardini, was at the heart of the Liturgical Movement, was also the (re-?)awakening of an intensely feminine image of the Church. As Ildefons Herwegen emphasized, "Woman and Church is to a certain extent an equation. For the Church has always remained feminine . . . the Church is the archetype of the Christian Woman."[47]

The specific ideal of "woman" as proposed by the Liturgical Movement on the basis of the liturgical image of the Church was a traditional and conservative one. It characterized women primarily by sexual functions, their absence, or their consequences: woman is "virgin," "bride," or "mother." The conviction that the Christian woman as virgin, bride, or mother is the most profound image of the Church was at the heart of the Liturgical Movement's woman-script (fundamental to this conviction was, of course, the idea of the Church as the bride of Christ, while being at the same time both virgin and mother).

---

[46] Löhr, "Priestertum der Frau," 349.

[47] Herwegen, "Kirche und Frau," 131f. One result of the intense feminization of ecclesiology (the other side of the ecclesiazation of woman) was a highly charged erotic liturgical discourse. This was particularly noticeable in the orbit of Maria Laach. The Church was seen as the "lover of the Triune God," "born to spousal intercourse with God in prayer" (Aemiliana Löhr). The liturgy became "the mysterious loving intercourse between Christ and the *Ekklesia*" (Odo Casel). For more on this, see Berger, *Liturgie und Frauenseele*, 60–64.

This ecclesiological woman-script of the Liturgical Movement found its most sustained expression in Athanasius Wintersig's *Liturgy and Woman's Soul*. The book was first published in 1925 and went through five editions in the following years. In 1932, a sixth and final edition was published. The fact that a book on women and worship by a Benedictine monk would go through six editions—and that in a time of economic depression—is a clear indication of *Liturgy and Woman's Soul* finding an eager audience.

As part of its liturgical ideal of "woman," the Liturgical Movement embraced the traditional gender dualism: the active creation of life belongs to man, the passive reception and nurturing to woman. The way in which this gender dualism was read liturgically is shown in the following quote from Athanasius Wintersig: "Only men are able to govern and teach in the Church, because only a man is able to represent Christ to the Church . . . only a man can beget life, and therefore a man alone can mediate anew to the Church divine life . . . a woman is perfected by becoming more and more like the Church which receives life."[48]

The traditional and conservative ideal of womanhood espoused by the Liturgical Movement was rooted in an intense gender dualism. One of the great threats of feminism for many leaders of the Liturgical Movement was the "masculinization" of women. The proponents of this liturgical woman-script were by no means only men. Aemiliana Löhr, for one, clearly embraced this liturgical ideal of womanhood. In a review of a book on "woman's priesthood," she wrote in 1934: "As the representative of Christ, man is by his very nature essentially priest, lord, and bridegroom; as the image of the *Ekklesia*, woman is by her very nature essentially sacrifice, servant, and bride."[49]

One counterpoint must be noted, though. This traditional (now liturgically based) woman-script developed a liturgical dynamic of its own, a dynamic quite contrary to the language of subordination and passivity. Through the traditional identification of woman with nurture and feeling (over against man's tendency toward rational thought), the Liturgical Movement ascribed to women a natural affinity

[48] Wintersig in a review of Neundörfer, "Bedingtes und Unbedingtes in der Stellung des hl. Paulus zur Frau," 281.
[49] Löhr in a review of Schneider, "Priestertum der Frau," 278.

with the liturgy: "woman . . . unless artificially repressed and distorted, craves for the spiritual in a degree far above that of the average man," wrote Virgil Michel.[50] Women therefore came to be seen as better able to appreciate the mystery that is worship than men. For Michel, woman—the "good Christian woman," that is—takes on sacramental qualities. She is "as it were a natural sacrament in the world, an external sign of inner grace radiating goodness."[51]

The natural affinity between women and the liturgy also serves to explain why there were far more women than men active in the Liturgical Movement. Pius Parsch noted:

"Everybody working at the center of the Liturgical Movement is able to see that woman is far more receptive to liturgical prayer and celebration than man. In our liturgical communities and celebrations, ninety out of a hundred worshipers are women. I have frequently wondered why this is the case, especially since Christ himself turned to men first. The reason probably is that, today, men are more shaped by individualism than women are. Communal worship is therefore not as attractive to men. Woman also has a natural tendency to turn inward and to contemplate, while man is too active to appreciate the regular forms of the liturgy. He does not have enough patience and calmness for them. Now we know why it is woman who shows such a deep appreciation of the liturgy. . . . Woman . . . is the best apostle of the liturgy. . . . Particularly young women . . . today are the primary bearers of liturgical renewal."[52]

A similar argument is made in the text "Liturgical Movement and Catholic Women" produced by the Catholic Women's Union. In fact, the wording between this text and Parsch's is so similar that the writer(s) almost certainly drew on Parsch. One reads:

"Experience shows us that, in almost every part of the world, the steadily growing Liturgical Movement has received greater and more whole-hearted support from women than from men. This may be due to the fact that man, in whom 'individualism' is more pronounced than in woman, is slower in embracing the 'corporate piety'

---

[50] Michel, "Liturgy and Catholic Women," 253.
[51] Ibid., 274. Cf. Michel, "Christian Woman," 253.
[52] Parsch, "Die Mitarbeit der Frau in der liturgischen Bewegung," 436f.

as contained in the liturgy. Man also is too active. He has not the patience and the quietness necessary for entering into the more tranquil forms and norms of the liturgy. Woman on the other hand is more disposed towards interior recollection and more susceptible, not only of liturgical piety, but of piety in general."[53]

Plagiarism or not, it is worth comparing these statements with the traditional picture of the invisibility of women in the Liturgical Movement!

4.3. Liturgical Ministries of Women

Convinced that women had a natural affinity with the liturgical mystery, the Liturgical Movement could not avoid the question of women's liturgical ministries. Initially, the question was approached through glorifying women's traditional roles[54] at the fringes of the liturgy, such as arranging flowers in church ("Who can care for the flowers in church better than a woman?"[55]). But the question of the "Role of the Christian Woman in the Liturgy"—as the Belgian priest Georges Malherbe (1865–1956)[56] raised it at the Liturgical Week at Malines in 1924—needed a more liturgically centered answer than glorifying women's care of paraphernalia in worship. Malherbe himself managed to produce the following short list: presence at worship, recitation of the prayers in union with the priest, sharing in communal liturgical singing, and encouraging children to join the

---

[53] "Liturgical Movement and Catholic Women," 565.

[54] Women throughout history had continued traditional forms of patronage as outlined in the previous chapter. An interesting example of women still building churches at the time of the Liturgical Movement is the Women's Peace Church (*Frauenfriedenskirche*) in Frankfurt am Main, Germany. Some of the money was raised by a key figure of the Catholic Women's Movement in Germany and member of the German parliament, Hedwig Dransfeld (1871–1925), traveling to the United States in 1923 and presenting the cause there, especially among German Americans. For more on Dransfeld, her visit to the United States, and the *Frauenfriedenskirche*, see Prégardier and Mohr, *Politik als Aufgabe*, 253–285. Sack, "Katholische Frauenbewegung, katholische Jugendbewegung und Politik in der Weimarer Republik," 132–138, rightly notes the tension between the patriotic-militaristic and the pacifist vision behind the *Frauenfriedenskirche*.

[55] Malherbe, "Le rôle de la femme chrétienne en liturgie," 186.

[56] Malherbe was a parish priest in Ronquières in the diocese of Tournai from 1905 to 1947.

choir.[57] The list is eclectic and haphazard—evidence of the fact that the author was struggling with a subject beyond his competence. What is noteworthy, however, is the fact that the question of women's liturgical roles surfaced at a Liturgical Week in 1924. There must have been a perceived demand for this issue to be addressed. In the long run, the Liturgical Movement could not avoid more central issues, including the priesthood of women.

4.3.1. *The Priesthood of Women*

Reflections on the priesthood of women were fueled in the Liturgical Movement, on the one hand, by the theological rediscovery of the notion of a (liturgical) priesthood of all believers. On the other hand, the ordination of women begun in some of the non-Roman Catholic communities of faith brought this topic to the forefront. Two other reasons contributed to the Liturgical Movement confronting women's ordination. First, in some parts of the Women's Movement, the exclusion of women from ordination was ammunition for the Feminist attack on the religious establishment. Second, some women in the Liturgical Movement themselves were beginning to name the pain of being excluded from ordination (with some men arguing that only the new brand of academic women would feel this way). Oda Schneider (1892–1987), an Austrian Catholic writer, acknowledged this pain of exclusion on the very first page of her book *On Woman's Priesthood* (1934). She described it as a pain every strongly religious woman experiences at some point in her life, a claim Aemiliana Löhr rejected in her review of the book for the *Jahrbuch für Liturgiewissenschaft*.

The Liturgical Movement as a whole displayed great diversity in reasoning about the exclusion of women from ordained ministry. While some writers pointed to the example of Christ, who chose only men as his apostles ("because he wanted to protect his Church from feminism"),[58] others saw woman as an image of the Church, not of Christ. Still others noted a discrepancy between the strongly feminine character of the Church and the exclusion of women from its altars. Josephine Mayer, a teacher and the wife of Anton L. Mayer, one of the editors of the *Jahrbuch für Liturgiewissenschaft*, asked in 1931: "Is

[57] Malherbe, "Le rôle de la femme chrétienne en liturgie," 181–186.
[58] Stenta, "Lebensweihe durch die Liturgie," 29.

94

this not a contradiction: Woman shall be most powerfully changed in her innermost devotional existence by the renewal of the spirit of the liturgy in exactly that Church which excludes her from ordained ministry and which forcefully maintains the maxim *Mulier taceat*?"[59]

In a similar vein, Aemiliana Löhr noted: "A curious contradiction: The *Ekklesia*, who is a woman . . . she, the virgin-mother, who constantly birthes new children for her heavenly husband out of the pure baptismal font which is her virgin womb, and who nurses them with holy 'milk,' the divine blood of her lover . . . she, the *Ekklesia*, a woman, the woman of earth and of heaven . . . this woman, the earthly image of the heavenly wisdom,—she does not allow women at her altars? This seems contradictory."[60]

Löhr clearly marked a tension here between the image of the *Ekklesia* as a woman—even a "priestess"—and the exclusion of women from the priesthood. Löhr, of course, did not solve this contradiction by advocating women's ordination. Rather, she identified the priestly office of women in the liturgy with the sacrifice that is offered: "Woman, as an image of the *Ekklesia*, has the duty and the grace to be offered as sacrifice and to constantly reflect in her life the sacrificial self-giving of the *Ekklesia*."[61] Man, as the image of Christ, is called to be priest and to offer this sacrifice.

The diversity of arguments within the Liturgical Movement against the ordination of women evidenced the need for justification of this practice. Two points deserve further mention in this connection. There was, first, in the Liturgical Movement an attempt to delineate an exclusively and specifically feminine priesthood. Woman is the priest of the home and the family, particularly the children.[62] This, of course, was no invention of the Liturgical Movement. The stereotype of woman as the "priestess of the hearth" had risen to quite some prominence in the second half of the nineteenth century.[63] The Liturgical Movement

[59] Mayer, "Pflege liturgischer Gesinnung," 240.

[60] Löhr, "Vom Opfer, vom Zeugnis und von der Geduld," 56.

[61] Ibid., 57.

[62] This topic is by no means confined to Roman Catholicism. The topic was also present, for example, in Jewish devotional literature for women; see Kratz-Ritter, *Für "fromme Zionstöchter" und "gebildete Frauenzimmer": Andachtsliteratur für deutsch-jüdische Frauen*, 19, 43, 77, 145f.

[63] See, for example, McDannell, "Catholic Domesticity," 61.

simply rooted this stereotype liturgically. As Virgil Michel put it: "The mother is indeed a gardener of God doing a veritable priestly work in the Christian care of her children. . . . She is truly the priestess of the home; hers is the sacerdotal work of bringing the latent seeds of divine grace . . . to bud forth in the soul of the child."[64] Norbert Stenta (1900–1939), a close associate of Pius Parsch at Klosterneuburg, went so far as to interpret the churching of women after childbirth as a "mother's ordination to her priesthood." He wrote:

"Being a mother means being a priest. At a time when we talk increasingly about the ministry of the laity, when we stress increasingly the priesthood of all believers and are no longer afraid to be labeled Protestants because of this, we also need to talk more about the particular priesthood of women. Certainly, the wife already exercises a holy, sanctifying priesthood vis-à-vis her husband, but how much deeper, how much more intensely divinizing [*vergöttlichend*] is the priesthood of the mother . . . the mother-priesthood is the highest expression of the priesthood of all believers . . . Exercising pastoral care, being priest to the coming generation, this is the great and holy task of women today."[65]

Stenta went so far as to pin the fate of Western civilization on this "mother-priesthood" (the article was written in 1932/1933!):

"The fate of the Western world will be decided with the fulfillment or non-fulfillment of this most beautiful profession in the world of Christian woman. Will they be missionaries of the light or of darkness; saintly priestly mothers or easygoing destructive playgirls; priestesses aware of their calling in this century, or demons precipitating the downfall—on this hangs whatever will decide the fate of our culture in the near future."[66]

The topos of women as the saviors of the world was widespread both in the Liturgical Movement and beyond. Virgil Michel for one used it in the article quoted above on "Christian Woman."[67] Women

[64] Michel, "Christian Woman," 250f.

[65] Stenta, "Volksliturgie und Lebensweihe," 193–196.

[66] Ibid., 195.

[67] See Michel, "Christian Woman," 254: "woman has a high Christian apostolate to perform in the world, the neglect of which means the downfall of civilization itself."

themselves often put the emphasis elsewhere when talking about their own specific priesthood. This was particularly the case for women who had entered the work force outside the home. An anonyma, for example, claimed in an article in *Bibel und Liturgie* that she went to work after the early morning Mass "to continue her priestly ministry in the liturgy of life."[68] This woman clearly did not understand herself primarily as a priest of the home but as a priest in the liturgy of her professional life.

4.3.2. The Diaconate for Women

A second subject garnering attention in the Liturgical Movement in connection with women's liturgical ministries was the diaconate. Through its research, the Liturgical Movement knew of the ministry of deaconesses in the early Church. Due to the movement's high regard for the early Church, some argued, albeit gingerly, for the rediscovery of this office by the Church of their day. The question of women's diaconate was treated, mostly positively, by such key figures as Odo Casel, Ildefons Herwegen, Pius Parsch, Virgil Michel, and Athanasius Wintersig.

The most sustained theological argument for a renewal of women's diaconate came, however, from a woman, Josephine Mayer. In an article written in 1938, Mayer studied the office of deaconesses in the early Church (she published, in the same year, a collection of early Church sources related to deaconesses in the prestigious series *Florilegium Patristicum*). But Mayer's guiding interest was not antiquarian. The crucial issue for her was that of a "deaconess of the future," authorized ecclesially by sacramental consecration. Mayer herself advocated such a ministry of women in the Church.[69] Most other women authors in the Liturgical Movement were not as bold as Josephine Mayer. They instead tended to reinterpret already existing fringe involvements of women in the liturgy, such as care of liturgical vessels and vestments, as "diaconal."[70]

In conclusion, the "norm of the fathers" embraced by the Liturgical Movement could, in some instances, lead to something like a revolution by tradition. It forced the movement to acknowledge the existence

[68] Anonyma, "Leben mit der Kirche," 412.
[69] See Mayer, "Diakonat der Frau," 106.
[70] See, for example, Schneider, *Macht der Frau*, 342.

of women's liturgical ministries in the heart of what it considered a normative moment in the Church's life, that is, the earliest centuries of the Church.

4.3.4. Lay Liturgical Ministries for Women

Questions about other liturgical ministries for women also began to surface in the Liturgical Movement. Written evidence, however, is by no means as rich as it is for the question of diaconal and priestly ministries. There are a few indications of women serving as lectors (that is to say, they would read the vernacular version of what the priest read in Latin), veiled admissions on the part of one woman of the desire to minister as an altar server, and references to women forming a liturgical *schola*.[71] The latter is especially interesting, since the famed *motu proprio* on church music of Pope Pius X, *Tra le sollecitudini* (1903), had described women as *incapaci* of the *liturgical ministry* of singing.[72] If women did sing in worship, it was not to be considered a liturgical ministry. Pius Parsch, in his parish of St. Gertrud in Klosterneuburg, nevertheless formed choirs of young girls who sang in the liturgy (in white tunics and veiled—a case of retrogression by tradition).[73]

4.4. Women's Liturgical Communities

Throughout the history of Christian worship, women's religious communities provided spaces with a distinct and intense interplay of women and worship. For one, religious women had direct "access" to the liturgy on a daily basis as part of their expected way of life (without priests worrying about husbands and children waiting for breakfast while the woman attended Mass). Within the Liturgical

[71] For more, see Berger, *Liturgie und Frauenseele*, 88–90.

[72] In light of this, it is questionable that a women-specific read of the Liturgical Movement can hail this document as the influential seed of the Liturgical Movement (including its women) it is usually taken to be.

[73] This assessment of mine is, of course, not echoed in the Liturgical Movement. Indeed, in the cultural and ecclesial context of the movement, "veiling" had become something like a defining pointer to woman's identity. A reflection of this is found, for example, in a note in *Orate Fratres* 24 (1949/50) 136f., entitled "The Eternal Feminine." It discusses approvingly the book with that title by the Catholic writer Gertrud von Le Fort. Le Fort had argued that "[t]he unveiling of woman always means the breakdown of her mystery."

Movement, a number of women's communities stand out, each with a different kind of interplay between the movement and the religious women. I will briefly look at three in turn: the Benedictine convent Ancilla Domini on the Mont-Vierge at Wépion in Belgium, the Benedictine Abbey of the Holy Cross at Herstelle in Germany, and the convent of the Sisters of the Adoration of the Most Precious Blood in O'Fallon, Missouri.

4.4.1. The Benedictine Convent Ancilla Domini on the Mont-Vierge, Belgium

The Benedictine convent Ancilla Domini on the Mont-Vierge at Wépion in Belgium was a child of the Liturgical Movement's social location in relation to the "woman's question" of its time. The roots of this religious community, whose apostolate was to join the "modern woman" to the liturgy of the Church, lay in the early years of the Liturgical Movement. Dom Eugène Vandeur (1875–1968), a monk of the Abbey of Maredsous, became prior of the Abbey of Mont César in 1909. It was the year of Lambert Beauduin's (now a direct confrere of Vandeur's) famous address to the Congress at Malines. Vandeur began to envision a liturgical apostolate specifically for women. In a letter to Abbot Ildefons Herwegen of Maria Laach, Vandeur described the envisioned community of religious women as "Benedictines who . . . would seek to lay claim to the great and irresistible Feminist movement, who would penetrate[!] this feminism at the deepest level and this with the help of a religious teaching based on the liturgical life of the Church."[74]

In 1917, Vandeur founded a small religious community of women in Brussels. Five years later, the community was established as a Benedictine convent, Ancilla Domini, on the Mont-Vierge close to Wépion. The prioress, Emmanuel Amelin (1900–1972; she left the convent in 1935), described its apostolate as "the re-christianization of society by woman,"[75] a task that was to be achieved mainly through introducing "modern woman" to the holy liturgy. This grandiose apostolate, characteristic also of some other endeavors of the time, demanded a religious community open to "women of the world." The convent on the Mont-Vierge consequently welcomed

---

[74] Quoted in Morard, *Les Bénédictines d'Ermeton*, 2.
[75] Amelin, "L'éducation liturgique," 157.

women visitors and offered liturgical retreats for women. Presentations by various priests, monks, and liturgical scholars were part of these retreats. The community's reputation spread not only within Belgium but also to Germany and Austria. In the early 1930s, the convent even offered German-language retreats for German-speaking women. Through this openness toward women of the world, this Benedictine convent created a space for laywomen who wanted to immerse themselves in the world of the liturgy.

In various publications of the Liturgical Movement, women praised the work of the sisters on the Mont-Vierge. Not even the fact that laywomen were encouraged to wear dark clothes and a veil in the convent (dark blue for unmarried women, black for married ones) posed a problem. The liturgical apostolate of the sisters on the Mont-Vierge, however, came to a sudden end in the mid-thirties, although the sources do not reveal why (financial difficulties are hinted at). The convent moved to another location in 1936. A year earlier one of its key figures had left the community altogether.

Whatever the reasons behind this relatively short-lived apostolate for women in the Liturgical Movement, the convent on the Mont-Vierge reveals a network of liturgically active women, both religious and lay, working together to bridge the gap between "modern woman" and worship. Here the focus differed from the other well-known Benedictine convent in the Liturgical Movement, the Abbey of the Holy Cross in Herstelle. The latter nurtured the liturgical lives of women within the community but did little to reach women who lived outside its walls and wanted to remain there.

4.4.2. The Benedictine Abbey of the Holy Cross at Herstelle, Germany

In the early 1920s, the religious women's community at Herstelle found itself at a moment of crisis and redefinition of its spiritual vision. At the time, it was a convent of Benedictines of Perpetual Adoration. The convent's spirituality centered not in the liturgy but in various forms of private devotional exercises. There was, for example, always one sister tied to a "pillar of scourging" in the sanctuary as part of the *imitatio Christi* (Hans Ansgar Reinhold [1897–1968], who as a novice at Maria Laach visited Herstelle, mentioned this practice).[76]

---

[76] See Reinhold, "Timely Tracts," 366–368.

In 1922 the prioress, Margareta Blanché, invited Odo Casel to the convent to discuss a reorientation of the community's spiritual vision. As a result, the convent at Herstelle in 1924 became part of the Benedictine congregation of Beuron, and its entry into the heart of the Liturgical Movement had begun. The community at Herstelle, now renamed the Abbey of the Holy Cross, had a very particular presence in the movement as far as women were concerned. For one, this was not a community actively engaged in bridging the gap between laywomen and the liturgy of the Church, an apostolate that the convent on the Mont-Vierge clearly had made its own.

The community at Herstelle was present in the Liturgical Movement in another way. It nurtured in its midst a number of able women liturgical writers. Aemiliana Löhr is the best example of this monastic nurture of a woman liturgical author, but there were others, some of them entering the community from teaching professions, some coming with doctorates. Theophora Schneider and Paschasia Stumpf, for example, held doctorates in philosophy. Oda Hagemeyer was a lawyer, Kyrilla Spiecker a medical doctor. The community at Herstelle, then, had in its midst a number of academic women who, with their entry into the monastic world, concentrated their training and skills on religious, and often liturgical, subjects.

In the first part of the twentieth century, only a monastic community—and one that had access to the scholarly world of liturgical studies through its chaplain, Odo Casel—could give women the kind of space the Herstelle Benedictines had to study and write on matters liturgical. On the other side of this coin, the women of the Abbey of the Holy Cross were not really present to other women at worship outside the walls of their monastery.

4.4.3. The Convent of the Sisters of the Adoration of the Most Precious Blood in O'Fallon, Missouri

The Sisters of the Adoration of the Most Precious Blood were originally a German community of religious women who had settled in O'Fallon, Missouri, in 1875.[77] When Martin Hellriegel, himself born in Germany, became chaplain of the community in 1918, the convent was well established and staffed a number of schools in the surrounding

---

[77] All information on the community comes from Lake's *History of the Sisters of the Adoration of the Most Precious Blood*, see esp. 116–127.

areas. In 1920, Mother Wilhelmine Vogelpohl (d. 1946) became the first American-born superior general of the O'Fallon community.

With the able leadership of both Mother Wilhelmine and Father Hellriegel, the Sisters of the Most Precious Blood soon became a center of the North American Liturgical Movement. Laypeople, abbots, and bishops regularly visited the community to participate in its liturgical life. The Eucharist was restored to its central position in the spiritual lives of the sisters. As early as 1922, a dialogue Mass with a homily had been introduced. Offertory processions and Easter Vigil services were begun. A new chapel was constructed and dedicated. The Liturgy of the Hours according to the Roman Breviary was adopted, with the Hours being chanted at their appropriate times. Gregorian chant was promoted. The sermons, conferences, and instructions in the convent all breathed a liturgical spirit. A course in Church Latin was taught, in which the "lay" sisters also participated. Last but not least, the liturgical vestments produced by the sisters' ecclesiastical art department displayed proper liturgical symbols (effeminate lace was, no doubt, avoided). Liturgical practices such as novenas and blessings were revived and made an integral part of the spiritual life of the community.

As far as one can tell, the sisters did not perceive their liturgical apostolate as specifically women-oriented. The community at O'Fallon was open to visitors from a wide variety of backgrounds, and its influence in the Liturgical Movement consequently ranged broadly. The sisters clearly had a presence in the movement as a religious community of *women*, but gender does not seem to have been a key to their liturgical self-understanding.

As we have seen, there were a number of women's religious communities active at the heart of the Liturgical Movement, each with a slightly different vision of a liturgical apostolate of and for women. What Gerald Ellard had advocated for religious women's communities, namely, a "Big Sister Movement for Getting the Liturgical Movement Moving Locally,"[78] was a multifaceted vocation for the women's communities active in the movement.

---

[78] Ellard, "Sisters as 'Big Sisters' to the Liturgical Movement," 247.

4.5. Liturgical "Women's Studies"[79]

Given the previous analysis of women's presence in the Liturgical Movement, it may seem that women were particularly active in parishes but not in the scholarly world of liturgical research. This scholarly world, however, was of crucial importance in the Liturgical Movement. The movement was fueled theologically by a learned return to the formative and normative centuries of the early Church. Was there, then, a "dust ceiling" for women in the Liturgical Movement? Were they present on the parish level but not in the higher echelons of scholarly research? To some degree that was the case, and the reasons are readily obvious. Women had only begun to gain regular access to universities at the end of the nineteenth century. In theology, and particularly liturgical studies, it would take decades before a woman actually received a doctorate in this discipline. Nevertheless, the initial impression of a gendered divide in the activities of the Liturgical Movement is not the only truth, as the following examples show.

To begin with, women had a scholarly presence in the Liturgical Movement as translators of both primary and secondary liturgical texts. That is to say, the Liturgical Movement included women who not only had a command of the ancient languages (Greek and Latin) but also knew modern languages well enough for the tedious work of translation. These translations done by women in the Liturgical Movement range from liturgical texts like the *Missale Ambrosianum* or the *Missale Romanum* to books of liturgical research like Louis Duchesne's *Origines du culte chrétien*. The latter is an interesting case. One of Romano Guardini's close women friends, Maria Knoepfler, translated Duchesne's influential book into German, but even a Guardini was unable to find a publisher for Knoepfler's painstaking work.

Second, women were present in the Liturgical Movement as authors of articles on liturgical subjects. The breadth of liturgical subjects treated by Aemiliana Löhr well illustrates this point. This Benedictine nun wrote on, among other subjects, the eschatological

---

[79] I am using the term "Women's Studies" in the non-technical sense here. That is to say, I use it to describe scholarly work done by women long before "Women's Studies" became an established academic discipline.

vision of the breviary hymns, the blessing of the palm branches, the priesthood of women in light of the Catholic liturgy, and Christian symbolism in art. Her most famous publication, *The Year of Our Lord*, in an enlarged edition entitled *The Mass Through the Year*, went through several editions and was translated into English.

Aemiliana Löhr was not alone, however. Other women authors like Agape Kiesgen, Emmanuel Amelin, and Cecilia Himebaugh could be mentioned here. Naturally, women engaged in liturgical research most frequently were members of religious communities. All four women authors just mentioned were Benedictines. There was at least one scholar, however, who clearly defied the monastic dominance in the liturgical scholarship of women. This woman was neither a member of an order, nor was she a liturgist by training, and yet she had great influence within the field of liturgical studies. I am referring to Christine Mohrmann (1903–1988). Mohrmann was a classicist who taught early Christian Greek and Latin at universities in the Netherlands. Her sustained research into the languages of the early Christian communities commanded the attention and admiration of liturgical scholars of her time.[80] Another example of a well-known woman scholar, albeit outside the confines of the Roman Catholic Church, is the British author Evelyn Underhill (1875–1941). Her famous book, simply entitled *Worship*, was published in 1937 and immediately reviewed at length in *Orate Fratres*.[81]

Third, there was, at the time of the Liturgical Movement, a growing amount of research done by women. The rise of the Liturgical Movement coincided with women entering the world of academia in larger numbers. A growing body of research, particularly doctoral dissertations by women, therefore claimed the attention of scholars. The *Jahrbuch für Liturgiewissenschaft*, central to the scholarly side of the Liturgical Movement, meticulously reviewed these dissertations if they were in one way or another related to liturgical studies. The reviewers were free with criticism and, to a lesser degree, praise for this research done by women. One typical example of such a review patronizingly suggested: "This woman author is recommended

---

[80] For more on Mohrmann, see *Liturgy Digest* 1:2 (1994) 4–43 (the article is not signed).

[81] See *Orate Fratres* 11 (1936/37) 397–400.

strongly to consult the *Jahrbuch für Liturgiewissenschaft* if she at all intends to write about Catholic liturgy in the future."[82]

A fourth and last characteristic of "women's studies" within the Liturgical Movement is related to the content of women's liturgical writings. Certain areas of research and writing in the Liturgical Movement clearly were seen as the proper domain of women. These included private devotional life and catechesis in the family, the liturgical catechesis of girls, and the specific role of women in the worship of the Church.

An example of a woman writer who claimed this domain as her own is Therese Mueller (b. 1905).[83] A native of Germany, she and her husband fled Nazi Germany in 1937 and settled in the United States. Therese Mueller, influenced by the Abbey of Maria Laach, soon became one of the key women activists of the North American Liturgical Movement. She was a regular contributor to *Orate Fratres* and also published extensively in church bulletins, covering a wide range of topics, such as appropriate baptismal garments, the churching of women, recipes, advice on Christian life in the family, etc. At the second National Liturgical Week in 1941, Mueller presented a paper entitled "The Christian Family and the Liturgy." She also authored three booklets: *Family Life in Christ* (1941), *Our Children's Year of Grace* (1943), and *The Christian Home and Art* (1950). In her choice of subjects, then, Therese Mueller was the ideal representative of a woman author in the Liturgical Movement. She claimed as her own the domain that the movement considered the appropriate liturgical apostolate of women as far as the written word was concerned.

All these instances of women authors in the Liturgical Movement show that the gendered divide in the movement was not set in stone when it came to liturgical writing. At the same time, women authors were neither as numerous nor as visible as the men who wrote on liturgical subjects. This observation of yet another asymmetrical genderization leads directly to a concluding reflection on women's presence in the Liturgical Movement.

---

[82] Hilpisch in a review of Christa Müller, "Die Lehre des Johannes Brenz von Kirchendienst und Kirchengesang," 499.

[83] For a concise introduction to Therese and Franz Mueller, see the entry in Tuzik, *How Firm a Foundation: Leaders of the Liturgical Movement*, 239–244.

5. THE LITURGICAL MOVEMENT: "ANDROCENTRIC" AND "LIBERATING"

Having completed the analysis of women's presence in the Liturgical Movement, I return to the title of one of the sections, namely "The Liturgical Movement: Moved by Women." Clearly, the Liturgical Movement was moved also by women, just as the whole history of the Church and its liturgy has always been moved by women as well as men. In putting the matter this way, I do not intend to minimize the reality of an androcentric liturgical tradition. There are reasons for the asymmetry of men's and women's presence in the Liturgical Movement, even if this asymmetry is not as stark as the traditional narrative of the movement has suggested. Men were not the only movers of this liturgical renewal. With its high regard for ancient liturgical tradition, however, the Liturgical Movement did not challenge this tradition's androcentric character.

Nevertheless, to narrate the movement as primarily a male and patriarchal enterprise is to render invisible the women activists of the movement. Rendering these women invisible clouds the "liberating" effect of the Liturgical Movement for many women active in it. These women claimed ownership of the liturgy in ways largely unimaginable prior to the beginnings of the movement. Women activists also gained space for their own liturgical experience, work, and leadership, something generally not accessible to women at the time. Despite its overwhelmingly conservative woman-script, then, the Liturgical Movement also, at points, proved liturgically quite "liberating" for women. Many women appreciated it as such.

Describing the Liturgical Movement as both conservative *and* liberating for women points back to the liturgical lives of women in the early Church.[84] They too worshiped in a context that provided both hitherto unknown freedoms *and* wide-ranging constraints. One difference between women at worship in the early Church and their successors in the Liturgical Movement is that the latter inherited a long tradition of gendered asymmetry in Christian worship. By the

---

[84] Interestingly, in his article "The Liturgy and Catholic Women," 271, Michel lifted up "women of the type of the early Christian women, who were such powerful instruments in the spread of Christian ideals in human life" as examples for the women of his day.

106

twentieth century, this tradition was well established and looked, for all intents and purposes, almost God-given. It needed more than the Liturgical Movement had to offer in the first half of the century to break with this gendered asymmetry in worship.

The beginnings of this break, however, became visible in the movement, particularly in some of its women. My thesis is that by the time of the Liturgical Movement a new kind of "woman at worship" had emerged. It was this woman, these women, who would ultimately carry the impetus of the Liturgical Movement further into a specific Women's Liturgical Movement as it grew in the second part of the twentieth century. The "new" women I have in mind, briefly, were the young, educated, urban, professional, middle-class women. They are the ones who decisively gained from the first wave of the Women's Movement and were in a position to claim the Liturgical Movement's "liberating" potential.

These women were the product of social forces at the turn of the century. With the beginnings of the twentieth century, as mentioned above, the lives of some women underwent quite dramatic changes. These changes cannot but have had an impact on the interplay of women and worship. Women entered secondary and higher education and professional and semiprofessional careers in larger numbers. This produced a new kind of "woman at worship," and this woman made her presence felt in particular ways in the Liturgical Movement. Professional women and women authors writing on liturgical subjects began to probe the theological presuppositions behind the gendered nature of worship. Some of these women questioned the liturgical woman-script of the male leaders of the movement.

An example of such a questioning is provided by the philosopher, scholar, and (now) saint Edith Stein (1891–1942). A converted Jew and later Carmelite nun killed at Auschwitz, she had close connections with the Benedictine Abbey of Beuron. In one of her writings, Stein points to the liturgical image of the "strong woman" to defy the bourgeois ideal of the woman at the hearth.[85] This scholar's liturgical woman-script was nourished by a very different reading of the liturgy than that of, say, Athanasius Wintersig and the school of

---

[85] For more, see Berger, *Liturgie und Frauenseele*, 49, 123–129.

Maria Laach. Other professional women read the liturgical image of woman in similar ways as Stein. They began to draw on the liturgy not to support but to critique the traditional woman-script. These kinds of women will be the initial bearers of the Women's Liturgical Movement. The following chapter turns to this "other" key liturgical renewal movement of the twentieth century.

Chapter 4

Liturgical History in the Making:
The Women's Liturgical Movement

1. NARRATING THE NEW

If the twentieth century really is the "the century of worship" for the Church,[1] then one of its defining features will be the irruption of women into liturgical practice and discourse. The previous chapter treated the shape of this irruption in the Liturgical Movement in the first half of the century. The present chapter will examine the most marked expression of this irruption of women into liturgical practice and discourse in the twentieth century, namely, the Women's Liturgical Movement.

How to name and circumscribe this movement is only the first problem in constructing its narrative. I have chosen the term "Women's Liturgical Movement," preferring it over other options, such as the "Feminist Liturgical Movement"[2] or "feminist ritual project."[3] The choice signals my intention to analyze the movement as broader than the focus on Feminist liturgies alone allows (therefore the choice of the term "Women" over "Feminist"), while at the same time staying, to some degree, within the Catholic tradition (therefore the choice "Liturgical Movement" over such terms as "ritual practice" or "ritualizing"). Feminist liturgies are, of course, a crucial part of the Women's Liturgical Movement, which itself is part of a larger

---

[1] The German theologian Arno Schilson has suggested as much; see his "Christlicher Gottesdienst—Ort des Menschseins," 55.

[2] This is the title of the entry written by Rosemary Radford Ruether in the 1986 *Dictionary of Liturgy and Worship*, 240f.

[3] Collins, "Principles of Feminist Liturgy," 17–24.

movement of women's ritualizing.[4] But the movement I want to concentrate on is, on the one hand, broader than Feminist liturgies and, on the other hand, narrower than the Feminist ritual project (to which non-theist women's celebrations also belong).

The Women's Liturgical Movement, as I understand it, includes women's groups devising fairly traditional liturgies, but doing so consciously as and for women, and often giving these liturgies a women-specific focus (be it saints' days of holy women or Marian devotions with a new twist).[5] It also includes traditional Catholic women's organizations that discover the liturgy as an important area of concern. It includes many people in the Church, both women and men, who make issues of liturgical gender justice their own. It includes the minor and not so minor liturgical changes the Church has undertaken in response to the growing unease with the asymmetrically gendered nature of worship. Lastly, the Women's Liturgical Movement might also be said to include its opposition, that is, on the one hand, women's voices arguing against the Feminist agenda and for the traditional liturgy of the Church and, on the other hand, post-Christian Feminists arguing against Feminist liturgies as contradictions in terms (Mary Daly).

A second crucial factor in constructing a narrative of the Women's Liturgical Movement is the context in which this movement comes to be located.[6] I have chosen to see it as part of the interplay of women and worship since the earliest Christian communities took shape. I therefore understand this movement as one moment—even if a defining moment—within the overall development of liturgical per-

[4] Lesley A. Northup explores this larger movement of women's ritualizing in her recent book *Ritualizing Women: Patterns of Feminine Spirituality* (1997).

[5] Two examples are the collection of women's liturgies by the German priest Werner Ripplinger, *Lasst uns loben, Schwestern, loben* (1987), and the collection *Frauengottesdienste* by the Swiss author Elisabeth Aeberli (1987).

[6] For an attempt to read the Women's Liturgical Movement as a form of inculturation, see Berger, "Women's Movement as a Liturgical Movement," 55–64, and Brazal, "Inculturation," 124–134. I am, however, no longer convinced of the adequacy of this approach. For one, the conceptualization of what constitutes culture, and in particular, "women's culture," is too simplistic. Especially in light of post-structuralist Feminist theory, there simply is no such thing as *a* women's culture. With that, however, the whole argument in my article is in doubt. At the moment, I do not intend to attempt to resurrect this argument in a different form.

formances of gender in the history of the Church. With this choice comes the acknowledgment that the Women's Liturgical Movement is not an isolated phenomenon, and certainly no "accident." It is, rather, an integral part of a long history of women at worship in constantly changing cultural contexts, and therefore best understood and narrated as part of this history.

An example of such a consciously contextual and historical understanding of the Women's Liturgical Movement is the way the relationship between the Liturgical Movement of the first half of the twentieth century and the Women's Liturgical Movement of the second half of this century is depicted. Rather than majoring on the differences between the two movements and depicting the Women's Liturgical movement as unique, unprecedented, and *sui generis*, I see both as a continuous questioning, redefining, and reconstructing of women at worship in the twentieth century. In the Liturgical Movement, this took place in response to the first Women's Movement. In the Women's Liturgical Movement, this takes place in response to, and in dialogue with, the second Women's Movement. In other words, *the way in which* women at worship are redefined and reconstructed differs markedly from the first half of this century, not the fact that this is happening.

With this interpretive stance, I in no way want to deny differences between these two liturgical renewal movements. The differences are all too obvious. But if one understands the two movements' positions on women at worship as particular responses to the way gender issues were raised in their respective cultural contexts, the differences can be accounted for more accurately than the simple juxtaposition "patriarchal"—"liberating" allows for. One way to account for at least some of the differences is to realize that both movements faced and interacted differently with different forms of the Women's Movement.

2. THE EMERGENCE OF A WOMEN'S LITURGICAL MOVEMENT[7]

2.1. Cultural Context and Social Location

The Liturgical Movement of the first half of the twentieth century emerged at a time when the first wave of the Women's Movement

[7] The emergence of the Feminist Liturgical Movement (more narrowly understood) is narrated concisely by Radford Ruether's article under that name. The

was at its peak. The Women's Liturgical Movement emerged on the wings of the second wave. Both Liturgical Movements, then, are located culturally in the midst of two waves of "feminisms."

One difference between the Liturgical Movement and the Women's Liturgical Movement is their differing interactions with these two forms of the Women's Movement. The second-wave Women's Movement emerged in the 1960s and signaled a time of major cultural shifts in women's lives.[8] To some extent, it was their bearer. This was particularly the case for white middle-class women who began to work outside the home again in larger numbers after the Second World War. But there were other cultural shifts that affect virtually all women: the rise of sophisticated reproductive technologies, rapidly changing sexual practices, diversifying family patterns, and increasing awareness of women's marginalization and, more starkly, of pervasive violence against women.

One way to summarize the result of these shifts is to say that the normative and dominant narrative of "woman" broke off with the beginnings of the 1970s.[9] The second Women's Movement embodied this break and the search for alternative narratives. Particularly with its more militant wing, the Women's Liberation Movement, the search for alternative narratives of women's lives gained a radical edge. A whole Feminist counterculture was born, with its own literature, music, art, and lifestyles. Even if this Women's Liberation Movement with its radical edge was short-lived, the broader concerns of the Women's Movement found their way into the cultural mainstream.

The Church is not made up of women living in isolation from women in the wider cultural context. The cultural shifts in women's lives and their embodiment in the second Women's Movement soon made themselves felt within the Church.[10] Women, for example, began to enter the scholarly world of theology and soon developed a

---

Dutch Feminist liturgist Denise Dijk currently is completing her dissertation on the Feminist Liturgical Movement in the United States.

[8] Flora Davis, *Moving the Mountain: The Women's Movement in America since 1960* (1991) provides a detailed narrative of the movement.

[9] See Chopp, "In the Real World," 7–8.

[10] For a more detailed account, see Mary Jo Weaver's book *New Catholic Women* (1985).

Feminist way of theologizing. Women's organizations and movements that differed sharply from traditional ones formed within the Catholic Church. There is, for example, the Women's Ordination Conference. There is the Women's Alliance for Theology, Ethics, and Ritual (WATER). There is Women-Church. And there, in the midst of all this, a liturgical renewal movement growing among women who have been impacted by the Women's Movement—the Women's Liturgical Movement—comes into being. One key difference between this liturgical renewal movement and the earlier Liturgical Movement lies exactly in its relationship to the Women's Movement. For the Women's Liturgical Movement, there is no antagonism and no hostility here. On the contrary, the Women's Liturgical Movement borrows freely from the wisdom and practices of the Women's Movement.

2.2. Birthing a New Liturgical Movement

The classical Liturgical Movement had gained official ground in the Church particularly since the 1940s. With the Second Vatican Council (1962–1965) and its Constitution on the Sacred Liturgy (1963), the Liturgical Movement bore its most highly visible immediate fruit. At that time, the ecclesial level of "high visibility" was not one populated by women.[11] They remained, for Vatican II and the ensuing liturgical reforms, the "separated sisters," as they began to call themselves (this despite the fact that in 1963, Pope John XXIII had wisely discerned women's aspirations as one of the crucial signs of the time). But the self-description "separated sisters" already signaled a turning point. Women began to experience and describe their place in the Church in the language of pain and protest. With this, they were part of the wider cultural irruption of the second Women's Movement in the mid-1960s. In the Church, this movement found particular expression in the emergence of Feminist theology and the Women's Liturgical Movement.

It will always remain a strange example of ecclesial asynchronicity that a massive liturgical reform was put in motion just before the institutional Church found itself confronted in a sustained way with

---

[11] For an account of the twenty-three women auditors at Vatican II, see Carmel Elizabeth McEnroy's study *Guests in Their Own House: The Women of Vatican II* (1996).

women's liturgical voices. By the time the official liturgical changes came to be implemented, many of them were already outdated for women. The women who named themselves "separated sisters" at Vatican II today name themselves "aliens in the rituals of the Roman Catholic Church"[12]—and that after thirty years of sustained liturgical reform. What happened?

With the 1960s, women had begun to choose between what one might call "resignation" and "revolution." On the one hand, women in growing numbers simply left the Church in a silent exodus. On the other hand, women remaining in the Church became active in various expressions of "revolution." The Women's Liturgical Movement, and particularly Feminist liturgies, is one of them. With the emergence of a distinctive Women's Movement within the Church, dissatisfaction with the existing way of worship had begun to grow. Indeed, worship soon became a focal point of women's protests. By the early 1970s, the first practical proposals for *Sistercelebrations* were in print in North America and by the mid-1970s, European materials surfaced. Actual women's worship services obviously preceded these publications by a number of years.

Initially, the changes vis-à-vis the traditional (even if now reformed and reforming) liturgy were concentrated on individual liturgical elements, and the worship services tended to be designed as "special" events. Many of the liturgies did not find their way into official publications. They lived in the experiences and the memories of participating women, in loose-leaf collections, in copied and shared materials. These liturgies thrived in a wide variety of contexts: in women's groups in parishes, in adult education centers, in divinity schools, in independent Feminist liturgical communities, and in institutional centers. They grew in the Netherlands[13] and in Germany,[14] in the United States and in Australia, in Peru and in Korea.[15]

[12] Ware, "Easter Vigil," 103. For more voices of alienation from Roman Catholic women, see Winter, *Defecting in Place*, 65–117.

[13] See Dijk, "Developments in Feminist Liturgy in the Netherlands," 120–128.

[14] For the emergence of Feminist liturgies in Germany, see Leistner, *Lass spüren deine Kraft*, 16–26.

[15] For the latter, see the article "Women Church of Korea," 56f., with a brief description of the liturgies celebrated by this group. My information about Feminist liturgies in Peru comes from sustained conversations with Rev. Rosanna Panizo, a member of Talitha Cumi, a Christian Feminist group in Lima.

With the beginnings of the 1980s, a whole avalanche of publications[16] on "Sistercelebrations," "Women's Prayer Services," "WomanWorship," "Feminist Liturgies," and "Women Church Celebrations" became visible. This abundance of materials witnesses to the fact that a clearly discernible movement had evolved, discernible enough for publishers to begin to give the written form of Feminist liturgies a more permanent existence. By the 1990s, there was a clearly established tradition of worship services by and for women, or, more narrowly, a "Feminist Liturgical Tradition."[17] There are long-term committed Feminist liturgical communities, there are regular women's worship services in parishes, there are women celebrations at large gatherings of women, and there is lively networking between most of these women at worship. Moreover, a number of Feminist liturgical/ritual scholars now are a part of the Women's Liturgical Movement and accompany it with scholarly enthusiasm and critical solidarity.[18]

There is also by now a distinctive Feminist Liturgical Movement in the so-called Third World. Obviously, emphases differ according to geographical and social location. Latin American Feminist liturgies are developed in the context of a strong tradition of Liberation Theology done by male theologians. African women have a particular interest in cultural factors, for example, African tribal rituals and their significance for women.[19] Asian Feminist theologians work in

[16] I read the data differently here than does Mary Collins, "Principles of Feminist Liturgy," 12, 15. Collins suggests that there is a "scarcity of texts" of Feminist liturgists and "a failure to produce a full corpus of feminist ritual texts." For a substantiation of my own reading, I simply point to my two bibliographies on "Women and Worship." For the German-speaking context, there is also a bibliography by Dobbeler, "Feministische Liturgien," 1–24. An "avalanche" of publications does not, however, imply that the majority of Feminist liturgies celebrated are also published. There is a vast amount of materials beyond the published realm.

[17] See the subtitle of Procter-Smith's book *In Her Own Rite: Constructing Feminist Liturgical Tradition.*

[18] I mention in particular Charlotte Caron, Mary Collins, Denise Dijk, Ruth Duck, Kathleen Hughes, Lesley Northup, Marjorie Procter-Smith, Gail Ramshaw, Susan Roll, Catherine Vincie, and Janet Walton. I would also include myself here.

[19] See, for example, Oduyoye, "Women and Ritual in Africa," 9–24; Edet, "Christianity and African Women's Rituals," 25–39; Nasimiyu-Wasike, "Christianity and the African Rituals of Birth and Naming," 40–53.

the context of Christianity as a tiny minority religion. Their particular interest is focused on non-Christian religious traditions, myths, and stories and their importance in, or usability for, Christian Feminist liturgies.

The heart of the Women's Liturgical Movement is, of course, not described primarily by the historical development. In what follows, I want to discuss the characteristic features of these new liturgies to show what ultimately motivated their emergence and growth. I begin with an analysis of how the "problem" of the traditional liturgy came to be identified.

3. THE PROBLEM IDENTIFIED: "MAN'S LITURGY"

3.1. Women's Liturgical Disillusionment

The immediate starting point for the emerging women's liturgies was a painful experience. Women began to perceive and confront a growing sense of disillusionment and alienation vis-à-vis the liturgical life of the Church, and that at a time when wide-ranging liturgical reforms championed the active participation of all. To put it in a nutshell: the traditional liturgy came to be seen as a "Man's Liturgy."[20] "Women's Place" in this liturgy became increasingly questionable.[21]

Linguistically, the problem was identified in a variety of ways: the liturgy was exclusive, sexist, misogynist, patriarchal, androcentric, imperial, hierarchical—a critical terminology clearly borrowed from the Women's Movement. The liturgy thus became one of many cultural institutions the Women's Movement was encouraging women to approach with suspicion. Defining and experiencing the liturgical tradition as androcentric usually did not need much suspicion or encouragement. Women started with the basic acknowledgment that they were all but invisible as authoritative liturgical subjects. Although they would often be the majority of those present at worship, they were not represented as women. Easily recognized examples of this "liturgical invisibility" of women were the fact that leadership was reserved for men and that the language used in and

[20] See the early article by the Italian Catholic Adriana Zarri, "Woman's Prayer and a Man's Liturgy" (1970). For a later article on the subject, see Zarri, "Sensibilità femminile e liturgia attuale" (1981).

[21] See the early and remarkably open article by the Dutch priest and theologian René van Eyden, "The Place of Women in Liturgical Functions" (1972).

for the liturgical assembly was usually in the masculine. Androcentric language in the Roman Catholic liturgy became especially noticeable with the early translations of liturgical books into the vernacular.

But scrutiny of "Man's Liturgy" grew as Feminist tools of analysis grew sharper. The early problems noted—absence of women from liturgical leadership, exclusive language—soon were joined by more subtle ones. The limited and stereotypical selection of biblical stories about women in the Lectionary was one of those problems.[22] There was also the growing awareness that concerns specific to women were painfully absent in the traditional liturgy. From menarche to menopause, from pregnancy to nursing, from breast cancer to domestic violence,[23] the traditional liturgy seemed to know and acknowledge little of women's lives.

Added to the "absences" soon were problematic presences. Women began to resist certain Scripture passages read and then proclaimed unquestioningly from the pulpit. They also found little help in women saints stereotypically honored for their virginity, humility, and self-effacement.[24] On the other side of the spectrum of problematic liturgical presences, many women found the various confessions of sins, with their focus on pride, self-determination, and strong will power, distinctly male-oriented and detrimental to their own beginning discovery of self.[25]

Even the argument that worship at heart is primarily not about saints, sermons, or sins but about the Living God did not help for long. At the heart of worship, women began to confront a God who was imaged and addressed almost exclusively in the masculine. While acknowledging God's prerogative to choose the ways of revealing Godself, women soon found that the Christian tradition

[22] The literature on this topic by now is quite extensive. For critiques of the Roman lectionary in particular, see Boisclair, "Amnesia in the Catholic Sunday Lectionary," 109–135; Tafferner, "Leseordnung aus der Perspektive von Frauen," 148–154; and Janetzky, "Lesung für die Frauen befreien," 725–749. See also Reid, "Liturgy, Scripture, and the Challenge of Feminism," 124–137.

[23] See, for example, Procter-Smith, "Reorganizing Victimization: The Intersection Between Liturgy and Domestic Violence," 428–444, and "The Whole Loaf: Holy Communion and Survival," 464–479, and Redmond, "Remember the Good, Forget the Bad," 71–82.

[24] See the analysis by Pahl, "Eine starke Frau, wer wird sie finden," 433–452.

[25] See, for example, Duck, "Sin, Grace, and Gender," 55–69.

knew many female or non-male images for the Living God they sought to worship. Unfortunately, the liturgy did not seem to know these images or to be hospitable to them.

The list of elements of women's growing disillusionment with the traditional liturgy is long. For Catholic women, it culminates in the question, "Is the Eucharist Still a Source of Meaning for Women?"[26] However one defines the core of women's liturgical disillusionment, the development of this disillusionment is clear: a growing Feminist consciousness brought the recognition of wide-ranging gender asymmetry for women at worship. Beginning with individual elements, such as liturgical leadership, women soon confronted a pervasive problem. The traditional liturgy was a "Man's Liturgy." With this analysis, liturgical choices seemed limited, and a ritual exodus into a promised land of Feminist liturgies a worthwhile journey.

However, the analysis just presented is only one particular way of interpreting the emerging Women's Liturgical Movement.[27] That there was "a problem" for women at worship generally began to be acknowledged. But depending on how acute and pervasive it was seen to be, the responses differed widely. It is worth looking at some of these responses in turn. They make up the ecclesial landscape that brings into sharper focus the characteristics of the Women's Liturgical Movement.

3.2. A Range of Responses

The Church hierarchy initially saw the problem confined to the question of women's liturgical ministries. In the 1970s, this meant the question of women lectors, cantors, Eucharistic ministers, and acolytes. The early answer was to distinguish between permanent liturgical ministries (even lay ministries) from which women were excluded and certain liturgical functions which women were allowed to fulfill.[28] Questions about ordination were quickly answered in the negative. Growing attempts at in-depth discussion of women's ordination were discouraged and then silenced. In the

[26] See the article by Mary Collins with that title.

[27] One only needs to remember that at the same time as women experienced the liturgy as described above, traditionalist women mourned the demise of the Tridentine Mass. The alienation on both sides needs to be acknowledged.

[28] Such the argument in a statement in *Notitiae* 9 (1973) 164. See also the article by Neunheuser, "Die Frau in der Liturgie," 164–177.

1980s, a lively concern of the hierarchy was the question of female altar servers—another painful example of asynchronicity between Vatican and Feminist worlds.

The theological motivity of the hierarchy's concern was essentially canonical and authority-centered: what should be allowed liturgically, what not. On the basis of the largely canonical response to women's problems, Feminist liturgies came to be seen as "disobedience," rooted in radical Feminism running liturgically rampant in the Church. There was, then, no problem these liturgies legitimately address. This position can be detected also on a more recent battleground, namely, the issue of inclusive language. The Vatican's reaction to modest proposals for various inclusive language liturgical texts has been hesitant at best. Inclusive language is interpreted as a threat. It entails changing the text of Scripture, disowning the tradition, and legitimizing dissent.[29]

In the scholarly world of liturgical studies, (mostly) men began to take note of women's voices of protest in the early 1970s. These scholars did so with the particular tools of their trade. That is to say, women's issues in the world of liturgical studies initially surfaced in the form of questions about the history of women's liturgical ministries. The early Church was seen as a key testing ground, and widows and deaconesses once again attracted scholarly attention.

The questions raised by women's voices, however, were approached with traditional historical tools of analysis. As such, early Church evidence did not yield many new insights, as the finesse of argumentation over the kind of ordination deaconesses received shows. The theological motivity in these scholarly endeavors ultimately remains focused on liturgical authority, the "norm of the fathers" (norma patrum). Whatever can be legitimized by ancient liturgical practice is relevant today. Only with the entry in sizable numbers of women into the field of liturgical studies has this situation begun to change.[30] But change is slow, and Feminist liturgical discourse has not, as of yet, reconceptualized the discipline as a whole.

---

[29] See, for example, the article by Sokolowski, "Some Remarks on Inclusive Language," 9f.

[30] A witty critique of this authority-centered orientation of liturgical studies is provided by Grimes, "Liturgical Supinity, Liturgical Erectitude," 39–58.

At the level of liturgical reform administrators (for lack of a better word), the situation is slowly improving. With the entry of women into this world, there has been a growing openness to acknowledge Feminist concerns, particularly in relation to inclusive language.[31] The impact of the Feminist critique on liturgical reforms deserves to be mapped in greater detail than is possible here. Suffice it to say that proposals for reform slowly began to be affected by women's concerns in the 1970s, be it in relation to liturgical ministries and offices, liturgical space and its openness for all worshipers, liturgical times and seasons, saints' calendars, the Eucharistic Prayer, Lectionaries, or the shape and content of rituals as a whole.

Many actual communities at worship, however, could not wait for liturgists to decide what role exactly the early deaconesses played or for liturgical reforms to reach the point when "all men" were finally eliminated from the Eucharistic Prayer. In some circles, liturgical self-help became the solution to the pressing problems of women at worship. Self-help concentrated for the most part on the struggle for inclusive language. The theological motivity here was clearly pastoral. Often this self-help was generated *ad hoc*, by people simply changing liturgical texts and liturgical language on the spot. But there were also more sustained attempts to guide these efforts. A sub-committee of the Baltimore Task Force on the Status of Women in the Church, for example, composed a booklet entitled *Liturgy for All People*, which set the Eucharistic Prayers in inclusive language.

As hinted at above, there is also a group of women (and men) who see no problem for women at worship today. Or if they do, they locate it on the other side of the spectrum of Feminist concerns. The problem they perceive lies with Feminist concerns, spelled out as modern anti-Christian discontent with the liturgy of the Church.[32] The theological motivity here is concern for tradition,[33] with "tradi-

---

[31] The "International Commission on English in the Liturgy" (ICEL) is a good example; see Henderson, "ICEL and Inclusive Language," 257–278.

[32] Essays in the book *The Politics of Prayer: Feminist Language and the Worship of God* (1992) are a good example of this. The book was edited by Helen Hull Hitchcock, the director of Women for Faith and Family.

[33] With this term, I do not want to discredit but simply name a theological motivity. I wonder whether traditionalist women are not the real challengers of Feminist liturgies rather than, say, the Vatican. What would a space have to look

tion" usually narrowly understood as a Vatican-centered and Tridentine-shaped enterprise.

Meanwhile, many women ever more sharply experienced "The Dilemma of Celebration."[34] No scholarly liturgical reflection on early deaconesses, no linguistic self-help, no growing presence of women in lay liturgical functions, no disappearance of "men" from the Eucharistic Prayer really "solved" the androcentric nature of the liturgical tradition as a whole. The "add-women-and-stir" approach to worship was experienced by these women as inadequate.

4. FEMINIST LITURGIES: RE-INVENTING WOMEN AT WORSHIP

Out of this dilemma, the new women's liturgies were born. Clearly, the theological motivity behind these liturgies is neither traditional, traditionalist, canonical, nor pastoral, if by that is meant a focus on the parish liturgy. Rather, the theological motivity essentially is Feminist. These liturgies do not attempt to start with the traditional liturgy and add women where possible. Their starting point is the (liturgical) flourishing and well-being of women themselves. As such, the new women's liturgies respond to the realization that the beginning changes in liturgical practice were too few, too cosmetic, too haphazard, and too slow. Clear alternatives to "Man's Liturgy" as a whole were needed.

Surveying the broad range of new women's liturgies, one can detect characteristic features even while acknowledging widely divergent practices. These common features together provide a picture of the particularities of a liturgy shaped by women and for women in the cultural context of the second Women's Movement. In what follows, I want to highlight these features in order, first of all, to grasp the center of the Women's Liturgical Movement, and second, to identify the points of departure from, and criticism of, the traditional liturgy. The following ten clusters can be identified as distinctive

---

like that could engender encounter between traditionalist women and Feminist liturgists? I share Mary Jo Weaver's concern that Feminists need to "listen to anti-feminist women in the Catholic church and attempt to see, in their own faithfulness to the tradition, a solution that works for them in ways we might not fully appreciate" (Weaver, *Springs of Water in a Dry Land*, 9).

[34] The expression is taken from a 1975 article by Nelle Morton in the book *Women in a Strange Land*.

features of liturgies shaped by women for women in the Women's Liturgical Movement.[35] So as not to create too uniform a picture, I will, whenever applicable, indicate tensions and differing options taken by different Feminist liturgical communities.

4.1. Women as Authoritative Liturgical Subjects

In the new women's liturgies,[36] women are authoritative subjects of the liturgy. They initiate, shape, lead, and celebrate worship. At first this may seem rather unremarkable, but the significance of this liturgical subjecthood of women is immense. Women as authoritative liturgical subjects all but turn on its head the traditional gender hierarchy in worship. In Feminist liturgies, women suddenly experience themselves as creators and shapers of a sphere that was traditionally not open to their ritual authority. In these new liturgies, women are full subjects of the liturgical celebration, and that not only in a generalized "active participation" but also in the very authorizing, shaping, and leading of worship.

Three points deserve mention in this connection. First, most Feminist liturgies are designed to be highly participatory. Against the background of centuries of women at worship simply "watching" and "hearing," Feminist liturgies put a high priority on every single worshiper actively participating in one way or another. Often participation-intense rituals are given preference to ensure every one's involvement: processions, clapping, meditative writing for the whole assembly, biblical reflections in small groups. Participation in Feminist liturgies is not dependent on someone's traditional liturgical expertise, that is, how to navigate in traditional sacred space, when to stand or kneel, what response to give when, etc. Rather, many of the ritual

[35] For other ways of narrating the characteristics of Feminist liturgies, see Neu, "Women Revisioning Religious Rituals," 158–167; Collins, "Principles of Feminist Liturgy," 11–15; and Procter-Smith, "Marks of Feminist Liturgy," 69–75. For an analysis of common patterns in women's ritualizing as a whole, see Northup, *Ritualizing Women*, 28–52.

[36] In what follows, I will mostly use the term "Feminist liturgies" for the sake of conciseness and for variety's sake (the term "women" is already present in most sentences, even without referring again and again to "women's liturgies"). Feminist liturgies exhibit many of the characteristics mentioned in starker form than (the broader) new women's worship services, but I definitely do not want to exclude the latter from the description.

practices of Feminist liturgies do not presume more expertise than that of the moment. This does not mean that they are not demanding in terms of participatory involvement. Most Feminist liturgies are demanding ritual events, much more so than the traditional liturgy was, where a breathing body could be enough.[37] In worship services designed by women for women, there is typically a lot of group formation, movement, response, eye contact, and touching.

Second, all liturgical "ministries" are open to women in Feminist liturgies. The term "ministries" has to be qualified, because a good number of these liturgies are celebrated without a clear ministerial focus. As Mary Collins has put it, they are often "deliberately headless."[38] Liturgical leadership generally is shared and non-hierarchical. There is no distinction between those with "ritual power" and those without. Within self-consciously Roman Catholic Feminist liturgical communities, this may lead to some liturgical stretching. There are groups that simply forgo certain rites such as the celebration of the Eucharist. Others might engage in forms of creative reinterpretation such as blessing and sharing bread and wine, but without naming the meal a Eucharist. Yet others opt for alternative meal celebrations such as the sharing of milk and honey. Some groups practice what might be called "prevenient obedience." They practice now what they consider the Church will one day mandate as its own practice, namely, not letting gender determine who is excluded from liturgical presidency.

Third, it is clear by now that in the creation of Feminist liturgies women once again have become bearers of liturgical traditioning. The "Feminist Liturgical Tradition" can be seen particularly in liturgies that are "handed on": from the United States to Belgium, to Germany, to the Philippines, to Chile. Particularly between the First and the Third World, there is a liberal borrowing and sharing of rituals.[39]

---

[37] This non-demanding character of, say, the Tridentine Mass in terms of participatory involvement could have its own beauty and attractiveness, as my mother never tired of reminding me. Exhausted from housework, children, and entertaining guests, she relished the early Sunday morning Latin Mass. According to her memory, it was the one space in her life where for an hour she could just "be" without anybody demanding anything of her, including God.

[38] Collins, "Principles of Feminist Liturgy," 14.

[39] See, as one example, *Woman and Religion*, edited by the Filipina Feminist theologian Mary John Mananzan, O.S.B. The book contains a number of

4.2. Liturgical Tradition and Liturgical Innovation

4.2.1. The Tension of Tradition and Crisis

In a Feminist ritual of the laying on of hands, Diann Neu of
WATER lets a narrator say: "I am a child born of the union of tradition and crisis."[40] This is an apt description of a perennial tension evident in many Feminist liturgies. In the majority of cases, traditional
forms are not abandoned altogether but accepted as framework and
background. Often, however, they are filled with new, women-
centered content. A ritual of anointing can be offered to a victim of
rape. An exorcism can be directed at the evils of patriarchy. A Good
Friday liturgy can center on women's suffering.

The tension between tradition and innovation provides a scale
from "light" to radically Feminist in the new women's liturgies vis-à-
vis the traditional liturgy. The scale is broad indeed. Where a liturgy
is located on this scale depends to some degree on its own ecclesial
location. Parish-based women's liturgies tend to be somewhat less
radical than those of their independent sisters. For the most part,
though, Feminist liturgies treat traditional liturgical forms relatively
freely. Stamped with the "norm of the fathers," these traditional
forms are not a priori normative for women's ways of worship but
rather are approached with suspicion.

4.2.2. Ritual Recipes

Suspicious of the liturgical tradition, Feminist liturgies generate a
host of new ritual practices. Thus, for example, liturgical dance is
(re)discovered, and meditative exercises become part of worship. But
there are also new liturgical celebrations specific to women, particularly rites around the cycles of women's bodies, from a "Celebration
of Pregnancy" or a "Healing Ritual Following Stillbirth and
Miscarriage" to a "Celebration at the Start of Menses" and a
"Celebration at the Onset of Menopause."[41]

Alienation from the liturgical tradition invites a look at other ritual
traditions. In some North American Feminist liturgies, there is liberal
borrowing from Native American ritual practices. Other Feminist

---

"contextualized liturgies" by women, many of them modeled on North American
Feminist liturgies.

[40] Neu, "Our Name Is Church," 78.

[41] All these can be found in Sears, *Life-Cycle Celebrations for Women*.

communities, however, worry about "ritual theft" and prefer to abstain from ritual borrowing, particularly from peoples who have experienced colonial expropriation in the past. Third World Feminist liturgies confront the question of whether and how to draw on indigenous, non-Christian ritual traditions. Korean Women Church, for example, uses traditional Korean forms of ritual drama,[42] and rice cakes and chilled ginger tea as part of its liturgies.[43] A women's group in Nicaragua struggles with Mayan symbols for God,[44] while a creation liturgy can include a prayer from the *Popul Vuh*, the Mayan Book of the Dawn of Life.[45] A Feminist liturgical community in Peru might choose to incorporate into its worship an offering to *pachamama*, the indigenous earth mother.

However these tensions between liturgical tradition and innovation are resolved in individual Feminist liturgies, one thing is clear: these liturgies cover new ritual ground. As such, they are experimental, playful, flexible, and momentary. They are never written in stone. Behind them stand no monumental ecclesial buildings, but liturgical assemblies of exploration and uncertainty. Obviously, then, the process of creating these liturgies, as well as celebrating and then assessing them, is part and parcel of the ritual.[46] The image of a recipe book taken up in a number of collections of Feminist liturgies[47] illustrates this characteristic well. There is no reproduction of ritual here, only suggestions of ingredients to stimulate other women's own ritual creativity.

4.2.3. Consciously Contextual

Feminist liturgies are highly contextualized. They cannot be celebrated in New York, Santiago, Frankfurt, and Manila without profound changes. None of these liturgies is designed to last for the next fifteen hundred years, nor are they designed as liturgies for everyone. They are consciously contextual and, as such, consciously limited

---

[42] See "Korean Woman Jesus: Drama Worship," 45.

[43] See "Women Church of Korea," 57.

[44] See Ramírez, "El poder de los simbolos," 36.

[45] See "Creation Story," 21.

[46] See, for example, Neu, "Women Revisioning Religious Rituals," 158: "Feminist rituals value both the process and the product."

[47] Two examples are Procter-Smith, *Praying with Our Eyes Open*, 13, and for a look beyond the Christian spectrum, Walker, *Women's Rituals*, 2.

celebrations. When a Filipina liturgy, for example, names "the prostitutes of Olongapo and Angeles and other women who are victims of the rest and recreation industry brought about by the US military bases," this liturgy very consciously and explicitly is rooted in the lives of women in the Philippines.[48]

4.2.4. Feminist Liturgies and the Liturgy of Life

For many Feminist liturgical communities, the liturgy and life are indivisible: "celebration, sacrament, ritual, worship are not so different and distracting a part of life as the patriarchal split would have us think,"[49] claims Mary Hunt from WATER. Also indivisible for many are the liturgy and the struggle for justice. This connection between liturgy and social justice, however, is not true for all new women's liturgies. Some of them are clearly more introspective and "consumerist" than others.[50] How much the liturgy and the struggle for justice are intertwined impacts the celebration significantly. The "Feminist Liturgy Circle" in Münster, Germany, for example, has integrated a "solidarity collection" into all its celebrations.[51] In Feminist liturgies from the Third World, the lines between the liturgy and the liturgy of life can become transparent as protest marches, demonstrations, and fasts merge with liturgical celebrations.

4.3. The Pleasure of Symbols

4.3.1. The Ordinary as Sacred

Feminist liturgies for the most part are stamped with an intensive predilection for symbols: rose-scented water, freshly baked bread, milk and honey, fragrant oil, burning incense, flowers, candles, branches, ashes, earth, grain, bulbs, straw, wine, fruit—yes, even apples.[52] All these symbols appear much more frequently than in traditional liturgies. Indeed, a natural symbol can easily be the focus of a

[48] See Mananzan, *Woman and Religion*, 197, 207.

[49] Hunt, "Women as Religious Agents," 9.

[50] Schüssler Fiorenza uses this term to describe groups whose primary focus is on "fulfilling the religious consumer needs of women"; see her article "Spiritual Movements of Transformation," 224f.

[51] See Hojenski, *Meine Seele sieht das Land der Freiheit*, 199.

[52] For the latter, see, for example, Radford Ruether, *Women-Church*, 145, and Henry, *The Book of Ours*, 25–28.

Feminist liturgy, as is the case, for example, in rituals centering on water.[53] But it is not only the natural symbols that come alive in worship. Women also bring their social worlds and its materials to the liturgy: weavings, photos, ribbons, mirrors, yarn, fabric, bowls, spices, paper tissue, children's toys, chiffon scarves. Women's liturgies, then, are intensely and vibrantly symbolic.[54] The symbols used appeal to all the sensory perceptions, and women's bodies themselves often become the key symbolic focus of a liturgy. This is the case, for example, in a "Birthing Preparation Liturgy," in a "Menopause Liturgy," and in "Menstrual and New Moon Rituals."[55]

The pleasure of the symbolic, so evident in Feminist liturgies, is rooted in women's newly found power to generate for themselves the symbolic world of the liturgy. Women experience themselves as liturgical symbol-breakers in the refusal of the uncritical acceptance of traditional symbols and as liturgical symbol-makers of their own.[56] In this Feminist symbol-making, a very direct and immediate intersection between liturgical symbols and women's lives is evident. The "ordinary" of women's lives becomes the "matter" for liturgical symbols. Feminist liturgies thrive on symbols that speak to and of the experiences of women. There is no fear here of bringing women's daily world into the liturgy—the more the better.

Symbols, of course, always image a world. The above list of symbols (weavings, photos, ribbons, mirrors, yarn, fabric, bowls, spices, paper tissue, children's toys, chiffon scarves) speaks particularly of and to the experience of white, middle-class North Atlantic women. In contrast, the central symbolic focus in a Mujerista liturgy might be a home altar,[57] holy cards, or rosaries.[58] In Womanist worship, overturned pots might be a key symbolic ingredient.[59] In an Asian

[53] See, for example, Kalven and Buckley, *Women's Spirit Bonding*, 349f., and Winter, *WomanPrayer*, 37–47.

[54] For a perceptive interpretation of some of these symbols, see Roll, "Traditional Elements in New Women's Liturgies," 43–59.

[55] See Radford Ruether, *Women-Church*, 200–206, 217–222.

[56] One of the earlier collections of Feminist liturgies, edited by Linda Clark and others, was entitled *Image-Breaking/Image-Making* (1981).

[57] See Isasi-Díaz, "On the Birthing Stool," 195.

[58] See Isasi-Díaz, "Mujerista Liturgies and the Struggle for Liberation," 104–111.

[59] See Williams, "Rituals of Resistance," 221.

Feminist liturgy, a Zen bell might be used as a symbol of prayer.[60] In a Nicaraguan women's liturgy in an urban settlement, a piece of zinc siding used in construction can become part of the offertory.[61] In Peru, a Feminist liturgy might make use of indigenous musical instruments, of *chicha*, a traditional indigenous corn drink, and of coca leaves.

4.3.2. *The Redefinition of Sacred Space*

As part of the Feminist attention to symbol, women's liturgies also redefine sacred space, and that on several levels. For one, Feminist liturgical communities typically gather in the round. They opt for a circle as the preferred configuration of the liturgical community over and against all other possibilities of gathering. The circle signals the conviction that all participants are ritually equal. Feminist liturgical communities also typically do not gather in institutional ecclesial space but in private homes or in other non-ecclesial gathering space. Depending on the particular celebration and the season, the community may gather outside. Most Feminist liturgical gatherings are also oriented horizontally rather than vertically throughout the celebration. Lesley Northup, a Feminist ritual scholar, sees this as a characteristic of women's rituals by which they differentiate themselves from "bonds of verticality." Northup writes: the "inherent horizontality of religious ritual experienced by, developed by, and reclaimed by women frees it from the bonds of verticality and allows it to spread out."[62]

Holy ground in Feminist liturgies, then, is not established by gathering in a "church." Holy ground is created and honored by women gathering together to celebrate worship, by women taking off their shoes before one another, by women hallowing the space they choose for their ritualizing with their own presences.

In the last few years, some Feminist liturgical groups have experienced the need to re-emerge from private liturgical space. As part of their struggle for a committed identity for the group, they have begun to search for a permanent, public, and visible space for their

---

[60] See Mananzan, *Woman and Religion*, 206.
[61] See Ramírez, "El Poder de los simbolos," 36.
[62] Northup, "Claiming Horizontal Space," 98.

liturgies.[63] Rosemary Radford Ruether has provided suggestions and a sketch for the architecture of a Women-Church building.[64]

4.4. Women's Liturgical Language: Inclusive and Imaginative

In many parishes and other institutional pastoral settings, the struggle over inclusive language is the most visible part of the Women's Liturgical Movement. In most new women's liturgies themselves, the issue of "inclusive language" is a crucial but also a multifaceted and complex one that goes far beyond the avoidance of "men" and "brothers" in prayers and hymns.

First of all, women have found their own voices in Feminist liturgies. It is women who speak (and usually only women). After the experience of being "liturgically voiceless"[65] in the traditional liturgy, women experience Feminist liturgies as a space that lets them raise and hear one another's voices. This is particularly important when it comes to interpreting the Scriptures. Women as preachers have generated not only a new "sound" but also new ways of reading the Word, new images, illustrations, and homiletic concerns.

Beyond the basic issue of whose voice(s) the liturgical assembly hears, there is the issue of the kind of language that is spoken. Naturally, the new women's liturgies opt for women-friendly language. But the spectrum of what women-friendly might mean is broad indeed. The Feminist liturgical scholar Marjorie Procter-Smith has helpfully distinguished between three kinds of women-friendly language: non-sexist, inclusive, and emancipatory.[66] The first one avoids gender-specific terms. The second one seeks gender balance in references. The third, emancipatory language, according to Procter-Smith, "seeks to transform language use and to challenge stereotypical gender references."[67] For Procter- Smith, only the third kind of language is truly Feminist. But in the new women's liturgies, all three kinds are found, the first two particularly in earlier liturgies.

A second characteristic of the language used in Feminist liturgies is the predilection for poetic language. I use the term loosely, wanting

---

[63] See, for example, Gess, "Christian Feminist Worshiping Community," 3.

[64] See Radford Ruether, *Women-Church*, 146f.

[65] Schaumberger, "Wir lassen uns nicht länger abspeisen," 48.

[66] See Procter-Smith, *In Her Own Rite*, 63–71.

[67] Ibid., 63.

primarily to highlight the difference of language in traditional liturgy and in new women's liturgies. If the Roman liturgy, with its Latin style of liturgical prayer, was hailed as a model of conciseness and clarity, Feminist liturgies delight in poetic prose. Hardly any of them glory in terse liturgical language, be it in prayers, hymns, or readings. Related to this is the fact that the Feminist liturgical vocabulary is not that of the language of dogmatic theology, as is the case in much of traditional worship (see, for example, the collect for Trinity Sunday). Rather, the Feminist liturgical vocabulary reflects the language of women's longings, fears, dreams, pains, and hopes. Traditional liturgical language is experienced as aseptic as far as women's lives are concerned. It has few if any words for what matters to women as women.

4.5. Liturgical Themes: "Women's Experiences"

In terms of content, Feminist liturgies initially were concerned with reversing the pervasive invisibility of women in the traditional liturgy—and that meant women's stories, women's bodies, women's voices, women's pains and longings. A powerful shorthand for these concerns was the category "women's experience." In Feminist liturgies, the androcentric silencing of women's experiences was to be corrected.

The emphasis on the experience of women necessarily led to an anthropological concentration in Feminist liturgies. In that, Feminist liturgies were not alone. They shared this anthropological concentration with many other "liturgies from below" as they emerged since the 1970s, be they liberation liturgies, political prayers, or children and youth liturgies. However, in Feminist liturgies the anthropological focus is on that half of humankind that often remains invisible even in an anthropological concentration: women. This anthropological focus on women gave rise to the fear that in Feminist liturgies women primarily celebrate and romanticize themselves. Certainly the emphasis on the significance of women in these liturgies easily assumes therapeutic functions. It empowers[68] women by strengthening feelings of self-esteem and solidarity. An Asian liturgy, for example, created by the Filipina Feminist theologian Virginia Fabella, includes this self-affirmation:

[68] See Neu, "Women's Empowerment Through Feminist Rituals," 185–200.

130

"We are women.
We are Asian.
We are alive.
We are struggling.
We are hoping.
We are created in the image of God."[69]

In a similar vein with this self-affirmation, books on Feminist liturgies entitled *Celebrating Women*[70] or *Worshiping Women*[71] characteristically beg a linguistic and theological question: Are women the worshipers or the ones being worshiped? It is easy to criticize this tendency of Feminist liturgies. I have done so myself.[72] The harder question to ask is, What truth is spoken about traditional liturgies in this counteremphasis? Does this counteremphasis not point to traditional liturgies as apparently detrimental to women's well-being?

The specific experiences of women highlighted in Feminist liturgies often are experiences of suffering: everyday forms of discrimination and harassment, the exploitation of women in the domestic and the work sphere, and the many forms of violence against women, from the subtle violence of advertising to wartime mass rapes. A characteristic example of such painful experiences in Feminist liturgies is the "Litany of Women in Pain." To each pain named (there are twenty altogether!), the liturgical community responds with "We stand with you." Here are just three of the voices of "women in pain":

"I am the voice of the woman who has been beaten, threatened, and abused.

I am afraid you will blame me for the choices I have made, even when I felt I had no choice.

I speak for the elderly women. I feel our society wants to throw me away—no one will hire me . . .

I speak for the one who was too shy to be heard, and for all women who are afraid to speak out, who block the pain from their memories, who hide their pain from others."[73]

---

69 Fabella, "Morning Worship," 5.

70 The book is edited by Hannah Ward, Jennifer Wild, and Janet Morley (1995).

71 The author is Heather Murray Elkins (1994).

72 See Berger, "Women as Alien Bodies in the Body of Christ," 116.

73 Published in Kalven and Buckley, *Women's Spirit Bonding*, 65f. Many other examples could be added. Suffice it to mention two: the "Litany in Remembrance of

Here is another example from a different liturgical genre, a "Call to Celebration" focusing on women's pain:

"Let the spirit inside you rage like an angry storm.
Let the spirit inside you blaze like a fiery torch.
Women-spirit is hurting and is in pain!
Women-spirit is broken and crushed!
Women-spirit has been battered and smothered!"[74]

Other indicators of the painful reality women bring to worship are the resurgence of lament as a dominant form of prayer[75] and the many rites of healing in Feminist liturgies. Examples of the latter would be a "Ritual of Healing for an Incest Victim," a "Rite of Healing for Wife Battering," a "Rite of Healing from Rape," and a "Rite of Healing from an Abortion."[76]

The definition of "women's experiences," so crucial in early Feminist liturgies, underwent changes in later years. As voices within the Women's Movement diversified, problems with the category "experience" emerged. "Whose experience?" became the key question as African American women, Native American women, Mujerista women, Lesbian women, and Third World women challenged the white Feminist discourse.

Two developments followed directly for many Feminist liturgies. First, women began to acknowledge and name divergent and conflictual experiences among themselves. Second, First World white Feminist liturgies are confronting the fact that the privilege of making gender more important than other markers of identity might belong to the culturally dominant. In other words, Womanist, Mujerista, and Third World Feminist liturgies typically cannot make gender the one and only focus of oppression. Gender justice in these liturgies is always linked to other justice struggles.

These insights have led to new themes in more recent Feminist liturgies, such as oppression among women, diversity of experiences, and the acknowledgment of particular forms of suffering in particu-

---

Violated Women," in Winter, *WomanPrayer*, 147–149, and the "testimonials" of women "bent over" in Crumby Clipson, *Liberating Liturgies*, 20f.

[74] Hunt and Neu, *Women of Fire*, 28.
[75] See Vincie, "Birthing Lament," 1–11.
[76] Radford Ruether, *Women-Church*, 151–162.

lar contexts. Disappearances and martyrdom, for example, are not daily experiences and crucial categories in most liturgies in the First World.[77] They are exactly that, though, for some communities in Central and South America.

4.6. Re-Defining (Liturgical) Tradition

4.6.1. Biblical Women

The initial concentration on women's "experience" lead to a re-reading of both biblical and post-biblical history through women's eyes. At the most basic level, God's story could no longer be told as simply the story of Abraham, Isaac, and Jacob. It was also the story of God with Sarah, Rebekah, and Rachel. God was no longer just the God of the fathers but also the God of our mothers.[78] At a deeper level, God also became the God of Hagar—the slave girl, the foreigner, the woman oppressed by another woman, the one invisible even in the first gaining of visibility of biblical women.[79] More recently, other women have surfaced, not just the exemplary or marginalized ones. "Biblical" women, after all, also means Jezebel, Salome, and Sapphira.

Good examples of the *anamnesis*[80]—the making present through remembering—of women in Feminist liturgies are the many and various "Litanies of Naming." The following such litany is from a liturgy "In Memory of Women of the Gospel Traditions" designed by Diann Neu. The congregational response to each "naming" is "Our time is now."

"Eve and Lilith, you claimed your power by reaching for knowledge and found that it was good. Your time was then . . .

Aseneth, Egyptian wife of Joseph, you were visited by an angel who told you what Metanoia, daughter of God, was doing on your behalf. Your time was then . . .

---

[77] An exception are liturgies commemorating the four U.S. women missionaries murdered in El Salvador in 1980; see, for example, Leistner, *Lass spüren deine Kraft*, 130–134.

[78] An example is the liturgy "God of the Matriarchs," in Swidler, *Sistercelebrations*, 1–8.

[79] See, for example, the two liturgies "Sarah, Our Mother in Faith" and "Hagar, Used and Abused" in Kirk, *Celebrations of Biblical Women's Stories*, 14–25.

[80] I follow the example of Procter-Smith, *In Her Own Rite*, 38–54, in daring to use this technical liturgical term in my analysis of women's liturgies.

Mary, you were a Galilean Jew, mother of us all, who listened, pondered and knew that you had been chosen to give birth to Jesus, one who is Powerful Liberator. Your time was then . . .

Mary Magdalene, you are the foundation of Women-Church, the apostle to the apostles, who shared with them the first news of the resurrection. Your time was then . . ."[81]

This liturgical naming of women is complemented by women being inscribed into the Scriptures in a variety of ways. One of these ways is the reading of Scripture against the grain. The following is an example of an adapted reading of certain passages from the Book of Isaiah. The reading is part of a "Lament for Women Recovering from Abuse in Childhood" designed by Nonie Wales, a member of the Uniting Church in Australia:

"Woman was despised and rejected by men,
a woman of sorrows and acquainted with grief
she was despised and they esteemed her not.

Surely she has borne his griefs and carried his sorrows
yet they esteemed her stricken by God and afflicted,
she was wounded for his transgressions
bruised for his iniquities . . .
who has laid upon her the iniquity of these men?"[82]

Here is a powerful transformation of a traditional biblical text. Abused women are read into the Suffering Servant accounts and become Christ-figures in this liturgical lament.

The most immediate result of the struggle with the scriptural tradition in the Women's Liturgical Movement, however, is embodied in other alternative ways of reading the Scriptures. I am thinking here of inclusive language Lectionaries,[83] supplementary collections of readings for the liturgical year,[84] and alternative collections alto-

---

[81] Neu, *Women and the Gospel Traditions*, 2f.

[82] Wales, "Lament for Women Recovering from Abuse," 10.

[83] Especially the *Inclusive-Language Lectionary* (1985–1987) and the *Lectionary for the Christian People* (1986–1988).

[84] An example is Barbara Rowe and others, eds., *Silent Voices, Sacred Lives: Women's Readings for the Liturgical Year* (1992).

gether.[85] There are also Feminist liturgies that consciously abstain from a reading of the Scriptures and instead read a variety of women's texts of the Christian and other traditions.

4.6.2. A New Communion of Women Saints and Heroines

What applies to the Scriptures also applies to the history of the Church. Early Feminist liturgies speak not of Church fathers but of Church mothers as part of God's story with God's people. Well-known women saints initially played a major role in new women's liturgies. Teresa of Avila and Catherine of Siena especially, the first two women officially designated "doctors" (i.e., teachers) of the Church, were again and again remembered in women's liturgies.[86] Interestingly, the third woman recently named a doctor of the Church, Thérèse de Lisieux, has not received any attention in new women's liturgies. Thérèse's spirituality, or rather the way it has been depicted, so far has not attracted sustained Feminist reconsideration.[87]

Quite often the liturgical commemoration of women saints in Feminist liturgies came to include women who were important to women, sainthood or not, Catholic or not, within Christianity or without. These women are interpreted in Feminist liturgies as important signs of God's loving presence with the world; as such, they are appropriate for women's *anamnesis* in the liturgy. Women celebrate the story of the liberation struggle of other women as part of their own story. The "Litanies of Naming" again provide good examples of this. In Miriam Therese Winter's *WomanPrayer*, there is a lengthy "Litany in Praise of Valiant Women" (it stretches over twenty pages!). Here are just some of the women named by Winter, a Roman Catholic Feminist liturgist:

---

[85] See, for example, the series of "Feminist lectionaries" by Miriam Therese Winter: *WomanWord* (1991), *WomanWisdom* (1991), and *WomanWitness* (1992), or the German inclusive lectionaries by Sabine Ahrens, ed. *Und schuf sie als Mann und als Frau. Eine Perikopenreihe zu den Lebenswirklichkeiten von Frauen und Männern für die Sonn- und Feiertage des Kirchenjahres* (1995), and Mieke Korenhof, ed., *Mit Eva predigen. Ein anderes Perikopenbuch* (1996).

[86] For a more recent Feminist liturgy centering on Teresa of Avila, see Leistner, *Lass spüren deine Kraft*, 126–130.

[87] Stuart, *Spitting at Dragons*, 54f., is one example of the few attempts at a Feminist reconsideration of Thérèse de Lisieux.

"Proba,
fourth-century theologian,
whose interpretation of tradition
was systematically ignored . . .

Maria Bartola,
sixteenth century,
Mexico's first female historian,
who recorded her experience
of the brutal Spanish conquest
of her Aztec civilization . . .

Phillis Wheatley,
who was purchased as a slave
at the age of eight,
became the first black poet
in America,
died in poverty
at the age of thirty-one
in 1784."

The naming of all the "valiant women" in this liturgy ends with the liturgist asking: "Who shall find a valiant woman?" The community responds: "Look! We are all around you."[88]

In Diann Neu's "Litany of Naming," this inclusion of "all women around us" is also marked. The liturgy begins with a women-centered "self-naming," such as: "I am Teresa, daughter of Hedwig, daughter of Hedwig, daughter of Clara." Then follows the invocation: "Mothers in our families, you have named us and given us life. Our mothers, move here with us; strengthen us as Church."[89]

There is another "inclusion" in women's liturgical *anamnesis* beyond the three mentioned here, that is, the saints, the heroines, and the women around us. With their particular sensitivities for women in pain, Feminist liturgies remember the "losers" in the dominant narrative, ecclesial and other. A telling example is liturgies focusing on the women tortured and burned as witches. *Sistercelebrations*, one of the earliest collections of Feminist liturgies, contains a worship service entitled "The Trial of the Halloween Six," which remembers

[88] Winter, *WomanPrayer*, 115–141.
[89] Neu, "Our Name is Church," 76.

136

women tortured and burned as witches.[90] In the same vein, Rosemary Radford Ruether provides a liturgical commemoration on October 31 of the women who were victims of witch-hunts, the "holocaust of women." The "Litany of Remembrance" includes the following names, among many others:

"Anna Rausch, burned 1628, 12 years old.

Sybille Lutz, burned 1628, 11 years old.

Emerzianne Pichler, tortured and burned together with her two children, 1679.

Agnes Wobster, drowned while her young son was forced to watch her trial by water, 1567.

Annabelle Stuart, burned alive 1678, 14 years old.

Veronica Zerritsch, compelled to dance in the warm ashes of her executed mother, then burned alive herself 1754, 13 years old.

Frau Dumler, boiled to death in hot oil while pregnant, 1630."[91]

4.7. Naming and Confronting Evil

With the previous "Litany of Remembrance" painfully in mind, it is not surprising that Feminist liturgies disavow the traditional understanding of sin and thus liturgically the confession of sin. As Feminist theologians noted early on, the dominant understanding of sin was shaped around "man" as the norm of this understanding (the groundbreaking article of Valerie Saiving was written two years prior to the beginning of Vatican II!). Sin primarily was identified with pride, self-will, and power. For women, who historically had been denied both power and self-will, this particular understanding of sin was singularly unhelpful. Feminist theology had to narrate anew.

In Feminist liturgies, the new narrative of what sin is becomes visible in a number of ways. First of all, confessions of women's sins simply are not staple diet in Feminist liturgies, particularly not in early ones. If there are confessions of sins, they obviously do not reiterate the traditional catalogue of women' sins (not enough humility, talked/gossiped too much, did not obey husband, etc.). Rather, the sins confessed in Feminist liturgies might be the lack of resistance to patriarchy, the lack of networking with sisters, and the lack of courage to say no.

[90] See Swidler, *Sistercelebrations*, 56–68.
[91] Radford Ruether, *Women-Church*, 226.

But in the Feminist liturgical universe as a whole, confessions of women's sins are not a central focus of worship. This, however, does not mean that sin does not loom large on the liturgical horizon. Feminist liturgies have a lot to say about sin, but not necessarily in confessions of sin. The sins that regularly appear in Feminist liturgies are usually sins *against* women. Behind the rite of anointing for a rape survivor stands a sin. Behind prayers for abused women stand sins. Behind recollections of women who died in the witch-hunts stand sins. In early Feminist liturgies, structural sins of the Church against women are often highlighted, particularly the many embodiments of androcentricity and misogyny. Thus, an Ash Wednesday Liturgy can become a liturgy of "Repentence [sic] for the Sins of the Church."[92] In more recent Feminist liturgies, such a focus on the sins of the Church against women is less noticeable. As women have begun to leave official ecclesial space behind, they have become "free not to be angry," as one Roman Catholic woman describes it.[93]

Considering the many evils Feminist liturgies confront, it is not surprising that exorcism can be a meaningful ritual element for women at worship. An early example of this is Radford Ruether's suggestion for an "Exorcism of Patriarchal Texts" of Scripture, among them Leviticus 12:1-5 (the uncleanness of women after childbirth) and 1 Timothy 2:11-15 (the command to women to be silent in church). Analogously, Radford Ruether offers a "Litany of Disaffiliation from Patriarchal Theology." After the reading of selected texts by Tertullian, Augustine, Aquinas, and others, the community prays: "From the evil power of this tradition, O Holy Wisdom, deliver us."[94]

Diann Neu offers an exorcism of women's "pains, hurts and alienations" during a Pentecost liturgy called "Women of Fire." Named as evil and then exorcised are, among others, the consistently male image of God, structures of racism and apartheid that separate black and white women, jealousy and aggression that separate woman from woman, all forms of patriarchy that suffocate women's spirits, unequal pay scales for women, and chains of classism, heterosexism, and ageism that bind women everywhere.[95]

---

92 Radford Ruether, *Women-Church*, 241.
93 Quoted in Winter, *Defecting in Place*, 89.
94 Radford Ruether, *Women-Church*, 137–140.
95 See Hunt and Neu, *Women of Fire*, 30.

This exorcism points to a characteristic feature of more recent Feminist confessions of sins. Women are not oblivious to their own sinfulness, particularly the sins against sisterhood, as one might call them. A "Rite of Mind-Cleansing from the Pollution of Sexism" suggested by Rosemary Radford Ruether names a whole array of such possible sins: "the hierarchical violence between middle-class white women and poor women of color; the economic power of privileged women over working-class women . . . the lateral violence between liberal and conservative women . . . the lateral violence between heterosexual and lesbian women . . . the lateral violence between separatist and liberal feminists."[96]

Another example of women confessing sins to other women comes from the closing worship service at the Consultation on Asian Women's Theology, held in Singapore in 1987. Women asked forgiveness of each other for the sins their countries had committed against women of other Asian countries. A Japanese delegate, for example, asked forgiveness of a Filipina, a white Australian begged forgiveness of a Core (indigenous) woman, an Indian delegate asked forgiveness of a Sri Lankan woman.[97] In a similar vein, in a Feminist liturgy of solidarity that appeared in the Asian Feminist journal *In God's Image*, the prayer of confession is split. "First World people" confess their apathy and indifference toward the Third World, their complicity, their betrayal of the poor, and their indulgence in consumerism. "Third World people" confess their anxiety and intimidation, their lack of confidence in the power of love, and their silence in suffering.[98]

All these examples show that the confrontation with evil in Feminist liturgies is a complex, multifaceted, rigorous, and self-critical way of naming the many powers of death in women's lives.

4.8. Healing and Hallowing Creation

Most Feminist liturgies display a positive emphasis on creation far more intensely than does the traditional liturgy. Feminist liturgies emerged in a time of heightened awareness of ecological crisis, and, with the 1980s, the development of an Ecofeminist theology. Where

---

[96] Radford Ruether, *Women-Church*, 133f.
[97] See "Closing Worship," 25f.
[98] See Rose, "Lima Liturgy," 28f.

Feminist liturgies are influenced by Ecofeminist theology, earth and nature come to be seen and venerated as the very Body of God. But the "earthiness" of Feminist liturgies is already obvious in the intensely symbolic nature of these celebrations as described above. From water to oil, from flowers to ashes, from earth to apples, these liturgies embrace and celebrate God's creation wholeheartedly. There are whole Feminist rituals that focus on water, on earth, or on fire. There are celebrations of Earth Day, seasons, and solstices. But the positive emphasis on the goodness of creation is also present in many individual liturgical elements, such as prayers. The following prayer by the Canadian Feminist theologian Mary Kathleen Speegle Schmitt gives an example of an image of God reminiscent of Ecofeminist theology:

"Mother of All Creation,
in the universe, your Womb,
we are sustained as of one body with You.
Protect us by your fierce love,
and assure us that we are safe with You:
that we radiate the strength and warmth
of your nearness to all the world;
One of Beauty,
Love-Child,
Spirit of Hope and Joy. Amen."[99]

Not surprisingly, the visions of the future developed in Feminist liturgies often join the liberation of women with the image of a healed and hallowed creation.

4.9. She Who Is[100] Worshiped

What distinguishes Feminist liturgies from other Feminist ritualizing is the divine center of worship they claim. However, being born of a Feminist suspicion of tradition, it is not surprising that in Feminist liturgies the God Who Is worshiped in and by traditional liturgies came under intense scrutiny. It soon became a hallmark of Feminist liturgies that they extend traditional images of God in order to take up feminine

[99] Speegle Schmitt, *Seasons of the Feminine Divine*, 44.
[100] I am indebted to Elizabeth A. Johnson for this naming of God; see her groundbreaking work *She Who Is: The Mystery of God in Feminist Theological Discourse* (1992). See also the collection by William Cleary, *Prayers to She Who Is* (1995).

images and forms of address. In early Feminist liturgies, there is often praise of God's motherhood, or God is spoken of quite specifically as "Mother God." The ritual "Mother Earth" by Miriam Therese Winter provides one example. A reader speaks the following text:

"God loved
the fruit of Her womb
with all its potential for good.
Intuitively,
She broke the silence,
singing:
Let there be light!
Her sunlight chased the shadows.
She danced with the moon and the stars.
She sang all life into being . . .
She taught earth all about motherhood,
about nurture,
about birth."

The ritual as a whole is interspersed with the following song: "Mother earth, sister sea, giving birth, energy, reaching out, touching me lovingly."[101] Both the reading and the song are characteristic of an emphasis on motherhood understood as nurturing and loving. After the initial enthusiasm for the image of mothering in Feminist liturgies, however, these definitions of motherhood themselves came under suspicion as part of the patriarchal ideology of "woman." The struggle over the meaning of motherhood in Feminist discourse is evident in some more recent works by Feminist liturgists. A good example is the following prayer by the Anglican liturgist Janet Morley:

"God our mother,
you hold our life within you,
nourish us at your breast,
and teach us to walk alone.
Help us so to receive your tenderness
and respond to your challenge
that others may draw life from us,
in your name, Amen."[102]

[101] Winter, *WomanPrayer*, 26.
[102] Morley, *All Desires Known*, 11.

Here God's motherhood is seen not only as nurturing but also as challenging, not only as comforting but also as liberating ("you . . . teach us to walk alone"). Together with the broadening of the image of motherhood in Feminist liturgies, a plethora of other images for God emerged, with *Sophia* (Wisdom) enjoying ever-growing popularity.[103] The following examples of other names for God are all taken from one publication, a collection of Christian Feminist prayers for the liturgical year. The author, Mary Kathleen Speegle Schmitt, utilizes an astounding wealth of images for God, among them: Mother of all Creation, Mother Eagle, Vigilant Mother, Divine Seamstress, Root of Wisdom, Weaver of the Web of Life, Divine Midwife, Passionate Sister, Shadow Sister, Bakerwoman, Shepherdess of the Universe, Divine Healing Woman, Queen of the Universe. The images mentioned for God so far are all feminine, but Speegle Schmitt offers a host of other names as well, including Inhabitor of both Dark and Light, Sourcewater of Life, Earth Dancer, Cloud of Radiance, Dawn of Glory, Fragrant Bread, Hidden Treasure, Potent Wine, Enticing Lifestream.[104] The wealth of images witnesses to the intensity of the search for new and authentic ways of naming God in women's liturgies.

Beyond these shared concerns of imaging God, however, "God" is no easy presence in Feminist liturgies. From the absence of specific God-references in some and the claim of God's presence in sisterhood in others; from the absence of Christ-references in some to the embracing of the title "Lord" in a few out of reverence for Womanist concerns;[105] from calling God "mother" to naming her *pachamama* to addressing God with "thee,"[106] there is a broad range of God-talk *and* God-silence in Feminist liturgies.

---

[103] See Edgardh Beckman, "Sophia," 36–43.

[104] For more, see all three volumes of Speegle Schmitt's *Seasons of the Feminine Divine*; Virginia Ann Froehle's *Called into Her Presence: Praying With Feminine Images of God* (1992); and Julie Howard's *We Are the Circle: Celebrating the Feminine in Song and Ritual* (1993).

[105] "Lord" may be a crucial and subversive way to address Christ if one's social location is that of slaves.

[106] Burmese women representatives to the Consultation on Asian Women's Theology, held in Singapore in 1987, prepared a morning worship that still addressed God in these terms; see Dunn and Thein, "Morning Worship," 13.

4.10. The Feminist Liturgical "Oikoumene"

Feminist liturgies practically always have an ecumenical orientation. The dividing lines between individual Churches fade in light of the gulf in all Christian communities between patriarchy and women's liberation. But the oikoumene of Feminist liturgies can also extend far beyond the Christian ecumenical world. Particularly in North America, Feminist liturgies can blur the lines between Christian, Jewish, Native, Wicca, and other women. More so than in Europe, the Feminist liturgical oikoumene easily tends to be broader than the ecclesial world. How far this oikoumene extends *in actu* often depends on geographic location. For a Feminist liturgical community in Latin America, the ecumenical openness to include both Protestant and Catholic women may be an achievement. For a Feminist community in Los Angeles, it in all likelihood is not. For Women Church in Korea, openness might mean inclusion of women shamans. For some of the above, embracing lesbian women is a call of ecumenical openness. Last but not least, for most Feminist liturgical communities, including men in liturgies is a question that causes much soul-searching and divergent answers.

What almost all groups share is a willingness to err on the side of inclusivity rather than exclusion. This erring on the side of Feminist inclusivity is an appropriate characteristic on which to draw this overview to a close. In some ways, one can subsume other characteristics under this one: Feminist liturgies will opt to err on the side of inclusivity whenever women's voices, stories, experiences of pain, symbols, traditions, and images of God are concerned.

5. GENDERED RESISTANCE: THE PARADOX OF THE WOMEN'S LITURGICAL MOVEMENT

Turning back from looking at individual characteristics to the development of the Women's Liturgical Movement as a whole, one notes growing diversity in the last decade or so. This development is parallel to developments in Feminist theology, Feminist theory, and the wider Women's Movement. One of these developments is the problematization of the initial identification of women's oppression with patriarchy. Three aspects deserve mention in this context.

First, there is growing recognition that the label "patriarchy" is too simple a conceptualization of the issue. Defining the issue for women as patriarchy masks the many interrelated oppressive structures that characterize women's lives. When hidden, however, these inter-related oppressive structures cannot adequately be challenged.

Second and related to the first, there has been a painful realization among women that within the complex web of oppressive structures, women themselves are agents of oppression of other women. Quick claims to global sisterhood, therefore, have become suspect.

Third, there is a growing awareness of women rendered invisible in the first wave of Feminist theologies and liturgies. These might be traditionalist women grieving over the loss of the Tridentine Mass, fundamentalist women appreciative of a male preacher expounding the Scriptures in traditional ways, or cloistered nuns experiencing the liturgy of the Church as life-giving and life-sustaining.

All these developments have impacted the Women's Liturgical Movement in a variety of ways. Some of the specific characteristics of more recent Feminist liturgies, as described above, have emerged in direct response to these developments.

There is a fourth and crucial shift in recent Feminist theory that has not impacted Feminist liturgies in any sustained way but will have fundamental consequences for their future. I am thinking of the destabilization of the subject "woman" and the suspicion surround-ing gender dualism in recent Feminist thinking. Under the impact of postmodern deconstructions, subjects such as "woman," the bedrock of early Feminist consciousness, have come to be interpreted as cul-tural (that is, constantly changing) constructs rather than as natural givens. Gender dualism, then, tends to be read as a highly charged cultural construct that in its starkest form is detrimental to the broad spectrum of actual women's lives.

What does this mean for the new women's liturgies? To answer this question, one needs to situate these liturgies within the whole history of women's ways of worship. As I have shown for early Christianity and the twentieth-century Liturgical Movement, Christian worship has had a starkly gendered script from its earliest beginnings. When viewed in this context, the Women's Liturgical Movement of our own time, with all its radical rethinking of women at worship, is no different. It, too, lets worship be a fundamentally gendered reality. The Women's Liturgical Movement embodies prac-tices of resistance to traditional liturgical genderization, not by abdicating the category gender, but by making gender a crucial de-

144

terminant of new liturgical practices. Rather than dislodging gender dualism, then, the Women's Liturgical Movement, and particularly Feminist liturgies, highlight gender dualism.

The problem Feminist liturgies confront is gender *hierarchy* in all its liturgical manifestations. These liturgies all but leave untouched the fundamental assumption of gender *dualism*. As distinctively women-centered liturgies in protest against a "Man's Liturgy," Feminist liturgies thrive on gender dualism. There is a paradox here if nothing else. Feminist liturgies struggle against an asymmetrically gendered liturgical tradition with liturgies far more asymmetrically gendered than ever before. In Feminist liturgies, gender openly becomes a, if not *the,* dominant feature of worship. In fact, the very existence of these liturgies is rooted in accepting the category of gender as a fundamental marker of human identity and of the Church's liturgical life.

Rather than reading this analysis as a critique of everything Feminist liturgies are about, I see this paradox of Feminist liturgies rooted in the paradoxical situation of women themselves. At the end of the twentieth century, with all the redefining of what "woman" means, women are nevertheless typically encouraged both to down-play gender (e.g., in their professional lives, where gender-specific pleading is suspect) *and* to uplift gender (especially when it comes to "feminine" appearance or such "woman tasks" as child-care) as a fundamental marker of identity. Feminist liturgies mirror this paradoxical situation by highlighting gender to protest traditional genderization in worship. There are three dynamics in the Women's Liturgical Movement that I want to comment on in light of this paradox.

First, I am not arguing that the Women's Liturgical Movement has brought nothing new. Located as it is within the Women's Movement, this liturgical renewal movement has opened up ritual space consciously gendered to the perspective of women, usually women impacted by various "feminisms." This space, for many women, has become a vibrant and authentic space of encounter with God. With that, the Women's Liturgical Movement is speaking a fundamental truth about liturgical tradition, presence and future: authentic worship ultimately cannot thrive with asymmetric liturgical constraints for women.

Second, the Women's Liturgical Movement embodies some liturgical practices for women that seem startlingly new but really are not.

This element in the movement is rooted in the absence to date of a thoroughgoing Feminist reconstruction of women at worship throughout history. We simply do not know liturgical tradition enough as of yet from the perspective of women to adequately judge the past. This can lead to misjudgments. Liturgical space is a case in point. Rather than marking the liturgical tradition space-wise as thoroughly androcentric and hostile to women, it would be more appropriate to acknowledge that the earliest liturgical space was, indeed, the "women's sphere" of the time. Feminist liturgies can then be seen as retrieving or reconnecting with the earliest "norm of the mothers"—no small feat, particularly in the Roman Catholic tradition.

There are other elements in Feminist rituals that deserve to be reinterpreted on the basis of a Feminist reconstruction of women at worship throughout history. Menstruation as a liturgical marker is a case in point, as might be the milk-and-honey-rituals that enjoy a certain popularity in Feminist liturgies. Both of these have in the past been elements of women's ways of worship. Feminist liturgies, in appropriating these elements, are not as alienated from liturgical tradition as some think. On the contrary, these Feminist liturgies are part of a long tradition of the interplay of women with worship and have to be understood as such. Knowing where, when, and how Christian women throughout history have encountered specific liturgical markers and rites that are now being reassessed and reappropriated in Feminist liturgies is crucial to such an understanding.

The ways in which some traditional elements of women's ways of worship are assessed and reappropriated in Feminist liturgies while others are discarded is a further indicator of the paradox I have identified in these liturgies. This fundamental paradox of the Women's Liturgical Movement has recently been exemplified in an article on the so-called churching of women. Natalie Knödel, in her Feminist reconsideration of this "obsolete rite," looks at one of the most gender-specific rites in liturgical history and discovers in it a liturgical space where women were taken seriously as women. This starkly gendered ritual therefore is claimed as potentially women-centered and submitted for Feminist reconsideration.[107] Knödel's article can serve to exemplify the paradox I have identified above. If the fundamental motivity of the Women's Liturgical Movement is to take gender—in

[107] See Knödel, "Reconsidering an Obsolete Rite," 106–125.

146

this case women—seriously and that on the basis of gender dualism, then even/especially a rite like the churching of women begins to look worthy of Feminist reconsideration.

The problem, then, is not liturgical genderization as such but the kind of genderization embodied in worship. In other words, gender as a marker in Feminist liturgies would be good, gender as a marker in traditional liturgies bad. Or, gender as a dominant liturgical marker is good if it is self-consciously embraced, self-defined, and self-actualized. To my mind, this is too simple a conceptualization of the issue. A more appropriate, if critical, reconceptualization of Feminist liturgies is suggested by the destabilization of the subject "woman" and the growing Feminist suspicion of gender dualism in recent Feminist theory. Looked at in light of these recent shifts in Feminist thinking, Feminist liturgies appear to live by gender dualism. Where would their subject be if the notion "woman" became unstable? What, on the other hand, if "women" have less in common than Feminist liturgies presuppose and necessitate? What if liberal inclusiveness of ever new women's voices and "experiences" is not enough? What about women who resist being included (the pleasure of a non-demanding encounter with God my mother experienced in "hearing" the Tridentine Mass prevents me from excluding from my narrative all non-Feminist women at worship).

I am posing these questions of the Women's Liturgical Movement, and of Feminist liturgies in particular, as a woman who has been at worship ever since her baptism at the ripe age of ten days.[108] I write as someone who celebrated her first communion in Latin. I also write as a liturgical scholar, and as someone who has been shaped profoundly by Feminist concerns. With this specific liturgical location of my own, I want to honor the new women's liturgies while not treating them as sacrosanct. The following, then, sketches my understanding of the Women's Liturgical Movement, of which I am a part.

I am convinced—and this has motivated the writing of *Women's Ways of Worship*—that reconstructing the history of women at worship will offer a new vision of the place of the Women's Liturgical Movement within liturgical history as a whole. I see this movement on a continuum of women at worship, a continuum of struggle with

[108] An alternative way of describing this is to conceive of a "catechumenate in the womb." I have explored this notion in Berger, "Katechumenat im Mutterleib," 61–66.

the historic marginalization of women in most liturgical contexts. This struggle has come to the forefront today with women themselves being agents of both the questioning and the transformation. There is clear correspondence, though, on the level of ever-changing constructs of women at worship, between "then" and "now." Indeed, the Church throughout history has struggled, in one way or another, with gender issues in its liturgy.

The paradox of Feminist liturgies highlighting gender to protest historical liturgical genderization is one facet in the complex history of gender representations in worship. Again, by naming this a "paradox," I do not want to deny its importance. I do, however, want to signal that the *future* role of gender in worship is a very open question indeed. For if gender dualism is acknowledged as a particular social construct in time rather than a God-given, then its place as a fundamental marker of liturgical identity is questionable, both for traditional *and* for women's liturgies.

The place of the Women's Liturgical Movement in the history of women at worship, nevertheless, is secure. The movement has brought to the forefront a crucial element of women at worship, one that has shaped women's liturgical lives since the very beginning, namely, their gender and the liturgical marginalizations based on it. The Women's Liturgical Movement, moreover, has imaginatively and effectively found ways to expose and to resist this liturgical marginalization. As such, it has confronted the rest of the Church with a provocative liturgical witness for our time.

Every way of worship is a liturgically embodied and practiced truth-in-fragment. With its very limitations it points beyond itself to Truth-in-fullness, the Living God who is worshiped. Feminist liturgies, as all others, are such practiced truth-in-fragment. The "fragments of truth" and the holes in between the fragments, however, differ from those in other liturgies. It is exactly in this difference that Feminist liturgies can be seen as a gift for the whole Church.[109]

There are several unique fragments of truth I see in Feminist liturgies.

First, these liturgies show that many women find ritualizing their faith together crucially important in their lives. These women very clearly do want to worship. The problem for many women, in other words, is not that liturgy is meaningless; the problem comes with the

[109] See Walton, "Challenge of Feminist Liturgy," 59.

148

kind of liturgies to which women are invited. The institutional Church has not extended appealing invitations to many women living at the end of the twentieth century. Feminist liturgies do.

Second, Feminist liturgies reveal that women are able symbol-makers, ritual experts, shapers of liturgical practices and narratives, and bearers of liturgical traditioning. How impoverishing if the liturgy of the Church has to live without this wealth of women's ritual charisms!

Third, women have found ways to authentically ritualize their dramatically changed lives in the second half of the twentieth century and are showing the rest of the Church possibilities of doing so. This is no small accomplishment. Who would have predicted that there are people gifted with creating meaningful liturgies, that is, ways of worshiping the Living God, for "postmodern" women? No official liturgical reform would have succeeded here. Altogether, Feminist liturgies witness to specific ways of liturgical well-being and flourishing for women in our times. As such, they are deeply significant if the Church wants to be more than a fellowship of "brothers" in the next century.

Granted that Feminist liturgies have engendered these "truths," like all liturgies they, too, remain truth-in-fragment. Where, then, are some of the holes in between the truths of these liturgies, and how will these non-truths be addressed in the future? This is the question for the last pages of this book, namely, the epilogue that follows.

Epilogue: Worship Beyond Gender?

Diann Neu, a leading Feminist liturgist, casts her sense of the Feminist liturgical enterprise in a wonderful story that begins with echoes of Scripture: "A woman revisioning ritual is like a woman who decides to make a quilt."[1] The woman gathers fabric in her house and begins to cut and arrange patches. When she discovers that she does not have enough fabric, she goes out to buy new materials. Then she calls on friends and strangers to help her sew. "The quilt grows larger and larger, brighter and bolder, more colorful and more diverse at every stitch. And the woman looks at the quilt which they are all making with their lives and she smiles and smiles and smiles, and she rejoices in her heart and is very glad. Let those who have ears to hear, hear. Let those who have eyes to see, see. Let those who have hearts to feel, feel."

It is tempting to end this study of *Women's Ways of Worship* with Neu's story, particularly with its intriguing echoes of Scripture. A gender-based liturgical narrative written at this time, however, when shifts in the interpretation of gender have become so marked, inevitably raises questions about the future. If my own sense of a basic paradox in Feminist liturgies is right, namely, that they ultimately underwrite a binary gender division counterproductive to the diversity of women's lives, then authentic worship for women in the future will lie even beyond the truths of Feminist liturgies.

Before looking to the future, though, I want to look back briefly. What has the above historical reconstruction of women at worship achieved? This first attempt at a gendered reading of the history of the liturgy leads to several conclusions. I want to draw attention to two in particular.

First, all future liturgical historiography will have to incorporate gender as a fundamental analytical category. There is no going back

---

[1] Neu, "Women Revisioning Religious Rituals," 156f.

to a (seemingly) gender-neutral narrative of the liturgy. Such a narrative serves to mask the powerful gender asymmetries in the history of worship.

Second, we need to recast the whole of liturgical history, not just individual parts of it, in gender-specific ways. Until this reformulation is accomplished, our knowledge of women's ways of worship remains eclectic and fragmentary. I hope to have provided a glimpse at such a redefined liturgical history, taking as examples early Christianity and the liturgical renewal movements of the twentieth century.

Beyond this historical reconstruction of women at worship, however, looms a fundamental theological question, and liturgical historiography alone cannot answer this theological question for us. The question concerns the future of worship and is, simply put: Should worship continue to be shaped by the binary division that the category of gender has provided (with or even without all the asymmetrical social constructs it entails)? Or do we need to look anew for a worship beyond gender,[2] and what would this mean?

As the previous chapters have shown, the liturgy historically has been a powerful script for, and embodiment of, gender roles. From the earliest gathering of the ecclesial assembly in women's space (i.e., private homes), through the growing marginalization of women at the liturgical "center" and a concomitant reorientation of liturgical practices by women to the "margins," to groups of women reclaiming ritual power for themselves as women in the twentieth century, gender has always shaped liturgical practices in fundamental ways. Whether this will and should be the case in the future, however, is indeed an open question. Two things are clear so far. First, asymmetrical gender relations, which shaped the liturgy essentially since the earliest times in a variety of ways, have forever been unmasked. We cannot return to a time of un-knowing the starkly and asymmetrically gendered nature of Christian worship. Second, the liturgical script for women has forever been enlarged by the Women's Liturgical Movement. Again, we cannot go back to a time of un-knowing the breadth of women's liturgical creativity and the riches of women's actual liturgical practices. With these two fundamental

[2] My concept of "worship beyond gender" owes its linguistic existence to Gail Ramshaw's book *God Beyond Gender* (1995).

shifts in women's liturgical lives in the twentieth century, how will worship appear in the next?

The charism of discernment is needed far beyond my limited possibilities to provide more than fragmentary reflections on this issue.[3] Possibly also, the time for grand visions of the future and magnificent unifying scripts is simply no more. My own sense of a yet-to-come liturgy beyond gender, then, leads in the following direction: The liturgical performances of gender in the future will have to differ fundamentally from an embodiment of the dominant social gender relations of the past. In other words, liturgy must be more, so much more, than the mirror or memory of gender relations in the surrounding culture. For many women in the Church, the horizon of expectations with which they approach worship has fundamentally changed with the passing of the twentieth century. Many women now experience worship against a cultural horizon that makes them live a different life and a different liturgy from, say, their mothers and grandmothers (and this quite apart from the liturgical reforms after Vatican II). It is painful for these women, and ultimately counterproductive to the gospel, if worship is one of the spaces where gender relations are still those of past dominations and marginalizations.

What, then, can the liturgical script for gender roles be in the future? Rather than liturgy embodying a past binary gender hierarchy, could the worship of the future be a space where multifaceted, vibrantly new, life-giving, God-sustained gender-roles are being practiced that allow all human beings and all creation to flourish? Could liturgy become a model of such gender roles rather than a stale mirror of past gender hierarchy?[4]

[3] One aspect I find very hard to assess, for example, is the influence of information technologies on our horizon of expectations as we approach worship in the future. How will *Women@Worship* live the liturgy in years to come? Their horizon of expectations will be powerfully shaped by the experience of "cyberspace," where such age-old anthropological constants as time, space, and gender are transformed beyond recognition. Another aspect of the changing horizon of expectations people will bring to worship in the future is the developments in medical technology. Transsexuals have been with us for decades, a hermaphrodite can accidentally "happen" through in vitro fertilization, and transgenetic human beings are on the horizon. Will the liturgy of the future openly welcome human beings who do not fit the binary gender division?

[4] Norbert Greinacher already suggested as much in his 1982 book on the Eucharist, *Im Angesicht meiner Feinde—Mahl des Friedens;* see particularly 66.

Such a vision, I suspect, will become true, paradoxically, when gendered identities no longer function as the key markers that they are in liturgies today, both in traditional *and* Feminist ones. This is the truth-in-fragment that, to my mind, poststructuralist Feminist theories hold as they deconstruct the very notion of gender as a fixed category. Rather than thinking of two separate fixed categories, "men" and "women," and continuing a binary gender division between human beings, these Feminist theories invite us to think of a broad spectrum of gendered beings and gender relations, with two polarities. Gender thus becomes fluid, unstable, complex, and constantly in flux and transition.[5] We "do" it, with different emphases at different times, rather than "be" it.[6]

Translating these theories into the world of the liturgy, the argument could be this: In worship, as a focal point of Christian existence, we are called to resist the absolutizing of sexed identity. One fundamental aspect of our baptismal practice of identity is that "there is no longer male and female" (Gal 3:28), a liturgical truth the apostle Paul named long before poststructuralist gender theory. The key liturgical question now becomes: How does the Church, how do we want to "do gender" liturgically so that the worship of the Church corresponds to the claim of the Christian community that it worships the God-With-Us, a God who created human beings male and female, in God's own image, but who also redeemed them so that there is no longer male and female?

I have quietly assumed in this Epilogue that the task for the future is to translate the truth-in-fragments in Feminist liturgies into transformative power for all who worship. In other words, I do not see the truths of Feminist liturgies ultimately best expressed in a continuously growing rift within the Church between women-defined liturgical communities and "others." One way to imagine such a translation of the Feminist truth-in-fragments is to think of a future *gender elasticity free of domination* in worship. Let me comment on the latter part of this double helix first. "Free of domination" imagines worship as a God-sustained space where social arrangements of gen-

---

[5] There are Feminists who have started critiquing these "post"-feminisms as disabling women from acting together.

[6] I am indebted for this phrase to McClintock Fulkerson, "Gender—Being It or Doing It," 188.

der hierarchy are not repeated but, on the contrary, challenged and confounded. The first part, "gender elasticity" in worship, imagines a God-sustained space that celebrates the whole gender spectrum without unnecessarily repeating and solidifying binary social gender arrangements. The liturgy, actually, embodies some experience in gender elasticity: At its heart is a God who became "man," but who now nourishes us with God's own body—a reality embodied by nursing mothers.

Holding both sides together—freedom from gender domination, and gender elasticity—involves both acknowledging a wide variety of gendered human beings and struggling against gender as a basis of ritual privilege and domination. I have found no better way to capture this new paradox than by rethinking a work by the African-American poet Pat Parker (d. 1989). Parker's poem "For the white person who wants to know how to be my friend"[7] caught my attention not only because of the truth it spoke to me as a white European woman living in the southern United States but also because it captured a paradox I sense in being a Catholic and a Feminist at worship at this point in time. My rethinking of Parker's poem could be called "For those who want to know how to worship with us":

"The first thing you do is to forget that we are women.
Second, you must never forget that we are women."

The ultimate paradox of the fundamental importance and final insignificance of gender lies at the heart of this new vision of authentic worship for the future.

[7] Published in Parker, *Womanslaughter*, 13.

Bibliography

Aeberli, Elisabeth. *Frauengottesdienste. Modelle.* Lucerne: Rex-Verlag, 1987.

Ahrens, Sabine, and others, eds. *Und schuf sie als Mann und als Frau. Eine Perikopenreihe zu den Lebenswirklichkeiten von Frauen und Männern für die Sonn-und Feiertage des Kirchenjahres.* Gütersloh: Gütersloher Verlagshaus, 1995.

Albrecht, Ruth. *Das Leben der heiligen Makrina auf dem Hintergrund der Thekla-Traditionen. Studien zu den Ursprüngen des weiblichen Mönchtums im 4. Jahrhundert in Kleinasien.* Forschungen zur Kirchen- und Dogmengeschichte 38. Göttingen: Vandenhoeck & Ruprecht, 1986.

Amelin, Emmanuel. "L'éducation liturgique dans les écoles, pensionnats et oeuvres de jeunesse." *La Femme Belge,* no. 2 (June 1924) 157–172.

Anderson, Jill. "Holy Women and the Cult of the Eucharist in the Early Irish Church." *Magistra: A Journal of Women's Spirituality in History* 3:1 (1997) 49–107.

Anonyma. "Leben mit der Kirche." *Bibel und Liturgie* 2 (1927/28) 411f.

Ansorge, Dirk. "Der Diakonat der Frau. Zum gegenwärtigen Forschungsstand." *Liturgie und Frauenfrage. Ein Beitrag zur Frauenforschung aus liturgiewissenschaftlicher Sicht.* Ed. Teresa Berger and Albert Gerhards, 31–65. Pietas Liturgica 7. St. Ottilien: EOS-Verlag, 1990.

Aston, Margaret. "Segregation in Church." *Women in the Church.* Ed. W. J. Sheils and Diana Wood, 237–294. Studies in Church History 27. Oxford: Basil Blackwell, 1990.

Aubert, Jean-Jacques. "Threatened Wombs: Aspects of Ancient Uterine Magic." *Greek, Roman, and Byzantine Studies* 30 (1989) 421–449.

Bagnall Yardley, Anne. "'Ful weel she soong the service dyvyne': The Cloistered Musician in the Middle Ages." *Women Making Music: The Western Art Tradition, 1150–1950.* Ed. Jane Bowers and Judith Tick, 15–38. Urbana, Ill.: University of Illinois Press, 1987.

Berger, Florence S. *Cooking for Christ: The Liturgical Year in the Kitchen.* Des Moines, Iowa: National Catholic Rural Life Conference, 1949.

Berger, Florence S. *Cooking for Christ: Your Kitchen Prayer Book.* Des Moines, Iowa: National Catholic Rural Life Conference, 1949.

157

Berger, Teresa. "The Classical Liturgical Movement in Germany and Austria: Moved by Women?" *Worship* 66 (1992) 231–251.

Berger, Teresa. "Katechumenat im Mutterleib?" *Glauben lernen—Glauben feiern.* Ed. Albert Gerhards and Gottfried Bitter, 61–66. Praktische Theologie heute 30. Stuttgart: Verlag W. Kohlhammer, 1998.

Berger, Teresa. *Liturgie und Frauenseele. Die Liturgische Bewegung aus der Sicht der Frauenforschung.* Praktische Theologie heute 10. Stuttgart: Verlag W. Kohlhammer, 1993.

Berger, Teresa. "Women and Worship: A Bibliography." *Studia Liturgica* 19 (1989) 96–110.

Berger, Teresa. "Women and Worship: A Bibliography Continued." *Studia Liturgica* 25 (1995) 103–117.

Berger, Teresa. "Women as Alien Bodies in the Body of Christ? The Place of Women in Worship." *Liturgy and the Body.* Ed. Louis-Marie Chauvet and François Kabasele Lumbala, 112–120. Concilium. Maryknoll, N.Y.: Orbis Books, 1995.

Berger, Teresa. "The Women's Movement as a Liturgical Movement: A Form of Inculturation?" *Studia Liturgica* 20 (1990) 55–64.

Betz, Johannes. "Die Eucharistie als Gottes Milch in frühchristlicher Sicht." *Zeitschrift für Katholische Theologie* 106 (1984) 1–26, 167–185.

Birnbaum, Walter. *Die katholische Liturgische Bewegung. Darstellung und Kritik.* Beiträge zur Förderung christlicher Theologie 30:1. Gütersloh: C. Bertelsmann, 1926. Rev. ed. *Die deutsche katholische liturgische Bewegung* as vol. 1 of *Das Kultusproblem und die liturgischen Bewegungen des 20. Jahrhunderts.* Tübingen: Katzmann Verlag, 1966.

Boisclair, Regina A. "Amnesia in the Catholic Sunday Lectionary: Women— Silenced from the Memories of Salvation History." *Women and Theology.* Ed. Mary Ann Hinsdale and Phyllis H. Kaminski, 109–135. The Annual Publication of The College Theology Society 40. Maryknoll, N.Y.: Orbis Books, 1995.

Botte, Bernard. *Le mouvement liturgique: témoignage et souvenirs.* Paris: Desclée, 1973. English trans. *From Silence to Participation: An Insider's View of Liturgical Renewal.* Washington: The Pastoral Press, 1988.

Bouyer, Louis. *Liturgical Piety.* Liturgical Studies 1. Notre Dame, Ind.: University of Notre Dame Press, 1955.

Bradshaw, Paul F. "Redating the Apostolic Tradition." *Rule of Prayer, Rule of Faith.* Festschrift Aidan Kavanagh. Ed. Nathan Mitchell and John F. Baldovin, 3–17. Collegeville, Minn.: The Liturgical Press, 1996.

Bradshaw, Paul F. *The Search for the Origins of Christian Worship: Sources and Methods for the Study of Early Liturgy.* New York: Oxford University Press, 1992.

Brazal, Agnes M. "Inculturation: An Interpretative Model for Feminist Revisions of Liturgical Praxis?" *Questions Liturgiques* 77 (1996) 124–134.

Briggs, Sheila. "A History of Our Own: What Would a Feminist History of Theology Look Like?" *Horizons in Feminist Theology: Identity, Tradition, and Norms.* Ed. Rebecca S. Chopp and Sheila Greeve Davaney, 165–178. Minneapolis: Fortress Press, 1997.

Brock, Sebastian P., and Susan Ashbrook Harvey, eds. *Holy Women of the Syrian Orient.* The Transformation of the Classical Heritage 13. Berkeley: University of California Press, 1987.

Brooten, Bernadette J. *Women Leaders in the Ancient Synagogue: Inscriptional Evidence and Background Issues.* Brown Judaic Studies 36. Chico, Calif.: Scholars Press, 1982.

Brown, Alden V. *The Grail Movement and American Catholicism, 1940–1975.* Notre Dame Studies in American Catholicism 9. Notre Dame, Ind.: University of Notre Dame Press, 1989.

Brown, Peter. *The Body and Society: Men, Women and Sexual Renunciation in Early Christianity.* Lectures on the History of Religions 13. New York: Columbia University Press, 1988.

Brown, Peter. *The Cult of the Saints: Its Rise and Function in Latin Christianity.* Chicago: The University of Chicago Press, 1981.

Bruit Zaidman, Louise. "Pandora's Daughters and Rituals in Grecian Cities." *A History of Women in the West.* Vol. 1: *From Ancient Goddesses to Christian Saints.* Ed. Pauline Schmitt Pantel, 338–376. Cambridge, Mass.: The Belknap Press of Harvard University Press, 1992.

Bruzelius, Caroline A. "Hearing Is Believing: Clarissan Architecture, ca. 1213–1340." *Gesta* 31 (1992) 83–91.

Burton, Katherine, and Helmut Ripperger. *Feast Day Cookbook: The Traditional Feast Day Dishes of Many Lands.* New York: David McKay Company, 1951.

Campbell, Debra. "The Heyday of Catholic Action and the Lay Apostolate, 1929–1959." *Transforming Parish Ministry: The Changing Roles of Catholic Clergy, Laity, and Women Religious.* Ed. J. P. Dolan and others, 222–252. New York: Crossroad, 1990.

Casel, Odo. "Zur Einführung." *Jahrbuch für Liturgiewissenschaft* 1 (1921) 1–3.

"Catholic Women are Studying the Liturgy." *Orate Fratres* 7 (1932/33) 30f.

Chopp, Rebecca S. "In the Real World: A Feminist Theology for the Church." *Quarterly Review* 16 (1996) 3–22.

Clark, Elizabeth A. "Ideology, History, and the Construction of 'Woman' in Late Ancient Christianity." *Journal of Early Christian Studies* 2:2 (1994) 157–184.

Clark, Elizabeth A. "The Lady Vanishes: Dilemmas of a Feminist Historian after the 'Linguistic Turn.'" *Church History* 67 (1998) 1–31.

Clark, Elizabeth A. "Patrons, Not Priests: Gender and Power in Late Ancient Christianity." *Gender & History* 2 (1990) 253–273.

Clark, Gillian. *Women in the Ancient World*. Greece & Rome: New Surveys in the Classics 21. New York: Oxford University Press, 1989.

Clark, Gillian. *Women in Late Antiquity: Pagan and Christian Life-styles*. Oxford: Clarendon Press, 1993.

Clark, Linda, and others, eds. *Image-Breaking/Image-Making: A Handbook for Creative Worship with Women of Christian Tradition*. New York: Pilgrim Press, 1981.

Cleary, William. *Prayers to She Who Is*. New York: Crossroad, 1995.

"Closing Worship and Reflection of the Consultation on Asian Women's Theology." *In God's Image* (December 1987/88) 25–29.

Cohen, David. "Seclusion, Separation, and the Status of Women in Classical Athens." *Women in Antiquity*. Ed. Ian McAuslan and Peter Walcot, 134–145. Greece & Rome Studies 3. New York: Oxford University Press, 1996.

Cohen, Shaye. "Menstruants and the Sacred in Judaism and Christianity." *Women's History and Ancient History*. Ed. Sarah B. Pomeroy, 273–299. Chapel Hill, N.C.: University of North Carolina Press, 1991.

Collins, Mary. "Is the Eucharist Still a Source of Meaning for Women?" *Living in the Meantime: Concerning the Transformation of Religious Life*. Ed. Paul J. Philibert, 185–196. New York: Paulist Press, 1994.

Collins, Mary. "Principles of Feminist Liturgy." *Women at Worship: Interpretations of North American Diversity*. Ed. Marjorie Procter-Smith and Janet Walton, 17–24. Louisville: Westminster/John Knox Press, 1993.

Combe, Pierre M. *Justine Ward and Solesmes*. Washington: The Catholic University of America Press, 1987.

Cooper, Kate. *The Virgin and the Bride: Idealized Womanhood in Late Antiquity*. Cambridge, Mass.: Harvard University Press, 1996.

Corley, Kathleen E. *Private Women, Public Meals: Social Conflict in the Synoptic Tradition*. Peabody, Mass.: Hendrickson Publishers, 1993.

Cott, Nancy F. *The Grounding of Modern Feminism*. New Haven, Conn.: Yale University Press, 1987.

"Creation Story: Latin American Reflection." *In God's Image* (Summer 1991) 20f.

Croegaert, Auguste. *La femme chrétienne et la restauration liturgique*. Brussels: Vromant & Co., 1922.

Crumby Clipson, Elaine Marie, and others, eds. *Liberating Liturgies, Created by Members of the Women's Ordination Conference*. Fairfax, Va.: Women's Ordination Conference, 1989.

Cunningham, Agnes. "Women and Preaching in the Patristic Age." *Preaching in the Patristic Age: Studies in Honor of Walter J. Burghardt, S.J.* Ed. David G. Hunter, 53–72. New York: Paulist Press, 1989.

Davis, Flora. *Moving the Mountain: The Women's Movement in America since 1960.* New York: Simon & Schuster, 1991.

Delumeau, Jean, ed. *La religion de la mère: les femmes et la transmission de la foi.* Paris: Éditions du Cerf, 1992.

Dienst, Heide. "Zur Rolle von Frauen im magischen Praktiken und Vorstellungen—nach ausgewählten mittelalterlichen Quellen." *Frauen in Spätantike und Frühmittelalter. Lebensbedingungen—Lebensnormen—Lebensformen.* Ed. Werner Affeldt, 173–194. Sigmaringen: Jan Thorbecke Verlag, 1990.

Dijk, Denise J. J. "Developments in Feminist Liturgy in the Netherlands." *Studia Liturgica* 25 (1995) 120–128.

Dobbeler, Stephanie von. "Feministische Liturgien. Eine Bibliographie." *Archiv für Liturgiewissenschaft* 37 (1995) 1–24.

Dobhan, Ulrich. "Der Name Teresa." *Edith Stein Jahrbuch* 2 (1996) 138–151.

Dorcas. "Nothing Ventured—." *Orate Fratres* 15 (1940/41) 492–495.

Douglass, Laurie. "A New Look at the *Itinerarium Burdigalense.*" *Journal of Early Christian Studies* 4 (1996) 313–333.

Duck, Ruth. "Sin, Grace, and Gender in Free-Church Protestant Worship." *Women at Worship: Interpretations of North American Diversity.* Ed. Marjorie Procter-Smith and Janet Walton, 55–69. Louisville: Westminster/John Knox Press, 1993.

Dunn, Mary, and Nyunt Nyunt Thein. "Morning Worship." *In God's Image* (December 1987/88) 13–15.

Edgardh Beckman, Ninna. "Sophia: Symbol of Christian and Feminist Wisdom?" *Feminist Theology* 16 (1997) 32–54.

Edet, Rosemary N. "Christianity and African Women's Rituals." *The Will to Arise: Women, Tradition, and the Church in Africa.* Ed. Mercy Amba Oduyoye and Musimbi R.A. Kanyoro, 25–39. Maryknoll, N.Y.: Orbis Books, 1992.

Egeria. *Diary of a Pilgrimage.* Trans. and annotated by George E. Gingras. Ancient Christian Writers 38. New York: Newman Press, 1970.

Eisen, Ute E. *Amtsträgerinnen im frühen Christentum. Epigraphische und literarische Studien.* Forschungen zur Kirchen- und Dogmengeschichte 61. Göttingen: Vandenhoeck & Ruprecht, 1996.

Ellard, Gerard. "Sisters as 'Big Sisters' to the Liturgical Movement." *Orate Fratres* 17 (1942/43) 246–255.

Eyden, René van. "The Place of Women in Liturgical Functions." *Liturgy: Self-Expression of the Church.* Ed. Herman Schmidt, 68–81. Concilium 72. New York: Herder and Herder, 1972.

Fabella, Virginia. "Morning Worship: In God's Image." *In God's Image* (September 1987) 4–6.

Fantham, Elaine, and others. *Women in the Classical World: Image and Text.* New York: Oxford University Press, 1994.

Feistner, Edith. *Historische Typologie der deutschen Heiligenlegende des Mittelalters von der Mitte des 12. Jahrhunderts bis zur Reformation.* Wissensliteratur im Mittelalter 20. Wiesbaden: Dr. Ludwig Reichert Verlag, 1995.

Fenwick, John R. K., and Bryan D. Spinks. *Worship in Transition: The Twentieth Century Liturgical Movement.* Edinburgh: T&T Clark, 1995.

Fonay Wemple, Suzanne. "Women from the Fifth to the Tenth Century." *A History of Women in the West.* Vol. 2: *Silences of the Middle Ages.* Ed. Christiane Klapisch-Zuber, 169–201. Cambridge, Mass.: The Belknap Press of Harvard University Press, 1992.

Franklin, R.W., and Robert L. Spaeth. *Virgil Michel: American Catholic.* Collegeville, Minn.: The Liturgical Press, 1988.

Frioux, Mary. "One Lay Woman Speaks Up." *Orate Fratres* 17 (1942/43) 224–226.

Froehle, Virginia Ann. *Called into Her Presence: Praying with Feminine Images of God.* Notre Dame, Ind.: Ave Maria Press, 1992.

Gerl-Falkovitz, Hanna-Barbara. "'dass die Frau sich wirklich selbst finde.' Romano Guardinis Wahr-nehmung der Frau." *Wie Theologen Frauen sehen—von der Macht der Bilder.* Ed. Renate Jost and Ursula Kubera, 127–141. Frauenforum. Freiburg: Herder, 1993.

Gess, Sandy. "The Christian Feminist Worshiping Community: An Interview." *Newsletter. The Center for Women and Religion, The Graduate Theological Union, Berkeley* (February/March 1996) 1–4.

Gilchrist, Roberta. *Gender and Material Culture: The Archaeology of Religious Women.* New York: Routledge, 1994.

Greinacher, Norbert. *Im Angesicht meiner Feinde—Mahl des Friedens. Zur politischen Dimension des Herrenmahls.* Gütersloh: Gütersloher Verlagshaus Mohn, 1982.

Grimes, Ronald L. "Liturgical Supinity, Liturgical Erectitude." *Reading, Writing, and Ritualizing: Ritual in Fictive, Liturgical, and Public Places,* 39–58. Washington: The Pastoral Press, 1993.

Gryson, Roger. *The Ministry of Women in the Early Church.* Trans. Jean Laporte and Mary Louise Hall. Collegeville, Minn.: The Liturgical Press, 1976.

Guardini, Romano. "Frauenart und Frauensendung." *Die christliche Frau* 19 (1921) 33–37, 52–57.

Guardini, Romano. *Vom Geist der Liturgie.* Ecclesia Orans 1. Freiburg: Herder, 1918. English trans. *The Spirit of the Liturgy.* London: Sheed & Ward, 1937.

Hamburger, Jeffrey F. "Art, Enclosure and the *Cura Monialium:* Prolegomena in the Guise of a Postscript." *Gesta* 31 (1992) 108–134.

Handmaids of the Lord: Contemporary Descriptions of Feminine Asceticism in the First Six Christian Centuries. Trans. and ed. by Joan M. Petersen. Cistercian Studies Series 143. Kalamazoo, Mich.: Cistercian Publications, 1996.

Hegemann, Edith. "Liturgische Gedanken zur Enzyklika *Quadragesimo Anno.*" *Liturgische Zeitschrift* 3 (1930/31) 385–392.

Hegemann, Edith. "Zu einem Aufsatz über 'Das Priestertum der Frau.'" *Liturgische Zeitschrift* 3 (1930/31) 256–279.

Henderson, J. Frank. "ICEL and Inclusive Language." *Shaping English Liturgy.* Festschrift Dennis Hurley. Ed. Peter C. Finn and James M. Schellman, 257–278. Washington: The Pastoral Press, 1990.

Henry, Kathleen M. *The Book of Ours: Liturgies for Feminist People.* Jamaica Plain, Mass.: Alabaster Jar Liturgical Arts, 1993.

Herwegen, Ildefons. "Zum Geleit." Maura Böckeler, *Das grosse Zeichen. Apokalypse 12,1. Die Frau als Symbol göttlicher Wirklichkeit*, 9–13. Salzburg: O. Müller, 1941.

Herwegen, Ildefons. "Kirche und Frau." *Vom christlichen Sein und Leben. Gesammelte Vorträge*, 131–153. Berlin: Sankt Augustinus Verlag, 1931.

Hilpisch, Stephan. Review of Christa Müller, "Die Lehre des Johannes Brenz von Kirchendienst und Kirchengesang." *Jahrbuch für Liturgiewissenschaft* 4 (1934) 499.

Hojenski, Christine, and others, eds. *Meine Seele sieht das Land der Freiheit. Feministische Liturgien—Modelle für die Praxis.* Münster: edition liberación, 1990.

Howard, Julie. *We Are the Circle: Celebrating the Feminine in Song and Ritual.* Collegeville, Minn.: The Liturgical Press, 1993.

Hughes, Kathleen, ed. *How Firm a Foundation.* Vol.1: *Voices of the Early Liturgical Movement.* Chicago: Liturgy Training Publications, 1990.

Hull Hitchcock, Helen, ed. *The Politics of Prayer: Feminist Language and the Worship of God.* San Francisco: Ignatius Press, 1992.

Hunt, Mary E. "Women as Religious Agents: A Feminist/Womanist Approach." Mary E. Hunt and Diann Neu, *Women of Fire: A Pentecost Event*, 3–15. Silver Spring, Md.: WATERworks Press, 1990.

Hunt, Mary E., and Diann Neu. *Women of Fire: A Pentecost Event.* Silver Spring, Md.: WATERworks Press, 1990.

Ilan, Tal. *Jewish Women in Greco-Roman Palestine: An Inquiry into Image and Status.* Texte und Studien zum Antiken Judentum 44. Tübingen: J. C .B. Mohr, 1995.

Inclusive-Language Lectionary Committee, ed. *An Inclusive-Language Lectionary: Readings for Years A–C.* Atlanta: John Knox Press and others for The Cooperative Publication Association, 1985–1987.

Irvin, Dorothy. "The Ministry of Women in the Early Church: The Archaeological Evidence." *The Duke Divinity School Review* 45 (1980) 76–86.

Isasi-Díaz, Ada María. "On the Birthing Stool: Mujerista Liturgy." *Women at Worship: Interpretations of North American Diversity*. Ed. Marjorie Procter-Smith and Janet Walton, 191–210. Louisville: Westminster/John Knox Press, 1993.

Isasi-Díaz, Ada-María. "Mujerista Liturgies and the Struggle for Liberation." *Liturgy and the Body*. Ed. Louis-Marie Chauvet and François Kabasele Lumbala, 104–111. Concilium. Maryknoll, N.Y.: Orbis Books, 1995.

Janetzky, Birgit. "Die Lesung für die Frauen befreien. Alttestamentliche Frauenperikopen im erneuerten Lektionar aus der Sicht feministischer Befreiungshermeneutik." *Streit am Tisch des Wortes? Zur Deutung und Bedeutung des Alten Testaments und seiner Verwendung in der Liturgie*. Ed. Ansgar Franz, 725–749. Pietas Liturgica 8. St. Ottilien: EOS-Verlag, 1997.

Jensen, Anne. *God's Self-confident Daughters: Early Christianity and the Liberation of Women*. Trans. O. C. Dean, Jr. Louisville: Westminster/John Knox Press, 1996.

John, Sabine. "Kindelwiegen." *Marienlexikon*, vol. 3. Ed. Remigius Bäumer and Leo Scheffczyk, 552–555. St. Ottilien: EOS-Verlag, 1991.

Johnson, Elizabeth A. *She Who Is: The Mystery of God in Feminist Theological Discourse*. New York: Crossroad, 1992.

Kalven, Janet, and Mary I. Buckley, eds. *Women's Spirit Bonding*. New York: Pilgrim Press, 1984.

Karle, Isolde. "'Nicht mehr Mann noch Frau.' Die Form 'Geschlecht' im Gottesdienst." *Feministische Impulse für den Gottesdienst*. Ed. Renate Jost and Ulrike Schweiger, 25–35. Stuttgart: Verlag W. Kohlhammer, 1996.

Kirk, Martha Ann. *Celebrations of Biblical Women's Stories: Tears, Milk, and Honey*. Kansas City: Sheed & Ward, 1987.

Knödel, Natalie. "Reconsidering an Obsolete Rite: The Churching of Women and Feminist Liturgical Theology." *Feminist Theology* 14 (1997) 106–125.

Koenker, Ernest Benjamin. *The Liturgical Renaissance in the Roman Catholic Church*. Chicago: Chicago University Press, 1954. 2nd ed., St. Louis: Concordia Publishing House, 1966.

Kolbe, Ferdinand. *Die Liturgische Bewegung*. Der Christ in der Welt 9:4. Aschaffenburg: Paul Pattloch Verlag, 1964.

"Korean Woman Jesus: Drama Worship." *Journal of Women and Religion* 13 (1995) 45–50.

Korenhof, Mieke, ed. *Mit Eva predigen. Ein anderes Perikopenbuch*. Düsseldorf: Presseverband der Evangelischen Kirche im Rheinland e.V., 1996.

Kraemer, Ross S. "Jewish Women in the Diaspora World of Late Antiquity." *Jewish Women in Historical Perspective*. Ed. Judith R. Baskin, 43–67. Detroit: Wayne State University Press, 1991.

Kraemer, Ross S., ed. *Maenads, Martyrs, Matrons, Monastics: A Sourcebook on Women's Religions in the Greco-Roman World*. Philadelphia: Fortress Press, 1988.

Kraemer, Ross S. *Her Share of the Blessings: Women's Religions among Pagans, Jews, and Christians in the Greco-Roman World*. New York: Oxford University Press, 1992.

Kratz-Ritter, Bettina. *Für "fromme Zionstöchter" und "gebildete Frauenzimmer." Andachtsliteratur für deutsch-jüdische Frauen im 19. und frühen 20. Jahrhundert*. Haskala 13. New York: Olms 1995.

Krause, Jens-Uwe. *Witwen und Waisen im frühen Christentum*. Stuttgart: Franz Steiner Verlag, 1995.

Krüger, Elke. "Überlegungen zum Quellenwert der irischen Bussbücher für Historische Frauenforschung." *Frauen in der Geschichte*. Vol. 7: *Interdisziplinäre Studien zur Geschichte der Frauen im Frühmittelalter. Methoden—Probleme—Ergebnisse*. Ed. Werner Affeldt and Annette Kuhn, 154–170. Düsseldorf: Schwann, 1986.

Küchler, Max. *Schweigen, Schmuck und Schleier. Drei neutestamentliche Vorschriften zur Verdrängung der Frauen auf dem Hintergrund einer frauenfeindlichen Exegese des Alten Testaments im antiken Judentum*. Novum Testamentum et Orbis Antiquus 1. Freiburg: Universitätsverlag, and Göttingen: Vandenhoeck & Ruprecht, 1986.

Laeuchli, Samuel. *Power and Sexuality: The Emergence of Canon Law at the Synod of Elvira*. Philadelphia: Temple University Press, 1972.

Lake, Jean Thomas. *A Time to Sow: A History of the Sisters of the Adoration of the Most Precious Blood of O'Fallon, Missouri*. N.p., n.d. [1972?].

Larson-Miller, Lizette. "Women and the Anointing of the Sick." *Coptic Church Review* 12:2 (1991) 37–48.

Lascar, Maria Louise. "Abendländische und griechisch-orthodoxe Mönchsprofess als Tauferneuerung." *Liturgische Zeitschrift* 2 (1930) 205–213.

Lascar, Maria Louise. "Die Sorge der Kirche für Mutter und Kind." *Bibel und Liturgie* 5 (1930/31) 312–315.

Lascar, Maria Louise. "Von der Würde und Weihe der christlichen Jungfräulichkeit." *Bibel und Liturgie* 5 (1930/31) 504–507.

Lathrop, Gordon, and Gail Ramshaw-Schmidt, eds. *Lectionary for the Christian People: Cycles A–C of the Roman, Episcopal, Lutheran Lectionaries*. New York: Pueblo Publishing Company, 1986–1988.

"Le rôle des femmes dans la liturgie." *Notitiae* 9 (1973) 164.

Leistner, Herta, ed. *Lass spüren deine Kraft. Feministische Liturgie. Grundlagen—Argumente—Anregungen*. Gütersloh: Gütersloher Verlagshaus, 1997.

Leonard, John K. "Rites of Marriage in the Western Middle Ages." *Medieval Liturgy: A Book of Essays.* Ed. Lizette Larson-Miller, 165–202. Garland Medieval Casebooks 18. New York: Garland Publishing, 1997.

Leyerle, Blake. "Appealing to Children." *Journal of Early Christian Studies* 5 (1997) 243–270.

L'Hermite-Leclercq, Paulette. "The Feudal Order." *A History of Women in the West.* Vol. 2: *Silences of the Middle Ages.* Ed. Christiane Klapisch-Zuber, 202–249. Cambridge, Mass.: The Belknap Press of Harvard University Press, 1992.

"Liturgical Movement and Catholic Women." *Orate Fratres* 8 (1933/34) 564–568.

Löhr, Aemiliana. *Das Herrenjahr. Das Mysterium Christi im Jahreskreis der Kirche.* Regensburg: Pustet, 1940. English trans. *The Mass Through the Year.* Trans. I. T. Hale. Westminster, Md.: Newman Press, 1958.

Löhr, Aemiliana. *Das Jahr des Herrn.* Regensburg: Pustet, 1934. English trans. *The Year of Our Lord: The Mystery of Christ in the Liturgical Year.* Trans. by a monk of St. Benedict. New York: P. J. Kenedy & Sons, 1937.

Löhr, Aemiliana. "Das Priestertum der Frau im Lichte der kath. [sic] Liturgie." *Die Seelsorge* 8 (1930/31) 346–354.

Löhr, Aemiliana. Review of Schneider, "Priestertum der Frau." *Jahrbuch für Liturgiewissenschaft* 14 (1934) 278.

Löhr, Aemiliana. "Vom Opfer, vom Zeugnis und von der Geduld." *Frau und Mysterium. Festgabe der Hersteller Benediktinerinnen zum 25jährigen Weihejubiläum von D. Theresia Jackisch.* Ed. Theodor Bogler, 55–70. Liturgie und Mönchtum 5. Maria Laach: Verlag Ars Liturgica, 1950.

Loley, Maria. "Liturgische Exerzitien in Poysdorf." *Bibel und Liturgie* 3 (1928/29) 306f.

M., Lina. "Wie ich zur Liturgie kam." *Bibel und Liturgie* 5 (1930/31) 324.

Maas-Ewerd, Theodor. *Die Krise der Liturgischen Bewegung in Deutschland und Österreich. Zu den Auseinandersetzungen um die "liturgische Frage" in den Jahren 1939 bis 1944.* Studien zur Pastoralliturgie 3. Regensburg: Verlag Friedrich Pustet, 1981.

Maas-Ewerd, Theodor. *Liturgie und Pfarrei. Einfluss der Liturgischen Erneuerung auf Leben und Verständnis der Pfarrei im deutschen Sprachgebiet.* Paderborn: Bonifacius-Druckerei, 1969.

MacDonald, Margaret Y. *Early Christian Women and Pagan Opinion: The Power of the Hysterical Woman.* Cambridge: Cambridge University Press, 1996.

MacMullen, Ramsay. *Christianizing the Roman Empire (A.D. 100–400).* New Haven, Conn.: Yale University Press, 1984.

MacMullen, Ramsay. "Woman in Public in the Roman Empire." *Historia. Zeitschrift für Alte Geschichte* 29 (1980) 208–218.

Malherbe, Georges. "Le rôle de la femme chrétienne en liturgie." *Cours et conférences des semaines liturgiques.* Vol. 3: *Congrès liturgique Malines 1924,* 181–188. Louvain: Abbaye du Mont César, 1925.

Mananzan, Mary John, ed. *Woman and Religion: A Collection of Essays, Personal Histories, and Contextualized Liturgies.* 2nd ed. Manila: Institute of Women's Studies, St. Scholastica College, 1992.

Martin, Dale B. *The Corinthian Body.* New Haven, Conn.: Yale University Press, 1995.

Mattila, Sharon Lea. "Where Women Sat in Ancient Synagogues: The Archaeological Evidence in Context." *Voluntary Associations in the Graeco-Roman World.* Ed. John S. Kloppenborg and Stephen G. Wilson, 266–286. New York: Routledge, 1996.

Mayer, Josephine. "Vom Diakonat der Frau." *Hochland* 36:1 (1938/39) 98–108.

Mayer, Josephine. "Die Pflege liturgischer Gesinnung an den höheren Mädchenschulen." *Zeitschrift für den katholischen Religionsunterricht an höheren Lehranstalten* 8 (1931) 238–247.

Mayer, Wendy. "The Dynamics of Liturgical Space: Aspects of the Interaction between St John Chrysostom and his Audiences." *Ephemerides Liturgicae* 111 (1997) 104–115.

McClintock Fulkerson, Mary. *Changing the Subject: Women's Discourses and Feminist Theology.* Minneapolis: Fortress Press, 1994.

McClintock Fulkerson, Mary. "Gender–Being It or Doing It? The Church, Homosexuality, and The Politics of Identity." *Que(e)rying Religion: A Critical Anthology.* Ed. Gary David Comstock and Susan E. Henking, 188–201. New York: Continuum, 1997.

McDannell, Colleen. "Catholic Domesticity, 1860–1960." *American Catholic Women: A Historical Exploration.* Ed. Karen Kennelly, 48–80. The Bicentennial History of the Catholic Church in America. New York: Macmillan Publishing Company, 1989.

McEnroy, Carmel Elizabeth. *Guests in Their Own House: The Women of Vatican II.* New York: Crossroad, 1996.

McGee, Lee, with Thomas H. Troeger. *Wrestling with the Patriarchs: Retrieving Women's Voices in Preaching.* Nashville: Abingdon Press, 1996.

Meens, Rob. "Ritual Purity and the Influence of Gregory the Great in the Early Middle Ages." *Unity and Diversity in the Church.* Ed. R. N. Swanson, 31–43. Studies in Church History 32. Cambridge, Mass.: Blackwell, 1996.

Meyer, Marvin, and others, eds. *Ancient Christian Magic: Coptic Texts of Ritual Power.* San Francisco: HarperCollins, 1994.

Michel, Virgil. "The Christian Woman." *Orate Fratres* 13 (1938/39) 248–256.

Michel, Virgil. "The Liturgical Movement and the Catholic Woman." *Proceedings of the Catholic Central Verein of America,* 57–59. St. Paul: National Federation of German-American Catholics, 1928.

Michel, Virgil. "The Liturgy and Catholic Women." *Orate Fratres* 3 (1928/29) 270–276.

Miles, Margaret R. *Carnal Knowing: Female Nakedness and Religious Meaning in the Christian West.* Boston: Beacon Press, 1989.

Moor, Geertruida de. "The Role of the Female Sacristan Prior to Trent." *Vox Benedictina* 10 (1993) 306–321.

Morard, Loyse. *Les Bénédictines d'Ermeton 1936–1986.* N.p., n.d. [1987?].

Morley, Janet. *All Desires Known: Inclusive Prayers for Worship and Meditation.* Harrisburg, Pa.: Morehouse Publishing, 1994.

Morton, Nelle. "The Dilemma of Celebration." *Women in a Strange Land: Search for a New Image.* Ed. Clare Benedicks Fischer and others, 119–127. Philadelphia: Fortress Press, 1975.

Mueller, Therese. *Our Children's Year of Grace.* St. Louis, Mo.: Pio Decimo Press, 1943.

Mueller, Therese. *The Christian Home and Art.* Kansas City, Mo.: Designs for Christian Living, 1950.

Mueller, Therese. *Family Life in Christ.* Popular Liturgical Library. Collegeville, Minn.: The Liturgical Press, 1941.

Murray Elkins, Heather. *Worshiping Women: Re-forming God's People for Praise.* Nashville: Abingdon Press, 1994.

Murray, Jane Marie. "Father Michel and 'The Christ Life Series in Religion.'" *Orate Fratres* 13 (1938/39) 107–112.

Muschiol, Gisela. *Famula Dei. Zur Liturgie in merowingischen Frauenklöstern.* Beiträge zur Geschichte des Alten Mönchtums 41. Münster: Aschendorffsche Verlagsbuchhandlung, 1994.

Muschiol, Gisela. "Liturgie und Klausur. Zu den liturgischen Voraussetzungen von Nonnenchören." *Kanonissenstifte.* Ed. Irene Crusius. Veröffentlichungen des Max-Planck-Instituts für Geschichte, Göttingen. Studien zur Germania Sacra. Göttingen: Vandenhoeck & Ruprecht, 1999 (forthcoming).

Muschiol, Gisela. "Reinheit und Gefährdung? Liturgie im Mittelalter." *Heiliger Dienst* 51 (1997) 42–54.

Nasimiyu-Wasike, Anne. "Christianity and the African Rituals of Birth and Naming." *The Will to Arise: Women, Tradition, and the Church in Africa.* Ed. Mercy Amba Oduyoye and Musimbi R. A. Kanyoro, 40–53. Maryknoll, N.Y.: Orbis Books, 1992.

Neu, Diann. "Our Name is Church: The Experience of Catholic-Christian Feminist Liturgies." *Can We Always Celebrate the Eucharist?* Ed. Mary Collins and David Power, 75–84. Concilium 152. New York: The Seabury Press, 1982.

Neu, Diann. *Women and the Gospel Traditions: Feminist Celebrations.* Silver Spring, Md.: WATERworks Press, 1989.

Neu, Diann L. "Women Revisioning Religious Rituals." *Women and Religious Ritual*. Ed. Lesley A. Northup, 155–172. Washington: The Pastoral Press, 1993.

Neu, Diann L. "Women's Empowerment Through Feminist Rituals." *Women's Spirituality, Women's Lives*. Ed. Judith Ochshorn and Ellen Cole, 185–200. New York: Harrington Park Press, 1995.

Neunheuser, Burkhard. "Die Frau in der Liturgie." *Notitiae* 15 (1979) 164–177.

Neunheuser, Burkhard. "Vorwort." Odo Casel, *Mysterium der Ekklesia. Von der Gemeinschaft aller Erlösten in Christus Jesus*. Ed. Theodora Schneider, 11–17. Mainz: Matthias-Grünewald, 1961.

Nolte, Cordula. *Conversio und Christianitas. Frauen in der Christianisierung vom 5. bis 8. Jahrhundert*. Monographien zur Geschichte des Mittelalters 41. Stuttgart: Anton Hiersemann, 1995.

Northup, Lesley A. "Claiming Horizontal Space: Women's Religious Rituals." *Studia Liturgica* 25 (1995) 86–102.

Northup, Lesley A. *Ritualizing Women: Patterns of Spirituality*. Cleveland: Pilgrim Press, 1997.

Northup, Lesley A., ed. *Women and Religious Ritual*. Washington: The Pastoral Press, 1993.

O'Brien, Mary B., and Patricia M. Miller, "A Woman of Vision: An Interview with a Founder of the Grail Movement in the United States." *U.S. Catholic Historian* 15:4 (1997) 95–106.

Oduyoye, Mercy Amba. "Women and Ritual in Africa." *The Will to Arise: Women, Tradition, and the Church in Africa*. Ed. Mercy Amba Oduyoye and Musimbi R. A. Kanyoro, 9–24. Maryknoll: Orbis Books, 1992.

Orsi, Robert A. *Thank You, St. Jude: Women's Devotion to the Patron Saint of Hopeless Causes*. New Haven, Conn.: Yale University Press, 1996.

Pahl, Irmgard. "'Eine starke Frau, wer wird sie finden?' Aspekte des Frauenbildes in den Messformularen der Heiligenfeste." *Liturgie und Frauenfrage. Ein Beitrag zur Frauenforschung aus liturgiewissenschaftlicher Sicht*. Ed. Teresa Berger and Albert Gerhards, 433–452. Pietas Liturgica 7. St. Ottilien: EOS-Verlag, 1990.

Parker, Pat. *Womanslaughter*. Oakland, Calif.: Diana Press, 1978.

Parsch, Pius. "Liturgie und Familie." *Bibel und Liturgie* 7 (1932/33) 161–167.

Parsch, Pius. "Die Mitarbeit der Frau in der liturgischen Bewegung." *Bibel und Liturgie* 7 (1932/33) 4–44.

Parsch, Pius. "Paramentenschule." *Bibel und Liturgie* 5 (1930/31) 19–22, 60–63, 246f., 345–347.

Paterson Corrington, Gail. "The Milk of Salvation: Redemption by the Mother in Late Antiquity and Early Christianity." *Harvard Theological Review* 82 (1989) 393–420.

Pecklers, Keith F. *The Unread Vision: The Liturgical Movement in the United States of America: 1926–1955*. Collegeville, Minn.: The Liturgical Press, 1998.

Pinsk, Johannes. *Frau im Beruf. Beiträge zur biblischen Theologie der Arbeit*. Ed. Hilde Herrmann. Düsseldorf: Haus der Katholischen Frauen, 1959.

Portefaix, Lilian. *Sisters Rejoice: Paul's Letter to the Philippians and Luke-Acts as Seen by First-century Philippian Women*. Uppsala: Liber, 1988.

Prégardier, Elisabeth, and Anne Mohr. *Politik als Aufgabe. Engagement christlicher Frauen in der Weimarer Republik. Aufsätze, Dokumente, Notizen, Bilder*. Annweiler: Plöger Verlag, 1990.

Procter-Smith, Marjorie. "Marks of Feminist Liturgy." *Proceedings of the North American Academy of Liturgy* (1992) 69–75.

Procter-Smith, Marjorie. *In Her Own Rite: Constructing Feminist Liturgical Tradition*. Nashville: Abingdon Press, 1990.

Procter-Smith, Marjorie. *Praying with Our Eyes Open: Engendering Feminist Liturgical Prayer*. Nashville: Abingdon Press, 1995.

Procter-Smith, Marjorie. "Reorganizing Victimization: The Intersection Between Liturgy and Domestic Violence." *Violence Against Women and Children: A Christian Theological Sourcebook*. Ed. Carol J. Adams and Marie M. Fortune, 428–444. New York: Continuum, 1995.

Procter-Smith, Marjorie. "The Whole Loaf: Holy Communion and Survival." *Violence Against Women and Children: A Christian Theological Sourcebook*. Ed. Carol J. Adams and Marie M. Fortune, 464–479. New York: Continuum, 1995.

Procter-Smith, Marjorie. *Women in Shaker Community and Worship: A Feminist Analysis of the Uses of Religious Symbolism*. Studies in Women and Religion 16. Lewiston, N.Y.: E. Mellen Press, 1985.

Quasten, Johannes. *Music and Worship in Pagan and Christian Antiquity*. Trans. Boniface Ramsey. Washington: National Association of Pastoral Musicians, 1983.

Radford Ruether, Rosemary. "Feminist Liturgical Movement, The." *The New Westminster Dictionary of Liturgy and Worship*. Ed. J. G. Davies, 240f. Philadelphia: The Westminster Press, 1986.

Radford Ruether, Rosemary. *Women-Church: Theology and Practice of Feminist Liturgical Communities*. San Francisco: Harper & Row, 1985.

Ramírez, Yeta. "El poder de los simbolos," *Con-spirando* 19 (March 1997) 35f.

Ramshaw, Gail. *God beyond Gender: Feminist Christian God-Language*. Minneapolis: Fortress Press, 1995.

Redmond, Sheila. "'Remember the Good, Forget the Bad': Denial and Family Violence in a Christian Worship Service." *Women at Worship: Interpretations of North American Diversity*. Ed. Marjorie Procter-Smith and Janet Walton, 71–82. Louisville: Westminster/John Knox Press, 1993.

Reid, Barbara. "Liturgy, Scripture, and the Challenge of Feminism." *Living No Longer for Ourselves: Liturgy and Justice in the Nineties.* Ed. Kathleen Hughes and Mark R. Francis, 124–137. Collegeville, Minn.: The Liturgical Press, 1991.

Reinhold, Hans Ansgar. "Timely Tracts: Odo Casel." *Orate Fratres* 22 (1947/48) 366–372.

Rhode, Irma. *Cookbook for Fridays and Lent.* New York: McKay, 1951.

Ripplinger, Werner. *Lasst uns loben, Schwestern, loben. Frauengottesdienste.* Würzburg: Echter Verlag, 1987.

Roll, Susan. "The Churching of Women after Childbirth: An Old Rite Raising New Issues." *Questions Liturgiques* 76 (1995) 206–229.

Roll, Susan. "Traditional Elements in New Women's Liturgies." *Questions Liturgiques* 72 (1991) 43–59.

Rose, Renate, and her women friends. "The Lima Liturgy: An Ecumenical Liturgy of Solidarity." *In God's Image* (December 1990) 27–34.

Rousseau, Olivier. *Histoire du mouvement liturgique: esquisse historique depuis le début du XIXe siècle jusqu'au pontificat de Pie X.* Lex orandi 3. Paris: Éditions du Cerf, 1945. English trans. *The Progress of the Liturgy: An Historical Sketch from the Beginning of the Nineteenth Century to the Pontificate of Pius X.* Westminster, Md.: Newman Press, 1951.

Rousselle, Aline. "Body Politics in Ancient Rome." *A History of Women in the West.* Vol. 1: *From Ancient Goddesses to Christian Saints.* Ed. Pauline Schmitt Pantel, 296–336. Cambridge, Mass.: The Belknap Press of Harvard University Press, 1992.

Rowe, Barbara, and others, eds. *Silent Voices, Sacred Lives: Women's Readings for the Liturgical Year.* New York: Paulist Press, 1992.

Rusch, Paul. "Erinnerungen an Pater Jungmann." *J. A. Jungmann. Ein Leben für Liturgie und Kerygma.* Ed. Balthasar Fischer and Hans Bernhard Meyer, 123–125. Innsbruck: Tyrolia, 1975.

Sack, Birgit. "Katholische Frauenbewegung, katholische Jugendbewegung und Politik in der Weimarer Republik: Standorte, Handlungsspielräume und Grenzen im Kontext des Generationenkonflikts." *Frauen unter dem Patriarchat der Kirchen. Katholikinnen und Protestantinnen im 19. und 20. Jahrhundert,* 120–138. Konfession und Gesellschaft 7. Stuttgart: Verlag W. Kohlhammer, 1995.

Sawyer, Deborah F. *Women and Religion in the First Christian Centuries.* Religion in the First Christian Centuries. New York: Routledge, 1996.

Schaumberger, Christine. "Wir lassen uns nicht länger abspeisen. Überlegungen zur feministischen Suche nach Liturgie als Brot zum Leben." *Meine Seele sieht das Land der Freiheit. Feministische Liturgien—Modelle für die Praxis.* Ed. Christine Hojenski and others, 43–58. Münster: edition liberacíon, 1990.

Scheid, John. "The Religious Roles of Roman Women." *A History of Women in the West.* Vol. 1: *From Ancient Goddesses to Christian Saints.* Ed. Pauline Schmitt Pantel, 377–408. Cambridge, Mass.: The Belknap Press of Harvard University Press, 1992.

Schilson, Arno. "Christlicher Gottesdienst–Ort des Menschseins. Fundamentalliturgische Überlegungen in ökumenischer Absicht." *Gemeinsame Liturgie in getrennten Kirchen?* Ed. Karl Schlemmer, 53–81. Quaestiones Disputatae 132. Freiburg: Herder, 1991.

Schneider, Oda. *Die Macht der Frau.* 4th ed., n.d. Salzburg: Otto Müller, 1938.

Schneider, Oda. *Vom Priestertum der Frau.* 4th ed., 1941. Wien: Seelsorgerverlag, 1934.

Schnitzler, Theodor. Review of Löhr, "Die Heilige Woche." *Liturgisches Jahrbuch* 7 (1957) 126f.

Schöllgen, Georg. "*Balnea Mixta.* Entwicklungen der spätantiken Bademoral im Spiegel der Textüberlieferung der Syrischen Didaskalie." *Jahrbuch für Antike und Christentum. Ergänzungsband* 22 (1995) 182–194.

Schüssler Fiorenza, Elisabeth. *In Memory of Her: A Feminist Theological Reconstruction of Christian Origins.* New York: Crossroad, 1985.

Schüssler Fiorenza, Elisabeth. "Spiritual Movements of Transformation? A Critical Feminist Reflection." *Defecting in Place: Women Claiming Responsibility for Their Own Spiritual Lives.* Ed. Miriam Therese Winter and others, 221–226. New York: Crossroad, 1994.

Sears, Marge. *Life-Cycle Celebrations for Women.* Mystic, Conn.: Twenty-Third Publications, 1989.

Sheppard, Lancelot C., ed. *The People Worship: A History of the Liturgical Movement.* New York: Hawthorn Books, 1967.

Sivan, Hagith. "Holy Land Pilgrimage and Western Audiences: Some Reflections on Egeria and Her Circle." *Classical Quarterly* 38 (1988) 528–535.

Sivan, Hagith. "Who Was Egeria? Piety and Pilgrimage in the Age of Gratian." *Harvard Theological Review* 81 (1988) 59–72.

Snyder, Graydon F. *Ante Pacem: Archaeological Evidence of Church Life Before Constantine.* Macon, Ga.: Mercer University Press, 1985.

Sokolowski, Robert. "Some Remarks on Inclusive Language." *L'Osservatore Romano* [English language edition], no. 9 (March 3, 1993) 9f.

Speegle Schmitt, Mary Kathleen. *Seasons of the Feminine Divine: Christian Feminist Prayers for the Liturgical Year, Cycles A–C.* New York: Crossroad, 1993–1995.

Stark, Rodney. *The Rise of Christianity: A Sociologist Reconsiders History.* Princeton: Princeton University Press, 1996.

Stenta, Norbert. "Lebensweihe durch die Liturgie: Von den Geschlechtern und Berufen im Gottesreich." *Lebe mit der Kirche* 7:31 (June 30, 1935) 26–30.

Stenta, Norbert. "Volksliturgie und Lebensweihe: Segnung der Mutter nach der Geburt." *Bibel und Liturgie* 7 (1932/33) 193–196.

Stuart, Elizabeth. *Spitting at Dragons: Towards a Feminist Theology of Sainthood.* New York: Mowbray, 1996.

Subcommittee of the Baltimore Task Force on the Status of Women in the Church, ed. *Liturgy for All People.* Hyattsville, Md.: Liturgy for All People, n.d.

Swidler, Arlene, ed. *Sistercelebrations: Nine Worship Experiences.* Philadelphia: Fortress Press, 1974.

Synek, Eva Maria. *Heilige Frauen der frühen Christenheit. Zu den Frauenbildern in hagiographischen Texten des christlichen Ostens.* Das östliche Christentum 43. Würzburg: Augustinus-Verlag, 1994.

Tafferner, Andrea. "Die Leseordnung aus der Perspektive von Frauen." *Bibel und Liturgie* 68 (1995) 148–154.

Tanner, Kathryn. "Social Theory Concerning the 'New Social Movements' and the Practice of Feminist Theology." *Horizons in Feminist Theology: Identity, Tradition, and Norms.* Ed. Rebecca S. Chopp and Sheila Greeve Davaney, 179–197. Minneapolis: Fortress Press, 1997.

Thébaud, Françoise. "The Great War and the Triumph of Sexual Division." *A History of Women in the West.* Vol. 5: *Toward a Cultural Identity in the Twentieth Century.* Ed. Françoise Thébaud, 21–75. Cambridge, Mass.: The Belknap Press of Harvard University Press, 1994.

Thraede, Klaus. "Frau." *Reallexikon für Antike und Christentum* 8 (1972) 197–269.

Trapp, Waldemar. *Vorgeschichte und Ursprung der liturgischen Bewegung vorwiegend in Hinsicht auf das deutsche Sprachgebiet.* Würzburg: R. Mayr, 1939. New ed., Münster: Stenderhoff, 1979.

Tuzik, Robert L., ed. *How Firm a Foundation.* Vol. 2: *Leaders of the Liturgical Movement.* Chicago: Liturgy Training Publications, 1990.

Underhill, Evelyn. *Worship.* New York: Harper & Brothers, 1936.

Vincie, Catherine. "Gender Analysis and Christian Initiation." *Worship* 69 (1995) 505–530.

Vincie, Catherine, and others. "Birthing Lament." *Liturgy* 14:1 (1997) 1–11.

Wales, Nonie. "Lament for Women Recovering from Abuse in Childhood." *Echoes: Justice, Peace, and Creation News* 10 (1996) 10.

Walker Bynum, Caroline. "Women Mystics and Eucharistic Devotion in the Thirteenth Century." *Fragmentation and Redemption: Essays on Gender and the Human Body in Medieval Religion,* 119–150. 3rd ed., 1994. New York: Zone Books, 1992.

Walker, Barbara G. *Women's Rituals: A Sourcebook.* San Francisco: Harper & Row, 1990.

Walton, Janet R. "The Challenge of Feminist Liturgy." *Liturgy* 6:1 (1986) 55–59.

Ward, Hannah, and others. *Celebrating Women.* New ed. Harrisburg, Pa.: Morehouse Publishing, 1995.

Ware, Ann Patrick. "The Easter Vigil: A Theological and Liturgical Critique." *Women at Worship: Interpretations of North American Diversity.* Ed. Marjorie Procter-Smith and Janet Walton, 83–106. Louisville: Westminster/John Knox Press, 1993.

Warren, F. E. *The Liturgy and Ritual of the Celtic Church.* Oxford: Clarendon Press, 1881.

Weaver, Mary Jo. *New Catholic Women: A Contemporary Challenge to Traditional Religious Authority.* San Francisco: Harper & Row, 1985.

Weaver, Mary Jo. *Springs of Water in a Dry Land: Spiritual Survival for Catholic Women Today.* Boston: Beacon Press, 1993.

Wegman, Herman. *Christian Worship in East and West: A Study Guide to Liturgical History.* Trans. Gordon W. Lathrop. New York: Pueblo Publishing Company, 1985.

Williams, Delores S. "Rituals of Resistance in Womanist Worship." *Women at Worship: Interpretations of North American Diversity.* Ed. Marjorie Procter-Smith and Janet Walton, 215–223. Louisville: Westminster/John Knox Press, 1993.

Wilson, Anna. "Female Sanctity in the Greek Calendar: The *Synaxarion* of Constantinople." *Women in Antiquity: New Assessments.* Ed. Richard Hawley and Barbara Levick, 233–247. New York: Routledge, 1995.

Winkler, Gabriele. "Überlegungen zum Gottesgeist als mütterlichem Prinzip und zur Bedeutung der Androgynie in einigen frühchristlichen Quellen." *Liturgie und Frauenfrage. Ein Beitrag zur Frauenforschung aus liturgiewissenschaftlicher Sicht.* Ed. Teresa Berger and Albert Gerhards, 7–29. Pietas Liturgica 7. St. Ottilien: EOS-Verlag, 1990.

Winter, Miriam Therese, and others. *Defecting in Place: Women Claiming Responsibility for Their Own Spiritual Lives.* New York: Crossroad, 1994.

Winter, Miriam Therese. *WomanPrayer, WomanSong: Resources for Ritual.* Oak Park, IL: Meyer Stone Books, 1987.

Winter, Miriam Therese. *WomanWisdom: A Feminist Lectionary and Psalter. Women of the Hebrew Scriptures, Part One.* New York: Crossroad, 1991.

Winter, Miriam Therese. *WomanWitness: A Feminist Lectionary and Psalter. Women of the Hebrew Scriptures, Part Two.* New York: Crossroad, 1992.

Winter, Miriam Therese. *WomanWord: A Feminist Lectionary and Psalter. Women of the New Testament.* New York: Crossroad, 1991.

Wintersig, Athanasius. *Liturgie und Frauenseele.* 6th ed., 1932. Ecclesia Orans 17. Freiburg: Herder, 1925.

Wintersig, Athanasius. Review of Neundörfer, "Bedingtes und Unbedingtes in der Stellung des hl. Paulus zur Frau." *Jahrbuch für Liturgiewissenschaft* 4 (1924) 281.

Witt, Reginald E. *Isis in the Ancient World.* Ithaca, N.Y.: Cornell University Press, 1971. Reprint, Baltimore: Johns Hopkins University Press, 1997.

Wittern, Susanne. *Frauen, Heiligkeit und Macht. Lateinische Frauenviten aus dem 4. bis 7. Jahrhundert.* Ergebnisse der Frauenforschung 33. Stuttgart: J. B. Metzler, 1994.

"Women Church of Korea." *In God's Image* (June 1990) 56f.

Young, William C. "The Ka'ba, Gender, and the Rites of Pilgrimage." *International Journal of Middle East Studies* 25 (1993) 285–300.

Zarri, Adriana. "Sensibilità femminile e liturgia attuale." *Rivista di Pastorale Liturgica* 19 (1981) 31–39.

Zarri, Adriana. "Woman's Prayer and a Man's Liturgy." *Prayer and Community.* Ed. Herman Schmidt, 73–86. Concilium 52. New York: Herder and Herder, 1970.

Index of Names

Editors of books are included in this index of names only if they or their edited book as a whole are of significance for the present study.

Abraham, 133
Aeberli, Elisabeth, 110n
Agatha, 64n
Agnes, 64n
Ahrens, Sabine, 135n
Albrecht, Ruth, 61n
Ambrose of Milan, 48, 49, 51, 60
Amelin, Emmanuel, 99, 104
Anastasia, 64
Anderson, Jill, 25n
Ansorge, Dirk, 42n
Apuleius of Madaura, 31
Aquinas, Thomas, 138
Artemis, 66
Asclepia, 45
Aseneth, 133
Ashbrook Harvey, Susan, 11n
Aston, Margaret, 55n
Aubert, Jean-Jacques, 53n
Augustine of Canterbury, 58
Augustine of Hippo, 51, 60, 138

Bagnall Yardley, Anne, 60n
Bartola, Maria, 136
Basil of Caesarea, 50–51, 61
Basilides, 56
Beauduin, Lambert, 72, 99
Berger, Florence S., 76, 87–88
Berger, Teresa, 1n, 2n, 10n, 69n, 70n, 78n, 83n, 90n, 93n, 107n, 110n, 115n, 131n, 147n
Betz, Johannes, 38n

Birnbaum, Walter, 80
Bishop, Edmund, 72
Blanché, Margareta, 101
Böckeler, Maura, 75
Boisclair, Regina A., 117n
Botte, Bernard, 80
Bouyer, Louis, 80
Bradshaw, Paul F., 6n, 17n, 56n
Brazal, Agnes M., 110n
Briggs, Sheila, 24n
Brock, Sebastian P., 11n
Brooten, Bernadette J., 29n
Brown, Alden V., 79n
Brown, Peter, 45n, 46n, 49n, 51n, 52n, 62n
Bruit Zaidman, Louise, 30n
Bruzelius, Caroline A., 19n
Buckley, Mary I., 127n, 131n
Burton, Katherine, 88

Caesarius of Arles, 58
Campbell, Debra, 86n
Caron, Charlotte, 115n
Casel, Odo, 71–72, 73, 74, 90, 97, 101
Catherine of Siena, 135
Cecilia, 64n
Chicago, Judy, 24
Chopp, Rebecca S., 112n
Chrysostom, John, 52, 53, 55, 66
Clark, Elizabeth A., 26n, 44n, 45
Clark, Gillian, 46n, 47n, 49n

Clark, Linda, 127n
Cleary, William, 140n
Clendenin, Mrs. John W., 83
Coddington, Dorothy, 76
Cohen, David, 47n
Cohen, Shaye, 56n
Collins, Mary, 109n, 115n, 118n, 122n, 123
Combe, Pierre M., 76n
Constantine, 13, 40, 41, 44, 45
Cooper, Kate, 64n
Corley, Kathleen E., 34n
Cott, Nancy F., 71n, 77n, 79n, 87n
Croegaert, Auguste, 75
Crumby Clipson, Elaine Marie, 132n
Cunningham, Agnes, 66n
Cyprian of Carthage, 12
Cyril of Jerusalem, 48, 60

Daly, Mary, 110
Damasus, 46
Davis, Flora, 112n
Day, Dorothy, 79
de Hueck Doherty, Catherine, 79
Diana, 32, 66
Dienst, Heide, 52n
Dijk, Denise J. J., 112n, 114n, 115n
Dionysius, 32
Dionysius of Alexandria, 56
Dobbeler, Stephanie von, 115n
Dobhan, Ulrich, 15n
Dorcas, 83n, 84n
Douglass, Laurie, 63n
Dransfeld, Hedwig, 93n
Duchesne, Louis, 103
Duck, Ruth, 115n, 117n
Dumler, Frau, 137
Dunn, Mary, 142n

Edgardh Beckman, Ninna, 142n
Edet, Rosemary N., 115n
Egeria, 60, 62–63
Eisen, Ute E., 12n
Ellard, Gerard, 73, 102
Enríquez, Teresa, 15
Ephraem, 60

Epiphanius of Salamis, 65
Eusebius, 50n
Eustochium, 63
Eva of St. Martin, 15
Eve, 66, 133
Eyden, René van, 116n

Fabella, Virginia, 130–131
Fabian Windeatt, Mary, 76
Fabiola, 63
Fantham, Elaine, 31n
Feistner, Edith, 64n
Felicity, 64n
Fenwick, John R. K., 80
Firmilian of Caesarea, 12
Fischer, Josepha, 71
Fonay Wemple, Suzanne, 9n
Fortune, 30
Franco, Francisco, 77
Franklin, R. W., 76n
Frioux, Mary, 85–86
Froehle, Virginia Ann, 142n

Galla Placidia, 44
Gerl-Falkovitz, Hanna-Barbara, 75n
Gess, Sandy, 129n
Gilchrist, Roberta, 19n, 20n, 55n
Gregory of Nyssa, 61, 66
Gregory the Great, 58
Greinacher, Norbert, 153n
Grimes, Ronald L., 119n
Gryson, Roger, 37n
Guardini, Romano, 73, 75, 78, 90, 103
Guéranger, Prosper, 72

Hagar, 133
Hagemeyer, Oda, 101
Hamburger, Jeffrey F., 20n
Hegemann, Edith, 77
Helena, 44, 63
Hellriegel, Martin, 73, 74, 87, 101
Henderson, J. Frank, 120n
Henry, Kathleen M., 20n, 126n
Herwegen, Ildefons, 73, 74, 75, 90, 97, 99

Hilpisch, Stephan, 105n
Himebaugh, Cecilia, 104
Hojenski, Christine, 126n
Howard, Julie, 142n
Hripsime, 65
Hughes, Kathleen, 77n, 115n
Hull Hitchcock, Helen, 120n
Hunt, Mary E., 126, 132n, 138n

Ilan, Tal, 28n
Irvin, Dorothy, 35n
Isaac, 133
Isasi-Díaz, Ada María, 127n
Isis, 30, 31, 38

Jacob, 133
Janetzky, Birgit, 117n
Jensen, Anne, 12n, 59n
Jerome, 49
Jezebel, 133
John III, Patriarch, 52
John XXIII, Pope, 113
John, Sabine, 22n
Johnson, Elizabeth A., 140n
Judith, 75
Juliana of Cornillon, 15
Jungmann, Josef Andreas, 73, 87

Kalven, Janet, 86, 127n, 131n
Karle, Isolde, 6n
Kersbergen, Lydwine van, 79, 86
Kiesgen, Agape, 104
Kirk, Martha Ann, 133n
Knödel, Natalie, 146
Knoepfler, Maria, 103
Koenker, Ernest Benjamin, 80
Kolbe, Ferdinand, 80
Korenhof, Mieke, 135n
Krabbel, Gerta, 75
Kraemer, Ross S., 10n, 28n, 29n, 52n, 56n
Kratz-Ritter, Bettina, 95n
Krause, Jens-Uwe, 46n
Krüger, Elke, 57n
Küchler, Max, 48n

Laeuchli, Samuel, 51n

Lake, Jean Thomas, 101n
Lampadion, 61
Larson-Miller, Lizette, 53n
Lascar, Maria Louise, 77
Lathrop, Gordon
Le Fort, Gertrud von, 98n
Leistner, Herta, 114n, 133n, 135n
Leonard, John K., 58n
Leyerle, Blake, 53n
L'Hermite-Leclercq, Paulette, 9n
Lilith, 133
Löhr, Aemiliana, 73, 74, 81, 90, 91, 94, 95, 101, 103–104
Loley, Maria, 85n
Lucia, 64n
Lucilla, 45
Lutz, Sybille, 137

M., Lina, 70n, 85
Maas-Ewerd, Theodor, 80
MacDonald, Margaret Y., 33, 36n, 37n
MacMullen, Ramsay, 27n, 47n
Macrina the Younger, 61
Malherbe, Georges, 93–94
Mananzan, Mary John, 123–124n, 126n, 128n
Marcella, 49
Marthana, 62, 63
Martin, Dale B., 36n
Mary, 22, 23, 63, 65, 66, 134
Mary Magdalene, 66, 134
Mattila, Sharon Lea, 33n
Maximilianus, 45
Mayer, Anton L., 94
Mayer, Josephine, 94–95, 97
Mayer, Wendy, 55n
McClintock Fulkerson, Mary, 6n, 154n
McConnell, Helen, 74n
McDannell, Colleen, 84n, 95n
McEnroy, Carmel Elizabeth, 113n
McGee, Lee, 25n
Meens, Rob, 58n
Melania the Elder, 63
Melania the Younger, 45, 63

Meyer, Marvin, 54n
Michel, Virgil, 73, 75, 76, 92, 96, 97,
   106n
Miles, Margaret R., 48n
Miller, Patricia M., 79n
Mohr, Anne, 93n
Mohrmann, Christine, 104
Monica, 51
Moor, Geertruida de, 20n
Morard, Loyse, 99n
Morley, Janet, 131n, 141
Morton, Nelle, 121n
Mueller, Franz, 105n
Mueller, Therese, 71, 76, 105
Murray Elkins, Heather, 131n
Murray, Jane Marie, 76
Muschiol, Gisela, 2n, 42n, 50n, 55n,
   57n, 61
Mussolini, Benito, 77

Nasimiyu-Wasike, Anne, 115n
Neu, Diann, 122n, 124, 125n, 130n,
   132n, 133, 134n, 136, 138, 151
Neunheuser, Burkhard, 74n, 118n
Nino, 59
Nolte, Cordula, 59n
Northup, Lesley A., 80n, 110n,
   115n, 122n, 128

O'Brien, Mary B., 79n
Oduyoye, Mercy Amba, 115n
Orsi, Robert A., 23n

Pachomius, 60
Pahl, Irmgard, 117n
Palladius, 50
Panizo, Rosanna, 114n
Parker, Pat, 155
Parsch, Pius, 73, 75–76, 81–82, 84,
   89n, 92–93, 96, 97, 98
Paterson Corrington, Gail, 38n
Paul, 62, 154
Paula, 63
Pecklers, Keith F., 76, 77n, 81
Perkins Ryan, Mary, 76
Perpetua, 64n

Phoebe, 34
Pichler, Emerzianne, 137
Pinsk, Johannes, 73, 75
Pius X, Pope, 98
Pliny, 37
Poemenia, 63
Pompeiana, 45
Portefaix, Lilian, 31n
Prégardier, Elisabeth, 93n
Priscilla, 35
Proba, 136
Procter-Smith, Marjorie, 2n, 80–81,
   115n, 117n, 122n, 125n, 129, 133n
Prudentius, 30n
Pulcheria, 44

Quasten, Johannes, 52n, 59n, 60n

Rachel, 133
Radford Ruether, Rosemary, 109n,
   111n, 126n, 127n, 129, 132n, 137,
   138, 139
Ramírez, Yeta, 125n, 128n
Ramshaw, Gail, 115n, 152n
Rausch, Anna, 137
Rebekah, 133
Redmond, Sheila, 117n
Reid, Barbara, 117n
Reinhold, Hans Ansgar, 100
Rhode, Irma, 88
Ripperger, Helmut, 88
Ripplinger, Werner, 110n
Roll, Susan, 57n, 115n, 127n
Rose, Renate, 139n
Rousseau, Olivier, 80
Rousselle, Aline, 9n, 29n
Rowe, Barbara, 134n
Rusch, Paul, 80n

Sack, Birgit, 79n, 93n
Saiving, Valerie, 137
Salome, 133
Sapphira, 133
Sara, 43-44
Sarah, 133
Sawyer, Deborah F., 30n, 32n, 49n

Schaumberger, Christine, 129n
Scheid, John, 30n
Schilson, Arno, 109n
Schneider, Oda, 91n, 94, 97n
Schneider, Theophora, 101
Schnitzler, Theodor, 74n
Schöllgen, Georg, 11n
Schüssler Fiorenza, Elisabeth, 36n, 37n, 126n
Sears, Marge, 124n
Sheppard, Lancelot C., 80
Sivan, Hagith, 63n
Snyder, Graydon F., 33n, 39n
Sokolowski, Robert, 119n
Sozomen, 49
Spaeth, Robert L., 76n
Speegle Schmitt, Mary Kathleen, 140, 142
Spiecker, Kyrilla, 101
Spinks, Bryan D., 80
Stark, Rodney, 27-28n
Stein, Edith, 107-108
Stenta, Norbert, 94n, 96
Stritch, Samuel A., 86
Stuart, Annabelle, 137
Stuart, Elizabeth, 135n
Stumpf, Paschasia, 101
Swidler, Arlene, 133n, 137n
Synek, Eva Maria, 44n, 65n, 66n

Tafferner, Andrea, 117n
Tanner, Kathryn, 25
Teresa, Mother, 1
Teresa of Avila, 135
Tertullian, 31, 48, 57, 138
Thébaud, Françoise, 78n
Thecla, 34, 62, 63, 66
Thein, Nyunt Nyunt, 142n

Theodoret, 49n
Thérèse de Lisieux, 135
Thraede, Klaus, 50n
Timothy of Alexandria, 56
Trajan, 37
Trapp, Waldemar, 80
Tuzik, Robert L., 77n, 105n

Underhill, Evelyn, 104

Vandeur, Eugène, 99
Vincie, Catherine, 48n, 115n, 132n
Vogelpohl, Wilhelmine, 102

Wales, Nonie, 134
Walker Bynum, Caroline, 25n
Walker, Barbara G., 125n
Walton, Janet R., 115n, 148n
Ward, Hannah, 131n
Ward, Justine, 76
Ware, Ann Patrick, 114n
Warren, F. E., 26n
Weaver, Mary Jo, 112n, 121n
Wheatley, Phillis, 136
Wild, Jennifer, 131n
Williams, Delores S., 127n
Wilson, Anna, 66n
Winkler, Gabriele, 38n
Winter, Miriam Therese, 114n, 127n, 132n, 135, 136n, 138n, 141
Wintersig, Athanasius, 74–75, 91, 97, 107
Witt, Reginald E., 30n
Wittern, Susanne, 66n
Wobster, Agnes, 137

Young, William C., 62n

Zarri, Adriana, 116n
Zerritsch, Veronica, 137